I AM THE LORD YOUR GOD

I AM THE LORD YOUR GOD

Christian Reflections on the Ten Commandments

Edited by

Carl E. Braaten and Christopher R. Seitz

William B. Eerdmans Publishing Company
Grand Rapids, Michigan / Cambridge, U.K.

© 2005 Wm. B. Eerdmans Publishing Co.

Wm. B. Eerdmans Publishing Co.
255 Jefferson Ave. S.E., Grand Rapids, Michigan 49503 /
P.O. Box 163, Cambridge CB3 9PU U.K.

Printed in the United States of America

10 09 08 07 06 05   7 6 5 4 3 2 1

Library of Congress Cataloging-in-Publication Data

I am the Lord your God: Christian reflections on the Ten commandments /
    edited by Carl E. Braaten and Christopher R. Seitz.
        p.   cm.
    Includes bibliographical references.
    ISBN 0-8028-2812-4
    1. Ten commandments.   I. Braaten, Carl E., 1929-
    II. Seitz, Christopher R.

    BV4655.I14   2005
    241.5'2 — dc22

                                                2004056403

www.eerdmans.com

Contents

III. Second Table of the Law

IV. The Divine Command

Contributors

Markus Bockmuehl, Reader in New Testament Studies, Fellow of Fitzwilliams College, Faculty of Divinity, University of Cambridge, Cambridge, England

Carl E. Braaten, Executive Director, Center for Catholic and Evangelical Theology; Coeditor of *Pro Ecclesia*, Sun City West, Arizona

William T. Cavanaugh, Assistant Professor of Religion, University of St. Thomas, St. Paul, Minnesota

David Bentley Hart, an Eastern Orthodox Theologian; he has taught at the University of Virginia, University of St. Thomas, Duke Divinity School, and Loyola College, Baltimore, Maryland

Reinhard Hütter, Associate Professor of Christian Theology, The Divinity School, Duke University, Durham, North Carolina

Robert W. Jenson, Associate Director, Center for Catholic and Evangelical Theology; Coeditor of *Pro Ecclesia*, Princeton, New Jersey

Gilbert Meilaender, Board of Directors Chair in Theological Ethics, Valparaiso University, Valparaiso, Indiana

Thomas C. Oden, Henry Anson Butz Professor of Theology, Drew University, Madison, New Jersey

Ephraim Radner, Rector, Church of the Ascension (Episcopal), Pueblo, Colorado

R. R. Reno, Associate Professor, Department of Theology, Creighton University, Omaha, Nebraska

Christopher R. Seitz, Professor of Old Testament and Theological Studies, St. Mary's College, University of St. Andrews, Scotland; President, Anglican Communion Institute

Philip Turner, Former Dean of Berkeley Divinity School at Yale; Vice President of the Anglican Communion Institute

Bernd Wannenwetsch, Tutor in Christian Ethics, Harris Manchester College, University of Oxford, Oxford, England

Robert Louis Wilken, William R. Kenan, Jr., Professor of the History of Christianity, University of Virginia, Charlottesville, Virginia

Preface

In 2003 the Society for Ecumenical Anglican Doctrine (now called the Anglican Communion Institute) and the Center for Catholic and Evangelical Theology jointly sponsored a series of theological conferences on the Ten Commandments. This volume contains the addresses given in Charleston, South Carolina, January 9-11; at Christ Church, Dallas, Texas, February 27–March 1; and at St. Olaf College, Northfield, Minnesota, June 15-17. Together, they bring fresh reflection to bear on general theological questions, such as the place of the Ten Commandments in civil society, their relation to natural moral law, their relevance for the Christian life, their use in catechetical instruction, as well as on particular ethical issues such as abortion, killing, homosexuality, lying, greed, and the like.

The Ten Commandments continue to stir controversy in both the church and society. Some would contest their relevance and validity in public life. Militant groups battle to expunge them from schoolrooms, law courts, and government offices, confining them instead to the sphere of private religion. More disturbing is the extent to which teaching the Ten Commandments in the church has been supplanted by the widespread heresy of antinomianism, the idea that if salvation is through "faith alone," Christians are free from the precepts of the moral law.

Jesus said to his disciples, "Come, follow me!" Following Jesus involves keeping the commandments of God. He said, "He who has my commandments and keeps them, he it is who loves me; and he who loves me will be loved by my Father, and I will love him and manifest myself to him" (John 14:21). The gospel has not abolished the law but is its fulfillment. Love lies at the heart of the commandments, and is not their antithesis. Jesus provided a succinct summary: "You shall love the Lord your God with all your heart . . . and your neighbor as yourself."

While Catholic and Protestant traditions make different use of the Ten Commandments, both agree on their divine authority and permanent validity. They agree that the Decalogue must be interpreted in light of the twofold commandment of love, and love in light of the Decalogue. Martin Luther, an Augustinian monk, followed his teacher Augustine in making the Commandments central in the education of children and prospective converts (cf. his *Large Catechism* and *Small Catechism*). The newly published *Catechism of the Catholic Church* devotes around one hundred of its seven hundred pages to the Commandments.

However, it is an uphill climb to reclaim the Ten Commandments for Christian teaching and give them their due in moral guidance. Sad to say, in many sectors of the contemporary church the teaching of the Ten Commandments has been supplanted by the postmodern rejection of objective standards, universal norms, and authoritative judgments. Religion that sells must satisfy the search for self-fulfillment; it must appeal to the sovereign self. Churches that define themselves in terms of biblical revelation, classical creeds and dogmas, divine commandments and moral codes seem to carry so much baggage, they find it hard to compete. It is useful to remember how H. Richard Niebuhr characterized the preaching of liberal Protestants: "A God without wrath brought people without sin into a kingdom without judgment, through the ministry of a Christ without a cross." Instead of preaching the Commandments of God, preachers who aim to make people feel good avoid negative talk about the wages of sin and the power of Satan, and substitute instead "Be Happy Attitudes" and the benefits of positive/possibility thinking.

The authors contributing to this book are calling the church to be the church, and not succumb to the temptation to serve as an agent of popular religion. The Ten Commandments are an indispensable part of the substance of the Christian faith. They stand alongside traditional creeds, rituals, symbols, and sacraments in equipping the church to be faithful in a new countercultural situation. The Ten Commandments make believers aware of the points of conflict between Christ and culture, between the city of God and the earthly city, of what it means to be in but not of the world. That is why we have entitled this book *I Am the Lord Your God*, because, as the chapters so eloquently affirm, the Commandments are above all about God, about the true worship of God and eschewing the worship of alien gods.

I. THE DECALOGUE
IN CHURCH AND SOCIETY

The Ten Commandments in the Church in a Postmodern World

Philip Turner

Introduction

The remarks that follow are meant to introduce the subject of this book — the Decalogue. It is perhaps a sign of the times that the Ten Commandments require introduction. Through most of the course of Christian history, this summary of the law, and Christ's summary of this summary ("You shall love the Lord your God with all your heart, soul, mind, and strength, and your neighbor as yourself"), would have required little introduction. They lay at the heart of Christian piety, standing there both as a standard of public behavior and as a means for individuals to examine conscience and direct their life's future course. Anglicans, Lutherans, and Calvinists all gave the Decalogue a prominent place in public life, public worship, and private devotion. My sense, however, is that within mainline Protestantism the Ten Commandments have been displaced in all these areas by more personal and subjective standards for measuring the health of society and the state of the soul. Indeed, the entire notion of commandments of this or any other sort, in the minds of many, has acquired an unattractive patina. Instead of suggesting the way people are to walk before God, instead of inscribing a common moral law, instead of being a light to the feet of lost humankind, they suggest unpleasant, even destructive, limitations on the lives of *individuals* that diminish the diversity of societies, constrain the freedom of *persons,* and inhibit the development of *selves.* The notion of commandments, in short, cuts across the very way in which we now describe ourselves as moral agents; i.e., as *individuals, persons,* and *selves* who are *free agents with rights* rather than *embodied beings* with *intellect, conscience,* and *will,* placed by God in a morally ordered universe in which we are to live in obedience to a moral law.

To this ecclesial and cultural downgrade of what for centuries had been taken as a summary of God's will for humankind, there came, not unsurprisingly, a reaction from individual officials and public interest groups that sought to inscribe the Ten Commandments in public places and imbed them in the curricula of public schools. That this effort to reestablish the Ten Commandments as a public standard has been led by Christians with Baptist roots is, to say the least, ironical. Baptists are supposed to stand for disestablishment, not establishment. One would have thought the old established churches would be the ones to cry out, but that has not proved to be the case. They have tended to follow the culture away from the notion of a public and common moral law, and toward a more individually centered ethic tied to social diversity and the flourishing of individuals. In this movement, they join more enlightened folk in seeking to "de-publicize" anything like a common morality. Matters of morals, as long as no unjustifiable harm is done to others, are said to be matters for individual conscience or matters for determination within interpretive communities, each of which may have its own take on things. The Ten Commandments do not fare well under the postmodern banners of personal flourishing and pluralism. And I say this even though the *New York Times* not long ago ran a series of articles on the Ten Commandments and their relevance (or lack thereof) to contemporary society. Careful reading of these presentations shows clearly that their author, Chris Hedges, could deal with the first table only by moralizing it, and with the second only in a most tentative manner. His articles leave one with the impression of a man whistling in the dark.

These observations led me to make a slight change in the original title of this chapter. I have decided to entitle it "The Ten Commandments in the Church in a Postmodern World" rather than "The Ten Commandments in the Church in Late Modernity." Modernity, be it late or early, held to the belief that there is something like a universal moral law. Modernity's most common representatives sought to root this common morality in some aspect of human nature rather than in either divine intellect or will, but they nonetheless held out for a universal moral law. It is precisely this universality that postmodernity rejects. We no longer look to an objective moral order that can be discerned by educated reason. Rather we look to communities of discourse, each with its own take on the world. In such a social world, epistemology is replaced by hermeneutics, and moral judgment is replaced by empathetic understanding.

So, if I am going to talk about the Ten Commandments in a "post" rather than "late" modern way, I must, at the outset, place them within an interpretive community, and so within the life of the church rather than within the life of humankind as such. The problem is that, though I want to do that, I do not want to do that alone. That is, I do not want to introduce the Ten Commandments as simply a Christian or Jewish thing. Neither, however, do I wish to introduce them simply as a generally negotiable form of moral wisdom. In respect to the Decalogue, I want to have my cake and eat it too. I want them to inscribe God's will for humankind as such, and I want them to have a special significance within the common life of both Judaism and the church. I have come to believe that unless I can do both those things, I will not have properly introduced our subject.

The question, of course, is how a universal law can at the same time be a particular one. In search of an answer, I propose first to do a bit of historical excavation, and then state why I believe that Christians need to hold to the view that the Decalogue inscribes a universal law laid down by God in creation, and that, at the same time, it has a special significance for Christian people.

In respect to the historical excavation, I propose to begin with a review of what the magisterial Reformers had to say about the issue I have posed, and then move behind the watershed of the Reformation to the period of the early church. There, in what I take to be the exemplary writings of Saint Augustine, I hope to display a focus that faded almost to the point of invisibility in the writings of the Reformers. In a final section I propose to address the question by means of a reading of the Sermon on the Mount, which I regard as the privileged perspective on the basis of which Christians should interpret the Decalogue.

An additional word is necessary as to why these historical excavations are necessary. They are necessary, to be sure, because despite our fear of influence and our desire to be innovative (especially in respect to religion and morals), it is simply the case that thought is possible only within a tradition. About this point postmodernists are absolutely correct. We cannot think about the Ten Commandments apart from a tradition of interpretation. The only question is which tradition we inhabit. However, there is a more important reason to begin with an account of a tradition of interpretation. Given the fact that we have roamed so far from this summary of God's will for our lives, we ought, I think, to regard ourselves, in respect to our knowledge of God and God's will, as less than children, as less even than toddlers. We ought to regard ourselves as infants who must learn to crawl, that we may learn to totter, that we may learn to walk, that we may learn to run. And so we ought, as infants and children must, to learn from our parents in the faith, and most of all from those parents who gave us the Holy Scriptures.

Historical Excursus: The Reformers and the Uses of the Law

Without exception, the Reformers took the Decalogue to be a written expression from the hand of God of the law of nature written also by the hand of God upon the human heart. As all know, they discussed both the natural law and the Decalogue in large measure by reference to their *uses.* The *uses* were two in the case of Luther and three in that of Calvin. For Calvin, in its first use (the *political use*) the natural law (and so the Decalogue) serves as a divinely mandated means to order social life. The Reformers all believed that human reason has access to the basic laws laid down by God in creation, and that these laws make social life possible. They believed also that these laws are inscribed in the Decalogue; i.e., that the Decalogue "republishes" the natural law written originally in the human heart. In its second use (the *pedagogical use*) Calvin held that the natural law (and so also the Decalogue) serves to remind people of their defection from the law inscribed upon their hearts. As such, the law serves to prepare the way for the gospel. Thus Luther, like Calvin, insisted that if the natural law was to be "reawakened," it had to be preached on the basis of Scripture. Anglicans were also made well aware of this second use by the placement of either the summary of the law or the Decalogue in the anaphora of the rite of Holy Communion in Cranmer's *Book of Common Prayer.* The idea was that conscience was to be examined in the light of the law so as to lead to a plea for mercy, and so also to a holy and effective reception of Christ's body and blood. Cranmer's rite incorporated Luther's pedagogical use into the structure of what he considered the church's central act of worship.[1]

The liturgical setting given to the Decalogue was not taken by any of the Reformers to mean that Christians alone had access to the natural law. There was, however, for them a sense in which Christians had access to *knowledge of* and *compliance with* God's law that was unavailable to nonbelievers. Luther and Calvin most certainly believed that both knowledge of God's law and the ability to keep it had been diminished by sin. Sin functions both to cloud the mind and bind the will. So the Decalogue, they argued, was given to an elected people in order that this people would know and follow what God in his wisdom had in creation made the law of all persons. Further, both held that Christ had made known depths of the law not previously grasped and had provided power to comply with its demands not previously possessed.

---

1. Richard Hooker, who (next to Thomas Cranmer) has had the greatest influence on the subsequent history of Anglicanism, in "Book One" of *The Laws of Ecclesiastical Polity,* extensively discusses law but not the Decalogue. Hooker believed in fallen reason's need for grace; however, in order to counter Puritan claims about the authority of Holy Scripture for the whole of life, he wished to establish an authority for reason independent of Holy Scripture. It is for this reason, I believe, that he discusses the natural law and reason's power to comprehend it, but not the republication of that law in the form of the Decalogue. Thus, though remaining orthodox in insisting on reason's fall, in order to counter the Puritan claims about the authority of Holy Scripture, Hooker gives authority to reason apart from Holy Scripture that is not to be found in either Calvin or Luther. Hooker is also different from Luther and Calvin in that he roots natural law in divine wisdom and not in divine will. He thus aligns himself with Thomas Aquinas rather than the nominalists from whom Luther and Calvin derived their notion of natural law. See esp. Frederick C. Beiser, *The Sovereignty of Reason: The Defense of Rationality in the Early English Enlightenment* (Princeton: Princeton University Press, 1996), pp. 46-83.

Historical Excursus: The Third Use of the Law

All of which brings us to the law's third use, namely, that a new (or deeper) knowledge of the law's meaning and new ability to keep it are given to those in Christ. Luther, unlike Calvin, was not happy about ascribing a third use to the law. Nevertheless, there lies within his writings something very much like a third use. Paul Althaus, in *The Ethics of Martin Luther*, points out that Luther regarded the Ten Commandments as "a summary of divine teaching," and that we should "value them above all other teachings as the greatest treasure God has given us."[2] He notes, however, that Luther's praise of the Decalogue does not refer to the Ten Commandments in their historical form, i.e., as found in Exodus 20. Rather he has in mind the Decalogue as it appears in the entire Bible, and as interpreted and fulfilled by the prophets and Christ. Luther even went so far as to say that Christ and the apostles established a "new Decalogue." In Althaus's words, "they have gone beyond, supplemented, deepened, and fulfilled the law of Moses through the new insights and understanding which Christ and his apostles, as moved by the Spirit of Christ, have brought."[3] Luther claims that "these Decalogues are clearer than the Decalogue of Moses, just as the countenance of Christ is brighter than the countenance of Moses."[4] Or, as Althaus says, "These new Decalogues express the intention of God's commandments better, more completely, and more deeply than the Mosaic Decalogue does."[5] The new Decalogue may thus be regarded as inscribing not only the natural law but also what Luther calls the "Christian law." In giving the new Decalogue, Christ gives new insights and new powers. Thus it would seem that this law provides more and demands more than the natural law and so also the Decalogue, at least in its original Mosaic form. It provides new knowledge of God's will and it demands love. More than that, it demands an extreme expression of love, namely, suffering.[6] Luther noted that even heathen, Turks and Jews must follow the natural law for the sake of peace. They must all practice some form of reciprocity in human relations. Nevertheless, such adher-

2. Paul Althaus, *The Ethics of Martin Luther* (Philadelphia: Fortress, 1972), p. 30.
3. Althaus, p. 31.
4. *LW*, 34:112-13.
5. Althaus, p. 31.
6. *LW*, 46:29, 40.

ence among Christians, though demanded, is different because it is done out of love, which allows obedience even in the midst of suffering.[7]

Even though I have *some* sympathy for Luther's worries about a righteousness based on works (and so also a third use linked to sanctification), I fail to see that there is a substantial difference between what he says about the natural law, the Decalogue, and the Christian law on the one hand, and Calvin's delineation of the natural law, the Decalogue, and the third use of the law on the other. Calvin, you will remember, like Luther, believed that the Decalogue is a republication of the natural law originally written on the human heart, but latterly on tablets of stone by the Holy Spirit. This republication was made necessary by the fall, which dulled and distorted moral knowledge and capacity. Nevertheless, even in the fallen state, both the natural law and its written version (the Decalogue) serve to order the unruly wills of people and convict them of sin in a manner that prepares the way for the gospel. These first two uses of the law are operative among unbelievers and believers alike. Reason still has power (and for Calvin considerable power) to discern this basic moral law, even if not in a perfect manner. Among believers, however, reason is corrected and will is empowered. Thus, the Decalogue takes on deeper meanings — meanings implicit from the outset, but revealed through the Spirit only to those who are in Christ.

Christians come to see that the law has at its apex the law of love, and at its base the purpose of God to gather the elect and order their lives within his kingdom. The natural law and the Decalogue in their manifold character are thus viewed as derived from this most basic principle and this most basic purpose. Calvin has no desire to develop a theory of either the natural law or its expression in the Decalogue that is self-contained or independent of Christian belief. As David Little has written, Calvin's theory of natural law "starts from the notion of love . . . as the central ethical principle embodied in Christian revelation, and then 'works back' to make room for those generalizations of human nature that Calvin considered the conditions or prerequisites for making the realization of love possible."[8]

7. *LW*, 46:29, 40.
8. David Little, "Calvin and the Prospects for a Christian Theory of Natural Law," in *Norm and Context in Christian Ethics,* ed. Gene Outka and Paul Ramsey (New York: Charles Scribner's Sons, 1968), p. 186.

Thus, when he exposits the particular commandments found in the Decalogue, Calvin pursues this theological agenda by providing both positive and negative explications. Or, to put the matter another way, "in Christ" he understands some of the commandments to contain more than prohibitions. Some of them enjoin positive obligations as well. Those "in Christ" understand, in a way others do not, that both the prohibitions and positive injunctions serve the law of love and so God's final purposes for the creation. Thus, for example, Calvin interprets the sixth commandment in this way. The prohibition of murder means not only that people are to refrain from murder; it means also that they are to go out of their way to enhance the physical and spiritual well-being of their neighbors. Calvin writes, "Scripture notes that this commandment rests upon a twofold basis: man is both the image of God and our flesh. Now, if we do not wish to violate the image of God, we ought to hold our neighbor sacred. And if we do not wish to renounce all humanity, we ought to cherish his as our own flesh."[9]

What we have here is an account of natural law and the Decalogue rooted not in independent human reason but in Christ, who both reveals and fulfills God's final design for the creation. Through Christ, men are set free not only to know God's law but also to obey God's will. The locus for this renewed and completed knowledge and for this new and completed obedience is the common life of the church. Within this fellowship "the cooperativeness and mutuality that is the end of God's design becomes the pattern of life."[10] As Calvin says in IV, 1 of the *Institutes,* "It is as if . . . the saints were gathered into the society of Christ on the principle that whatever benefits God confers upon them, they should in turn share with one another." Again, as Little says, "As the matrix of love, as the representative of the order of the gospel, the Church becomes an independent community that at once fulfills, and yet remains qualitatively different from, the natural world in which it finds itself."[11]

Now there are several things to be noted about this all-too-brief

9. John Calvin, *Institutes of the Christian Religion,* ed. John T. McNeill, 2 vols. (Philadelphia: Westminster, 1959), 2:8, 40.
10. Little, p. 184.
11. Little, p. 185.

account of Luther and Calvin. The first is that for them the Decalogue enshrines natural law or, if you will, the law of reason. The second is that the republication of the natural law in the form of the Ten Commandments was made necessary by the fall. The third is that both the natural law and the Decalogue are made more understandable and given deeper meaning by the coming of Christ and the Holy Spirit. The fourth is that, for Calvin, the Decalogue, in its third use, is given in respect both to understanding and compliance in a specifically ecclesial context. That is, though intended for all, it has the particular purpose under the providence of God of forming the life of a faithful and exemplary community.

These observations allow me to address my initial question in a tentative manner. For the Reformers the Decalogue, on the one hand, inscribes a universal law written originally in the hearts of all people by God in creation. On the other hand, the Decalogue has particular significance for Christians because they have been given knowledge of its deepest meaning and purpose; in the case of Calvin, this knowledge is of primary importance for the constitution of the common life of the church. The commandments are thus universal in that they inscribe what God wills for the life of all people. They are, however, particular in that their meaning is revealed for providential reasons to a particular people who are given power they did not previously possess to live in accordance with them.

Historical Excursus: Saint Augustine

All the elements mentioned above, save one, are to be found in Saint Augustine's famous discussion of faith and works in *A Treatise on the Spirit and the Letter*.[12] Nevertheless, the emphasis given them in this

12. I do not propose to write a thorough analysis of Saint Augustine's treatment of the Decalogue. Instead I have chosen one treatise as a means of highlighting a difference in focus between the early fathers of the church (of whom I take Augustine to be representative) and those of the Reformation. All quotations from Augustine's treatise that appear in the following text are taken from the translation of *A Treatise on the Spirit and the Letter* by Benjamin B. Warfield, D.D., in the Nicene and Post-Nicene Fathers, 1st ser., vol. 5, *St. Augustine, Writings against the Pelagians,* pp. 83-114.

treatise is very different from that to be found in the writings of the Reformers. Indeed, the place of the Decalogue in the life of a Christian is given an altogether different focus; namely, through the presence of the Holy Spirit in the heart of the believer, it is said to produce growth in holiness that leads individuals to their ultimate end — the vision of God.

For Augustine the true significance of the Decalogue lies in the fact that it maps the character of holiness. The emphasis on it as a summary of natural law written on the heart in creation is hardly to be found. If one looks in this treatise for an equivalent to the first use ascribed to the law by Calvin, one finds at best only ambiguity. In chapters 43 through 49, Augustine wrestles with the meaning of Paul's reference in Romans to Gentiles who do "by nature" what is contained in the law, and thereby show that the law is "written in their hearts."[13] In interpreting these verses he finds only two possibilities. Either Paul refers to Gentiles who because of sin have lost both the image of God and knowledge of the law, but through faith in Christ and the presence of the Spirit have been given a new heart and so a new nature; or he refers to Gentiles who, though sinners, have not lost the image of God utterly but retain some knowledge of the law. In this case, however, both the image and the knowledge have been weakened (though not utterly lost). Nevertheless, even in the case of a weakened image, for it to be said that the Gentiles do "by nature" what the law demands, they must believe in Christ and in consequence be given the Holy Spirit so that it may be said that the law is written on their hearts. Thus, in either case, whether the law has been blotted out or remains as a vestige, doing "by nature" what the law demands presupposes the grace of Christ.

In this discussion, Saint Augustine in no way wants to establish a natural knowledge of the law's demands. On this matter he remains neutral. His emphasis is not on a natural law written originally on the human heart, be it present or absent, but on the absolute need for grace if one is to know and do the good. In this treatise, at least, it is very difficult to establish anything like a first use of the law with its mutedly positive estimate of the powers of human reason and will. An equivalent to the second use of the law is more prominently displayed, however. Saint Augustine frequently refers to the power of the law, partic-

13. *Writings against the Pelagians,* pp. 101-4.

ularly in the form of the Decalogue, to convict of sin.[14] The Decalogue is not, however, presented as a summary of natural law. It is given to God's people, Israel, rather than to the nations, and it is given with the purpose of instructing them about God's will. The problem is that the law cannot produce the righteousness it demands, and so serves to judge rather than sanctify the people. The same is true for a Christian person. Save for Sabbath observance, there is no commandment that should not be kept by Christians. Yet, at best, the commandments, apart from grace, can be kept only out of servile fear and not freely. Only the presence of the Holy Spirit produces love that leads to free obedience and so to true righteousness.[15] In a pithy summary, Saint Augustine expresses the point like this: "The law was therefore given, in order that grace might be sought; grace was given, in order that the law might be fulfilled."[16]

Compliance with the law is not for Saint Augustine an end in itself. It leads to righteousness of life that is epitomized by loving God with all one's heart, soul, mind, and strength, and one's neighbor as oneself. When such love is perfected, one is granted a vision of God that produces final happiness.[17] Thus, to summarize Saint Augustine's treatment of the Decalogue: it expresses God's will for both Israel and the church. Apart from faith, grace, and the Holy Spirit, it leads to judgment. In the power of the Spirit, love for God is engendered in the mind, which in turn directs appetite and will to true obedience and righteousness. Obedience and righteousness are defined by obedience to the Decalogue that is summarized in the command to love God completely and one's neighbor as oneself. To be in such a state is to be holy, and so fit for God's greatest gift — a vision of himself as he truly is. Thus, it seems fair to say in summary that for Saint Augustine, the significance of the Decalogue is related almost univocally to a quest for personal holiness and achievement of life's telos.

14. For Augustine's discussion of the Decalogue, see *On the Spirit*, chaps. 23-31, in *Writings against the Pelagians*, pp. 93-96.

15. Saint Augustine believed that the Holy Spirit illumined the mind in such a way as to allow it to love God, and with the love of God the mind came to preside over the appetites and the will so as to produce an obedient and holy life. See, e.g., *On the Spirit*, chap. 36, in *Writings against the Pelagians*, p. 98.

16. *On the Spirit*, chap. 34, in *Writings against the Pelagians*, p. 97.

17. *On the Spirit*, chap. 64, in *Writings against the Pelagians*, p. 112.

The Witness of Scripture:
Saint Matthew and the Sermon on the Mount

To return to our original question, it would appear that for Saint Augustine (in contradistinction to both Luther and Calvin), the particular significance of the Decalogue is so prominent that it reduces its general significance to a mere and only possible shadow. What is one to make of this and other differences in emphasis to be found in the traditions by which the significance of the Decalogue has been measured? There are common themes, to be sure; but they are in no way given equal weight. There are, furthermore, themes to be found in one interpreter that are not even present in others. A plurality of understanding of this sort is not uncommon in Christian tradition. But when one is confronted with such a variety of voices, the proper thing to do is not to pick and choose among them according to taste, but to return to Holy Scripture with the questions tradition raises and *there* seek to resolve one's perplexities. And so it is with a return to Holy Scripture that I propose to end these remarks.

I carry the question about the universal or particular significance of the Decalogue to the Sermon on the Mount in Saint Matthew's Gospel. It is here that Christ is said to give the law (and the Decalogue in particular) an authoritative interpretation. In this sermon Jesus speaks not as a new Moses, but as the Son of the Father to whom the Father delivers all things, and who alone knows the Father (Matt. 11:25-27). The question, of course, is, to whom is Jesus speaking? Most commentators agree that Matthew here and in other places in his Gospel places Jesus before a double audience. There are the crowds and there are the disciples (5:1; 8:1). The entire bent of Matthew's account of Jesus' ministry makes it clear that the crowds include the Gentiles, and that the Gospel is intended for the Gentiles. Thus, there is a sense in which Jesus' interpretation of the Decalogue (5:17-37) is "spoken to the winds."[18] The Sermon on the Mount (and so also Jesus' interpretation of the law) is meant for everyone. Jesus' last words instruct his disciples not only to

---

18. I owe this phrase to Ulrich Luz, whose three-volume commentary on Matthew's Gospel has provided the inspiration for the interpretation of the Decalogue that follows. See Ulrich Luz, *Matthew 1–7: A Commentary,* trans. Wilhelm C. Linss (Minneapolis: Augsburg Fortress, 1989). See also Ulrich Luz, *The Theology of the Gospel of Matthew* (Cambridge: Cambridge University Press, 1995).

go into all the world "and make disciples of all nations," but also to teach these disciples "to observe all that I have commanded you" (28:19-20). What Jesus commanded is summed up in the Sermon on the Mount, and most certainly contains his authoritative interpretation of the Decalogue. One may choose for a variety of reasons to call the law Jesus enjoins by a term other than "natural law," but it does seem difficult to hold that Matthew holds no view that, independent of belief in Jesus, there is a divine law that holds for all people.[19] The law, even the law taught by Jesus, is the law of life and so the law of all people.

On the other hand, the Sermon on the Mount is intended to instruct the disciples in a form of righteousness that exceeds that of the scribes and the Pharisees (5:20). The law has special significance for them. The disciples have been instructed for a particular purpose. They are to be the "salt of the earth" and "the light of the world." Indeed, it is by the good works of the disciples that people (in general) will see the truth, and so give glory to God, the author of this truth. Thus, both at the outset and at the end of the Gospel, compliance with the law (understood as a righteousness that exceeds that of the scribes and the Pharisees) has an evangelical purpose.

A *community* of disciples, furthermore, shares this purpose. The higher righteousness (in which the Decalogue as interpreted by Christ plays a prominent, if not dominant, part) is not understood in the first instance (as in the case of Saint Augustine and most other church fathers) as a way to personal holiness. Rather it marks a road or exemplary way that a community of disciples is to follow so that God's law will be made known to the nations. If you will, the law, understood as a higher righteousness, displays life in the kingdom of God. The call to perfect obedience found at the conclusion of Saint Matthew's discussion of the law is a call for a community of disciples to enter a way that exemplifies the truth about God and human blessedness by means of their life together.

I can establish the communal focus of Christ's teaching by his explication of the prohibition against killing (5:21-26). Clearly, in his ex-

---

19. For example, Oliver O'Donovan has presented the notion of a divine will for creation which he does not wish to call natural law because of all the difficulties connected with the term — particularly the difficulty of establishing some common knowledge of this law. See Oliver O'Donovan, *Resurrection and Moral Order: An Outline for Evangelical Ethics* (Grand Rapids: Eerdmans, 1986).

position of the higher righteousness Jesus in no way lessens the prohibition. He lets it stand that anyone who kills will be "liable to judgment." The command seems to hold for anyone. Notice, however, that an immediate shift in vocabulary takes place. In his discussion of anger and its expression through various forms of insult, the word "brother" (or fellow believer) is introduced. The prohibition of killing is general, but it now is given a communal focus. This focus continues in the positive injunction to be reconciled with any "brother" who may have something against you. One cannot escape the conclusion that the injunction to seek reconciliation with the "brother" found here is linked to the injunction that concludes Christ's exposition of the law. This time the injunction is to love one's enemy — one who may have injured you rather than one you may have injured. The "you" used here is a plural "you," and is to be taken as an injunction to a missionary community concerning their attitude toward those who reject and persecute them (cf. 5:10-11).

Thus, we may take this first item in Christ's exposition of the Decalogue as having communal import. The search for reconciliation, along with love for one's enemy, is central both to the law and to the witness of the community of those who would enter the kingdom of heaven. The community of disciples is "salt and light" to the extent that its members seek reconciliation one with another and love those who persecute them and utter all sorts of evil against them on Christ's account. To the extent that they do not, they are without speech or dumb (this is the punned meaning of without taste), and so good for nothing but to be thrown out and trampled underfoot.[20]

Now, this is but a brief exposition of one element of the higher righteousness or what Luther called "the new Decalogue." I must presume that the full meaning of the various commands of the Decalogue as explicated in Christ's presentation of the righteousness that exceeds

---

20. It is important to note that Matthew's presentation of the communal character of the higher righteousness does not give license for a form of discipline that submerges the individual in a collective. For *Star Trek* fans, Matthew does not advocate a "Borg ethic." Rather, as is clear from this exposition of the sixth commandment, the free response of the community of disciples is to be joined by the free response of each disciple in love for both the brother and the enemy. The common life of the community of disciples gives expression to the summary of the law, as do the life and *heart* of each of its members.

that of the scribes and Pharisees will be contained in the chapters that follow this one. I wish to say in conclusion only that, as the early fathers of the church so clearly understood, Jesus' call to be perfect in obedience is not intended simply to remind people of how far they fall short of God's demands. Matthew believed that Christ's most important name was Immanuel, and that this name contained a promise that Christ would accompany his disciples along the way, and give them strength for growth in obedience (Matt. 1:23; 28:20). I must leave hanging, as did Matthew, how the stern demands of the higher righteousness, the threat of judgment, and the promise of forgiveness are related in God's economy. It is enough to say that Matthew most certainly viewed Christ's teaching about the law (and so also the Decalogue) as a part of the Gospel itself. In this respect, Calvin and Barth understand Matthew correctly, and in so doing they make contact again with the tradition to be found in the fathers of the church. One need only add that the way to be followed is not *in the first instance*, as the fathers thought, a way to personal holiness and the beatific vision. It is, as Calvin saw, a way of life that is to provide a distinctive (one might even say, evangelical) mark to the common life of a communion of saints — a mark that displays the character of life in the kingdom of God. Life in the kingdom is life as God intends it for the peoples of the earth. Thus, the particular and common law for the common life of the church makes manifest the universal law of God — the law that is to be taught to the nations as the law of their created nature.

The Ten Commandments: Positive and Natural Law and the Covenants Old and New — Christian Use of the Decalogue and Moral Law

Christopher R. Seitz

> *The light of nature is never able to finde out any way of obtayning the reward of blisse, but by performing exactly the duties and workes of righteousnes. From salvation therefore and life all flesh being excluded this way, behold how the wisedome of God hath revealed a way mysticall and supernaturall . . . concerning that faith hope and charitie without which there can be no salvation; was there ever any mention made saving only in that lawe which God him selfe hath from heaven revealed?*
>
> R. Hooker, *Lawes* 1.11.5, 6; 1.118.11-15, 119.12-15

The Governing Perspective of This Essay, in Three Statements

(1) God's personal law — his torah — is not a universal impingement, naturally perceived as such. (2) It is a special gift, given to a particular elect, and received as such by Gentiles adopted, through Christ's work, into a new covenant. (3) The terms of this giving and of this transferal must be recovered for the Christian church, now detached from Israel, and so prone to universalisms, in the wake of Kant, and confident or confused appeals to nature.

I. Statement of Intention

There is much I could do in an essay such as this. In the context of this book, I am not assigned specific commandments, but am free to think about the covenantal character of the Decalogue, in Israel and by extension to the Christian church. One concern will be to interrogate appeals to natural law as a way to commend the Ten Commandments for those outside the old covenant.[1] A second concern is with how moral laws not found in the Ten Commandments might rightly be taken as applicable in the Christian church. So I am trying to give an account of the Decalogue as Christian law, on the one hand; and I am seeking to understand the logic by which Christians have used certain of Israel's positive laws outside the Decalogue, often referring to them as "moral law." To show the complexity of the matter, consider an example from the early church. The *Didascalia Apostolorum* assumed a distinction between the commandments God spoke to all the people (that is, the Decalogue) and those Moses subsequently delivered. The "first legislation," it was argued, is to be maintained, while the latter, the "second legislation," is not.[2] It is important to interrogate this distinction in order to determine why Christians, especially in the early church, received with enthusiasm both the Ten Commandments and those laws in the second legislation called "moral."

1. Here a rough distinction can be made between premodern appeals to natural law, as a subset of a doctrine of creation and Christology (so early church; Aquinas, Calvin, et al.), and modern appeals, which lack a theistic a priori and take their bearings instead from scientific and empiricist epistemologies. See J. Porter, *Natural and Divine Law: Reclaiming the Tradition for Christian Ethics* (Grand Rapids and Cambridge: Eerdmans, 1999), and the important essay of N. Wolterstorff, "The Migration of Theistic Arguments: From Natural Theology to Evidentialist Apologetics," in *Rationality, Religious Belief, and Moral Commitment: New Essays in the Philosophy of Religion,* ed. R. Audi and W. J. Wainwright (Ithaca, N.Y., and London: Cornell University Press, 1986).

2. See W. Horbury, "Old Testament Interpretation in the Early Church," in *Mikra*, ed. J. Mulder (Assen and Maastricht: van Gorcum, 1988), p. 746: "a distinction is drawn within the Pentateuch between the true and moral law, including at least the decalogue, and the (ceremonial) 'second legislation' *(deuterosis)*" — this in the *Didascalia Apostolorum.* "Christ came 'that he might affirm the Law, and abolish the Second Legislation,' and the bishop must be 'a good discriminator between the Law and the Second Legislation' (*Didascalia* 6:17; 2:5)" (p. 746 n. 91).

II. Challenge: A Question Prior to Natural Law Appeals: Why Do Christians Retain the Ten Commandments?

In the New Testament we find restatements of the Ten Command-ments. We find summaries of the law. We find combinations of law. We find explicit commentary on bad ("you have heard that it was said") and good ("but I say to you") uses of Old Testament legal material. We find Jesus commending the Decalogue, in part or whole, in his re-sponse to the rich young ruler, and we find Paul concerned about cer-tain mistaken, Jewish and Gentile, appeals to law. Romans 13 has no trouble referring to explicit Decalogue injunctions (adultery, murder, theft, coveting), linked by Paul to the law of love which is said to en-close them. And certain of the Ten Commandments lie behind the for-mulation of Colossians 3:5-6.[3]

Why then do Christians set forth the Ten Commandments from the per se witness of the Old Testament, in catechesis, for ethical reflec-tion, and in church architecture, instead of these New Testament hear-ings of the Decalogue? Is our failure to follow the letter of the fourth commandment not a sign that we should stop setting forth the letter of the Old Testament in its specific presentation of the Ten Command-ments? Who can approach the commandment not to covet without some help from Paul? Wouldn't the Golden Rule be a more accurate summary for the Christian who stands outside the covenant with Is-rael? The catechism of the 1979 *Book of Common Prayer* (Episcopal Church in the United States of America) does not reproduce the letter of the Decalogue in explicit form, and in that is a recognition, I suspect, that the old law is old and requires abstraction into moral principles, which it obligingly provides.

In short, why do Christians make the Ten Commandments given

---

3. "Colossians iii.5-6 lists vices which bring the wrath of God; they are 'forni-cation, impurity, passion, evil desire, and the covetousness which is idolatry.' Is not this list based upon a combination of the sixth (fornication, impurity, passion) and tenth (evil desire, covetousness) commandments interpreted in relation to the first table of the Law (idolatry)? A subsequent reference (Colossians iii.20) to obedience to parents as pleasing to the Lord confirms the impression that Paul has the Decalogue in mind"; and "we can see how far Paul went to retain (recover) the sub-stance of the Decalogue" (Robert Grant, "The Decalogue in Early Christianity," *Harvard Theological Review* 60 [1947]: 6).

to Israel central in their literal form when there is no reproduction of them in the NT, but only forms of commentary and reflection?

Any account of the use of the Decalogue, by Israel within the old covenant or by the church within the new covenant, and a new cultural context, would be foolish if it did not assume these issues to be relevant. But more is at stake than simple relevance. To state the issue in terms of biblical theology, they force us to consider the authority of the Old Testament per se, as against an authority *in Novo receptum:* as the New represents the Old's letter. They force us to consider, at a time when it is unpopular to consider, the plain-sense authority of the Old Testament as Christian Scripture. One could conclude that much of the confusion over Christian sexual teaching stems from confusion over how to hear the per se voice of the Old Testament, in the Decalogue and in moral law more generally. So it is to that issue that we now turn.

III. The Law, Israel, and Gentiles

Let me state, then, a thesis which will remain basic to my treatment of covenant and law. It is: *The Ten Commandments are not ours in the nature of the thing.* By "ours" I refer to Christians who stand outside the old covenant; by "not in nature" I mean a related thing: not knowable apart from positive law, that is, law as commanded, in this case, by the God of Israel at Sinai. That especially the first four commandments, which deal with the revealed name and identity of God as personally disclosed to Israel, cannot be written off nature ought to be self-evident. If we think these are natural laws, we have probably not just misheard them but domesticated them as well.[4] It is impossible to square the late modern logic (which appears to be an argument from nature) that "we all worship the same God" with the holy God's personal self-disclosure in the first table of the Decalogue. Especially Anglicans, in recent days, have believed that the best way to get a hearing for the Old Testament and its law is to show that it naturally makes sense, or that the Old Testament is really a kind of natural law in dis-

---

4. See the insightful essay in this volume of Ephraim Radner, who attempts to show one instance of "naturalization" — that is, making oath-taking the chief burden of the third commandment, instead of reverence for the revealed name.

guise, if only we knew how to look. Not surprisingly, a corollary to this is that, where it cannot be shown to make natural sense (whatever that is!), it is the accidents of a deeper substance and can profitably be set aside.[5]

The scriptures of Israel, however, show us a positive law revealed by a named God to a people of election and promise. *It is only in the context of positive law* that the law is then secondarily extended and shown to exist in relationship to peoples who are not by nature part of the old covenant. Here we — Christians outside the older covenant relationship — may find a clue as to how "not ours" becomes "ours" after all; here the dynamic underlying natural law appeals might be discovered. As I have said, this essay is a modest effort to press beyond the inconsistent appeal to natural law in connection with the church's use of the Decalogue and other of Israel's legal and narrative legacies for the life and practice of Christian people. Virtually all of the church's present wrestling with sexuality stems from a confusion over how to hear Israel's plain-sense witness in matters of creation and law.

Uncharacteristically for most Christians perhaps, this will mean giving pride of place to Leviticus and especially chapters 17, 18, 19. At a moment of familiar candor the self-appointed radical, American bishop Jack Spong, declared Leviticus to be "an example of premodern ignorance."[6] In addition to a profound reflection on love of neighbor which we will look at below, the Decalogue also appears in Leviticus in modified form, and in connection with those outside the covenant relationship. If we are to understand how the law functions

5. In a book which seeks to commend "natural theology," James Barr nevertheless lodges this important disclaimer deep into his argument: "[The natural theology of the Bible] is not really 'autonomous' natural theology, but is itself derived from previous religion and is dependent on previous religion" (p. 147; here I take "religion" to mean some sort of positive law, though the term is unfortunately imprecise). He continues, "[There is a] proof, one may say, from *nature,* but it does not arise from any dispassionate examination of the natural world. It arises from religion, from the established religious belief that one deity had made the world and made it good" (*Biblical Faith and Natural Theology* [Oxford: Clarendon, 1993], pp. 147-48).

6. John S. Spong, *Living in Sin? A Bishop Rethinks Human Sexuality* (San Francisco: Harper and Row, 1988), p. 146. See my discussion in "Sexuality and Scripture's Plain Sense," in *Word without End: The Old Testament as Abiding Theological Witness* (Grand Rapids and Cambridge: Eerdmans, 1998), pp. 319-39.

for Christians, in the new covenant, it will be the surprising thesis of my paper that our best guides can be found in Leviticus. What we see there, moreover, is consistent with the logic of the New Testament and the early church. This includes, in Leviticus, the instinct to offer summaries of the law, to display appropriate combinations of different laws (and in distinction to inappropriate ones), and to introduce distinctions between kinds of laws in the old covenant which help guide the early church's attention to law as a critical category in Christian life. Leviticus is offering a figural guide to how the church later will reflect on law beyond the explicit covenant moment of God and Israel at Sinai.

I am not here seeking to diminish the creative interpretative power one might reasonably trace to Jesus, but rather am questioning whether "the creativity of Jesus" or a special spiritual lens used by him is what is at stake.[7] Almost all attenuation of law in Christian hands moves from a faulty understanding of Jesus' relationship to the Old Testament. Usually this takes the form of background noise rising from an extreme reading of Paul, but at other points it steps boldly into the foreground. In either case, Christian obedience to positive law from Israel's covenantal disclosure is threatened. No one reading very long in the literature of the early church will miss the signal importance Israel's law retained for the Christian assembly. That such an instinct has faded is not just the fault of an exaggerated Pauline emphasis; it belongs to the addiction to novelty and progressivism of our age, and its resistance to seeing positive law as a blessing and as foundational to life. We can speak lovingly of "Old Man River" or, in Saint Andrews, of the "Old Course" — but the existence of two testaments has raised the possibility of thinking of them developmentally rather than as figurally and intimately related. The result is to reduce God's laws given to old Israel to a former day and to regard them now as outmoded and replaced by a law of love.[8]

7. On the notion of Jesus as the bringer of "critical scriptural exposition," see my remarks in "Two Testaments and the Failure of One Tradition-History," in *Figured Out: Typology and Providence in Christian Scripture* (Louisville: Westminster John Knox, 2001), pp. 35-47.

8. C. Seitz, "Dispirited: Scripture as Rule of Faith and Recent Misuse of the Council of Jerusalem," in *Figured Out,* pp. 117-30.

IV. Not Ours by Nature

Many, I suspect, would accept that the Ten Commandments come to us only by way of some bridge.[9] They come from long ago. They use strange language. They are connected with a context, delivery from Egypt, which is not our own. And this is true even when we may all sense the wisdom in what the commandments command as somehow universal and pertinent to our own day, so, e.g., "Thou shalt not murder." Historical distance, different language, and different context, nevertheless, innocently conspire to remind us of the commandments' foreignness.

But there is a more specific way in which the commandments have been regarded as foreign. Luther touched on this in his essay "How Christians Should Regard Moses." Luther insisted, in a context of concern about what he called "enthusiasm" (viz., Christian application of Israel's law without sufficient discrimination), that the commandments were given *to Israel*, in the nature of the thing, and that this context would — indeed, should, must — remain critical for how outsiders conceived of their relationship to the commandments. His highly dialectical handling of the problem is beyond my competence to describe. Indeed, I sometimes wonder if it is beyond anyone's competence, though Heinrich Bornkamm gave it a serious try.[10]

Even if one wished to commend the commandments using a category like "natural law," as Calvin and Scotus and certain of the church fathers did, it would have to be granted that this amounts to a deduction, a second-order theological explanation, especially in the case of God's revealed name and the first table of the Decalogue, where respect for this revealed name is the subject of the third commandment. What needs to be pressed is whether second-order deductions conform to the logic and judgment of the plain sense of the OT witness, and if so, how.[11]

---

9. See John Barton (*Ethics and the Old Testament* [London: SCM Press, 1997]) for a recent statement of this.

10. "Law and Gospel," in *Luther and the Old Testament* (Philadelphia: Fortress, 1969), pp. 120-79. See the essays of Wannenwetsch and Hütter in this volume as well, where the theological brilliance of Luther's handling of the Decalogue is put on display.

11. For use of the term "judgment" see D. Yeago, "The New Testament and Nicene Dogma: A Contribution to the Recovery of Theological Exegesis," *Pro Ecclesia* 3 (1994): 152-64.

A category like "natural law" cannot easily move the epistemological boundary established by election and the covenantal relationship itself: rather, it sees law and nature from an angle of vision granted from outside the covenant relationship of God and Israel. What would it mean to take the boundary seriously — to honor positive law as given to Israel alone — and yet to see how and why that law spills out into creation more broadly?

Such an approach reckons with the fact that, within the letter of Torah itself, Israel receives a kind of positive law or commandment which God intends for those outside the covenant. One sees this clearly in Leviticus 17–19 where certain of the Ten Commandments are discussed, and where the sojourner with Israel comes into explicit view. That is, in the Torah broadly speaking a distinction is made between a law given to Israel and one given to and for Gentiles in their midst[12] (which Gentiles cannot know naturally, as it were, in their inherent Gentile-ness; only by coming into contact with Israel and learning of this Torah of the one God can knowledge be obtained — on this see especially Isaiah 40–48). At other places in the Old Testament, of course, examples are given of God's general governance of the Gentiles (or so Israel sees it in her specific witness), as in Amos 1–2, or Ruth, or Job, or even Jonah. One also thinks of Genesis 1–11 and the book of Genesis as a whole, which is prior to the giving of the Ten Commandments and the rest of the law. In this period of "ecumenical bonhomie" the general governance of the nations is matched by a general governance of Israel quite apart from *misvot* and *torot,* and so we have not moved from the same basic picture.

But in the context of Sinai lawgiving, and of God's declaration to Israel which now comprises what we call the Ten Commandments, it is clear that this is a law given to a people *in a covenant relationship,* and that this context cannot be removed when one outside the covenant seeks to hear the commandments as the scriptures of Israel set them forth. This would render void God's election and disclosure to a specific people.

---

12. On the importance of the Hebrew phrase "in the midst of" for Acts 15, see R. Bauckham, "James and the Jerusalem Church," in *The Book of Acts in Its Palestinian Setting,* vol. 4, ed. R. Bauckham (Grand Rapids: Eerdmans; Carlisle: Paternoster, 1995), pp. 415-80.

V. An Illustration of This: The Sabbath

An example of the subtle relationship between natural and disclosed law can be seen in the case of the Sabbath. The Sabbath is mentioned in the context of creation, that is, connected with God's ways with nature and universal governance (Gen. 2:2-3: "So God blessed the seventh day and hallowed it, because on it God rested from all his work which he had done in creation"), and so the reader is aware of it. Yet the ancestors are not portrayed as Sabbath-keepers.[13] And, in the brilliantly crafted story of the manna feeding (Exod. 16), which precedes the giving of the Decalogue and the covenant ceremony (Exod. 19–24), the readers and Moses learn of a special natural law for those with eyes to see it, already in place for regulating the food (Exod. 16:5), so that a rest can be kept on the Sabbath.

It is important to note that the story speaks of a test, which strictly speaking Israel (and Moses?)[14] failed ("I will prove them, to see if they walk in my law or not"). Although the Sabbath was naturally prepared for, the knowledge of this was not positively available. Moses would have to explain to the people what God had said privately to him (16:5: "On the sixth day, when they prepare what they bring in, it will be twice as much as they gather daily"); that is, they could on the day before the Sabbath get twice what they had previously got, not

13. For a creative analysis of this, see Walter Moberly, *The Old Testament of the Old Testament,* Overtures to Biblical Theology (Minneapolis: Fortress, 1992), and G. Wenham, who speaks of "an air of ecumenical bonhomie about patriarchal religion which contrasts with the sectarian exclusiveness of the Mosaic age and later prophetic demands" ("The Religion of the Patriarchs," in *Essays on the Patriarchal Narratives,* ed. A. R. Millard and D. J. Wiseman [Leicester: IVP, 1980], p. 184).

14. See the reading of Rashi at this key juncture: "They asked him (Moses), 'How is this day different from other days?' — From this we learn that Moses had not yet told them the section regarding the Sabbath which he had been commanded to say to them: (v. 5) 'And it shall come to pass on the sixth day that they shall prepare etc.' — he did not do this until they asked him, 'What is this?' Then he said to them, (v. 23) 'This is that which the Lord hath said' — this is that which I was commanded to say to you previously, but I forgot to do so (Cf. Ex.R. 25). On this account Scripture (God) punished him, in that He said to him, (v. 28) 'How long will ye refuse [to keep my commandments]', and He did not exclude him from the general body, by saying, 'how long will they refuse etc'" (*Exodus* [New York: Hebrew Publishing Company, n.d.), p. 85).

worry about it going bad, as they had discovered it would, and could therefore rest on the Sabbath and not labor. Some still went out, in a perverse demonstration of human love for "doing it our own way" even when it means more, not less, work (cf. Gen. 3:3). But the point was established by the failure of the test, and so no punishment was meted out (see the story's conclusion in vv. 28-30). God would have manifestly to command the Sabbath as constitutive to the covenant relationship (which he does immediately in the Decalogue's plain-sense delivery of 20:8). Thereafter, Sabbath-breaking could not take place without knowledge that it was God's publicly delivered law being broken.

More can be said here. Resting on the Sabbath, as Deuteronomy sees it, is tied to the special act of deliverance from Egypt, and by virtue of this it has the capacity to spill into the world outside the covenant (Deut. 5:14: "you shall not do any work, you . . . or the sojourner who is within your gates"). The Sabbath is for those in the midst of Israel as well. This "spilling into the world" outside the covenant takes a yet more detailed form in those portions of the Torah where Israel is told what law shall obtain for the Gentiles in their midst (see esp. Lev. 17–19). It is precisely awareness of this sort of interior Torah discrimination which sets the parameters for the decision in Acts 15 about what will be required of Gentile Christians.[15]

So, it is critical on any account of the Ten Commandments to keep our eye on the shifting contexts the Old Testament portrays. Failure to note this frequently means that a term like "natural law" is asked to cover categories too diverse for it to manage. It is critical that we keep this in mind, especially as we consider the way certain distinctions emerged in the postbiblical period to deal with the two-testament reflection on law for the Christian. I am speaking of the terms which, for example, appear in the Thirty-nine Articles, to choose an example within Anglicanism: "moral, civil and ritual." The use of these terms points to the need for distinguishing between kinds of Old Testament commands which are then to be received in Christ for the church. Yet recourse to these categories should not bypass too quickly the basic framework which gives rise to them; the result would be an

---

15. On this see M. Bockmuehl, *Jewish Law in Gentile Churches* (Edinburgh: T. & T. Clark, 2000); Bauckham (n. 12 above) and other commentators.

appeal not to the letter of Scripture, but to derivative abstractions meant to organize that letter. Appeals to virtues or abstractions apart from the plain sense of Scripture are always perilous, begging questions as to what we mean by love, or moral, or ritual, or whatever. The contexts in which the relationship between disclosed law and its natural extension is explored show this relationship to be subtle, but always riveted to positive law in the first instance.

The basic framework of epistemological extension is a familiar one in the Scriptures: God elects a people Israel, gives the law as an act of grace and an act of loyalty, and moves to the Gentile world only on the basis of that fundamental election, disclosure, lawgiving, and covenant. Even within the covenant itself we see the distinction of a law for Israel and a law for Gentiles, so that this distinction is part and parcel of the act of covenant making at its very heart. Christ does not render this framework void but accomplishes the purposes of God within it, as Israel, God's beloved, the Light to the nations and the Bringer of God's true Torah (Isa. 42).

When later distinctions are employed in order to commend some laws as binding in Christ and label others as not, the terms "moral," "ritual," and "civil" begin to be used.[16] Yet the distinctions which might best be used to describe the law within the Old Testament itself are those which apply to Israel, the obedience to which will mark her out as God's people, and those which extend beyond Israel and regulate the life of those in her midst. If we can get a better sense of this inner-Torah distinction, I think we will see why those in Christ, outside the covenant relationship with Israel, have felt it appropriate to hear the Ten Commandments as a new kind of law precisely for the Christian. And this in turn may help us understand why other commands in the old covenant — moral law — have been seen as crucial to any account of the new life in Christ given in the new covenant.

16. Irenaeus is one of the first to do this by distinguishing two kinds of legislation, the latter not from God directly, but through Moses. Horbury describes it thus: "distinguishing the abiding moral law of the decalogue from the further but temporary 'precepts of bondage' given through Moses, [Irenaeus] appealed to Deut 4:13f.; here the Lord himself 'declared . . . the ten commandments,' but also 'commanded *me* at that time to teach you statutes and judgements (Vulgate 'caerimonias et iudicia,' whence the term 'ceremonial law')" (Horbury, pp. 760-61).

VI. Decalogue in Its Old Testament Context
and Extension (Leviticus)

For scholar and general reader of the Old Testament alike, it is clear that the Ten Commandments are unique in their context. Unlike the more than six hundred laws mediated by Moses, these ten are given directly by God.[17] God spoke these words directly to the people of Israel, instilling in them awe and reverence; they knew with whom they had to do, and thereafter asked that Moses might speak for God to them. Second, the Ten Commandments are repeated in nearly explicit form in Deuteronomy. While it might be possible to contrast the law collections of Exodus with those of Deuteronomy or Leviticus (the stock-in-trade of higher criticism), the Ten Commandments are repeated verbatim. The minor differences are just that (e.g., the motive clause regarding the Sabbath, on which more below). Third, the Decalogue is in a distinct apodictic (ungrounded "thou shalt not") style, and in clipped form. Fourth, these laws stand at the head of all that follows, giving rise no doubt to the later concept of certain laws being foundational or summaries of the others, upon which they hang. Fifth, these laws are generated out of divine compassion, linked to the deliverance out of Egypt. Law is gift here, born out of God's saving and identifying purpose. The motive for their giving belongs integrally with them. In both Deuteronomy and Exodus the Ten Commandments stand in a signal position within the dramatic flow of the narrative and at the dramatic moment of deliverance and set-apartness.

It has been argued recently that Leviticus 19, which contains in nearly verbatim form eight of the Ten Commandments, is also set apart in a distinct way from its context in the so-called Holiness Code. That is, as the law collections of Exodus and Deuteronomy have their Decalogue, so to speak, so too Leviticus in a modified form. Rendtorff says, "I am personally convinced that the one who put Leviticus 19 where it is now, had in mind the Decalogue at Sinai."[18] Its location in Exodus 20 matches that of Leviticus 19.

---

17. A fact which some take to underscore their universality.

18. "Discussion," in *Reading Leviticus: A Conversation with Mary Douglas,* ed. J. F. A. Sawyer, Journal for the Study of the Old Testament — Supplement Series 227 (Sheffield: Sheffield Academic, 1996), p. 63.

What is striking for our purposes is that Leviticus 19 falls in that context of the larger book where reference is made to the so-journer. A simple glance at a concordance shows that most of the chapters of Leviticus are concerned solely with Israel and her deport-ment, in ritual, clean and unclean discrimination, offerings and sacri-fice, and so in these the term for sojourner *(ger)* is absent. But in the section comprising chapters 17–20 the term is abruptly in evidence. No wonder close readers of Acts 15, in search of the key for why cer-tain laws were laid upon the new Gentile Christians, realized the an-swer was to be found here in Leviticus. Chapter 17 places the so-journer within Israel under obligation to hold blood sacred; chapter 18 makes it clear that laws governing sexual relations (incest and ho-mosexuality) apply to the sojourner, who is therefore not to be like the Gentile when brought near to God's people. At this dramatic point in the chapter (18:24-30), we hear of the fate which awaited those who dwelt in the land: the land vomited them out. And it is not just Israel which is to stand aside from the laws and the ways of the nations: so too the sojourner.

When we enter chapter 19, then, and hear the Decalogue's laws set in a new context, what is striking is that the sojourner is still in view. This is the famous chapter which speaks of love of neighbor as oneself, which is cited as a summary of the law in the New Testament and in rabbinic literature. "You shall love your neighbor as yourself: I am the LORD" (19:18). Israel is to be holy as God is holy, and on this note the chapter opens. To obey the laws of the Decalogue is, Leviticus 19 has it, to be as God is in his character. What is often not noted is that love of neighbor applies in verse 18 to Israel; that is, we are still in that context of lawgiving which strictly speaking applies to Israel only. This makes the final movement of the chapter all the more striking, for there it is that the sojourner again appears.

"When a stranger sojourns with you in your land, you shall not do him wrong. The stranger who sojourns with you shall be to you as the native among you, and you shall love him as yourself; for you were strangers in the land of Egypt: I am the LORD your God" (vv. 33-34).

Several striking things require to be noted:

1. The book of Deuteronomy does not use the term "sojourner" very often, but in the context of its Decalogue presentation it grounds Sabbath rest not in creation but in recollecting Israel's sta-

30

tus of slave in Egypt, and therefore enjoins Israel to cease from labor, and extend that as well to the sojourner who is within her gates. As Leviticus extends divine law into the realm of the sojourner, so too does Deuteronomy, as a sort of *inclusio,* explicitly in the Decalogue itself.

2. Leviticus 19 contains eight of the Ten Commandments, but it cannot be said to be only about "moral law." The sojourner appears in this chapter as one who is to be treated as Israel is to treat her fellow Israelite. All this is grounded in the will of the one God of Israel. It is positive law, not natural law, even at the level of what we might judge to be the natural law in its most obvious guise: Wouldn't everyone agree that the Golden Rule makes natural sense? Israel learns what is God's will, from God's law, and in the context of that she learns something which may not be within range for the one she finds herself confronted with, the sojourner. She is to love the sojourner in her midst, as herself. This may be regarded as a kind of moral law, but it is not natural law in the first-order sense. And it exists within a context which does not distinguish between this sort of moral injunction and the rules, say, governing sacrifice of peace offerings.

3. Chapter 18 also ends with an extension to the sojourner, but here it is regulating the actual conduct of the sojourner, not Israel's attitude and behavior toward the sojourner, as in chapter 19. The laws governing Israel's life in the realm of appropriate sexual conduct apply in toto to the sojourner. It is not a chapter concerned with purity laws, as is sometimes held. Rather it is for the most part apodictic law. Male homosexual behavior is forbidden in the same context as concern over adultery, menstruation, Molech worship and child sacrifice, and bestiality. It is difficult to think of these under one simple rubric: purity. Add to this the long list of forbidden incestuous behaviors, which are grounded in nothing except the divine "No," and it would appear to be a chapter concerned with simply ruling out what cannot be tolerated without a natural outcome of disaster. Indeed, here it might be appropriate to discuss whether the positive law assumes a quite natural consequence. But the reverse logic, from natural to positive, does not emerge in the plain sense.

With these brief observations in place, it becomes immediately clear why a recent study of New Testament ethics[19] is required to run roughshod over two significant features of Leviticus.

1. For Countryman, it is crucial that internal distinctions, matters of literary context, structure, and formal organization must be ignored in the name of making Leviticus to be about purity in all its parts. Purity is the engine which generates the laws of Leviticus, not just in a chapter involving clean and unclean animals (Lev. 11), but even where purity is not being discussed. Here is a classic historical-critical instinct, assisted by anthropological insights wrongly applied, which seeks to unlock the logic of narrative or law and in so doing ignores genuine literary distinctiveness and organizational flow, "the canonical shape"; this is particularly critical to attend to in chapters 17–19, as we have seen. I believe it is a fair judgment to say that the longer Mary Douglas worked with her purity and danger scheme, in explicit exegesis of Leviticus and in conversation with Jewish and Christian exegetes, the more complicated and nuanced her take on Leviticus became.[20] Sadly, Countryman introduces a sort of master view of Leviticus and its logic which ignores the plain-sense presentation of the book in its artistry, subtlety, and range.

2. The section of Leviticus we are examining reveals the second major flaw in Countryman's work. One sees very early in his argument that it is absolutely necessary that the system he erects of Israel's alleged purity notions must stand in absolute contrast to any subsequent Gentile (non-Israelite, non-Jewish) use of it. It is Israel's Levitical

19. L. W. Countryman, *Dirt, Greed, Sex: Sexual Ethics in the New Testament and Their Implications for Today,* 2nd ed., SCM Classics (London: SCM Press, 2001). W. Houston comments, "When it comes to sex, the issue is relatively clear, despite Countryman's quixotic attempt to prove that Paul rejects all purity rules in relation to this as to all other subjects. The laws and ethical perceptions in Judaism about sex were rooted in cultural features that were seen (for the most part rightly) to be common to all humankind, and they were therefore held by *gerim* Jews to apply to all human beings, whether *gerim* or not. Even if such perceptions did in fact divide Jews from Greeks, they did so, in the Jewish view, because of pagan corruption, not because the rules in question were designed to make Jews distinctive. It is naturally to be expected that they should appear in the New Testament, for though purity-based they are inevitably seen as moral rather than 'ritual' rules" (*Purity and Monotheism: Clean and Unclean Animals in Biblical Law,* Journal for the Study of the Old Testament — Supplement Series 140 [Sheffield: JSOT Press, 1993], p. 270).

20. See, e.g., "Sacred Contagion," in *Reading Leviticus* (pp. 86-106).

world of purity and danger and taboo. What Jesus does is dismantle this, in the name of opening up God's new nonlegal or purity-constrained life for all. The problem can be immediately sensed in Leviticus 17–19. Already in the very delivery of it, Leviticus understands certain of its laws as having to do with non-Israelites. There is not a neat development, Israel and her purity here, Gentiles and their own life and law there, moving from Old to New Testament reflection.

It is for this reason that we are addressing in this context of Christian reflection on the Ten Commandments the way Israel's positive law, which in the nature of the thing is not ours, is *in Christ* (the faithful Israel) ours after all. It is a law and a life for us as we become sojourners in the midst of Israel, this Israel having come in the flesh and by his sacrifice fulfilled and completed the sacrifice wholly acceptable to God, for which Leviticus was a positive, full-slanting shadow and type. In those chapters where laws are extended to enclose the sojourner outside of Israel, we see examples of a kind of law that is not Israel-specific and is not taken up into the ritual, blood sacrifice of the man Jesus. The logic of this distinction explains how it is that the plain sense of the Old Testament, in the realm of law and commandment, was handled consistently by Jesus and the early church, which retained the Decalogue and alongside it offered a summary of the whole law of God given to Israel.[21]

It further explains how a category like "moral law" emerged, and why, traditionally, Christians have regarded the laws concerning homosexuality, bestiality, and other injunctions of Leviticus moral law extensions of the foundational law given by God to Israel at Sinai. Reference to these Ten Commandments in the New Testament does not include explicit restatement of the Decalogue on the per se terms we find it in Exodus and Deuteronomy. This has to do with the conviction that

21. "By means of a careful and literal exegesis of the context of the Decalogue early Christian interpreters were able to show that it was only the Decalogue which God had spoken, and that the rest of the Law had been added for various reasons. The Decalogue provided an extremely valuable means of catechetical instruction, as it does today. And yet it was realized that Jesus not only summed it up but went beyond it. But since he went beyond it only to reenforce it, Christians did not feel free either to reject the Decalogue or to call his interpretation impossible of fulfillment. Instead they recognized the existence of catechumens and of mature Christians as well, and expected progress in the practice of religion" (Grant, p. 17).

Christ is the law's end and fulfillment, thus allowing summaries of the law, such as existed within Judaism, to function within a new context of Christ's work among the nations. The Decalogue is heard with reference to these summaries, and the warrant for this is traced in the New Testament witness to the earthly Jesus himself. It is precisely because Christ's work spilled out into the world beyond the old covenant, and was calibrated to this task, that the instinct emerged as early as we can track it in the early church to regard the moral laws in the old covenant which apply to the sojourner as relevant as they were in the original context, and now a fortiori in the new covenant as well. Not just the Decalogue, but also moral laws which were applied to the Gentiles in Israel's midst, were seen as applicable in the church, "for Christ has brought us near who were once far off" — making us like those in the midst of Israel in the wilderness.

The very fact that in sections of the early church wide and quite direct application of Israel's law can be seen — for individual sexual behavior, calendar, priesthood, money, and so forth — indicates the very gradual way in which a subsequent two-testament perspective on law emerged.[22] Christians in time, after the parting of the ways with Israel, ceased living in strict conformity to the ruling of Acts 15, for example, which was derived from Leviticus. But the general logic of the sojourner in the midst was never abandoned, and the early church continued to hear the Decalogue and the moral law given by God to Israel and the sojourner as a law in Christ, as what Irenaeus called the *virtus decalogi* (the power of the Decalogue). He is one of the first to speak of natural precepts given within mankind from the beginning of creation, which are in time revealed explicitly in the Decalogue and in the moral law more broadly.[23] This "immanent" in-

22. See the very helpful survey of the period by Horbury in *Mikra*.

23. Irenaeus states, "The Decalogue, however, was not Mosaic. 'When God first admonished them through the natural precepts, which he had given men from the beginning within them — that is, through the Decalogue, disobedience to which deprives one of salvation — he asked of them nothing more'" (*Against Heresies* 4.115). Irenaeus demonstrates this by referring to Deuteronomy: "As Moses says in Deuteronomy (v. 22): 'These are all the words which the Lord spoke to the whole congregation of the children of Israel on the mountain.' . . . The patriarchs did not have the Decalogue because the 'power of the Decalogue *(virtus decalogi)* was written on their hearts and souls'" (4.15).

terpretation of an "economic" reality brought the Decalogue into greater, not lesser, prominence, and it allowed for the persistence of moral law as a category which would apply to Christians in the new covenant.

Conclusions

1. Revelation and "natural law." The idea that God and his will can be known satisfactorily and independently of revelation is nowhere assumed in the Bible; God cannot be known as he means fully to be known in nature.[24] Within the context of revelation and positive law, however, assumptions can be made by Israel of the ways in which the nations might know about justice and the divine will, and indeed such are often asserted to be in force. But nowhere does it appear obvious that the nations know the true God or his specific will through natural means alone.[25] Job discovered God in the whirlwind, it was an awesome experience, and he saw with the eye something he had known before only by hearsay. But the named God of Israel would wait patiently to reveal himself and his will, in the full sense, in his ways with Israel, in promise to the ancestors and as "the one who is as he is" in the events of the exodus. From within this specific series of disclosures of himself and his will, the Ten Commandments are set forth. From within this special relationship and from it outwards, Israel can speak of God's more natural governance. So, too, Paul can speak of the Athenians having witnesses in a vague way to the work of God in their midst. But when he seeks to fill out this natural intimation of God with

24. See n. 5 above, where Barr reflects on this from his own perspective, with his own biblical theological bearings and contraints.

25. Jon. 1:1-17 is a particularly subtle portrayal. The sailors know there is a divine reason for the rough seas: they pray "each one to his god" for relief. Noting Jonah's absence, they seek him out and demand that he too "cry to his god." When he reveals why the sea is as it is, the name of YHWH is mentioned for the first time in their hearing. Upon getting natural relief, by chucking Jonah overboard according to his own command, they then fear YHWH and act appropriately in religious terms. The account of Dan. 4 is also noteworthy. There the author resists letting the divine name come onto the lips of Nebuchadnezzar, however, in his confession (4:34-37). But his confession of the one God's ways in nature is clear nonethless (v. 35).

the full content of God's self and his will, from Israel and in Christ, the Athenians balk and must adjust their bearings (Acts 17:32). So too the confessing Nebuchadnezzar or the sailors with Jonah when he is bound for Nineveh. The movement is from a positive law context to a natural extension of that, and not the reverse.

2. Natural law and the "second legislation." By distinguishing between the sojourner brought near and the nations in general, it is possible for Leviticus to assert a kind of natural law which accompanies the breaking of basic moral laws, such as are enumerated in Leviticus 17–18. That is, from within the context of positive law, Israel is prepared to see God at work naturally, in the judgment of the nations. In a telling natural phrase, the land is said to have vomited them out, independently of their knowledge of God's positive commands (Lev. 18:28).

Moves at work in the early church to distinguish between the second legislation (all non-Decalogue law) and the Ten Commandments are straining at distinctions, in Christ, but the result is not entirely salutary. Not all law in the Decalogue is natural, and much law in the "second legislation" applies to the foreigner brought near; the application of such law to the Gentile converts in Acts 15 means that it is reasonable to think of the Decalogue as law in Christ, for the Christian, but also law as can be found in the second legislation. The emergence of "moral law" as a category reflects resistance to simple first- and second-legislation distinctions.

3. Harnack and Ebionism. The influence of Harnack on reconstructions of Christian doctrine in the first centuries has been mixed. One negative legacy is the assumption that doctrine had to fight two equal and opposing fronts: gnosticism and Ebionism. Christian doctrine is a measured and even rejection of both. This view is flawed for its functionalism, on the one side, as though doctrine is not pressured chiefly by Scripture's plain sense;[26] but also, it mishandles what it calls "Ebionism."[27] We are in great debt to those interpreters of the church

---

26. See my essay "'Our Help Is in the Name of the LORD, the Maker of Heaven and Earth': Scripture and Creed in Ecumenical Trust," in *Figured Out,* pp. 177-90.

27. Harnack does note the centrality of the scriptures of Israel in positive terms for the early church. See A. Harnack, *Bible Reading in the Early Church* (London: Williams and Norgate, 1912). "At first primitive Christianity was concerned exclusively with the Scriptures of the Old Testament. Even the apologists, when speaking of Scriptures, mean only these. What Wrede says of Clement . . . is true of all Christians

fathers who have shown us how widespread was the use of Israel's scriptures as first-order scripture, and this especially in the area of law.[28]

4. Appropriate and inappropriate coordinations of law. In Acts 15 the laws which apply to baptized Gentiles are drawn from Leviticus according to a principle of selection, having to do with the phrase "in the midst of my people."[29] Various summaries of the Ten Command-

---

of primitive times belonging to the Catholic Church: 'Clement's treatment of Scripture depends entirely upon the axiom, accepted by all Christians, that the Old Testament is the unique sacred book, given by God to Christians and properly to Christians alone, whose words could claim absolute authority and formed the first and the most important foundation of all Christian paradosis. From a historical point of view it would be altogether unsatisfactory to say that the Jewish Old Testament — as a whole or in part — continued in force for the Christians as if its recognition implied some kind of previous reflection, and as if the possession of this heavenly and infallible book were not in the eyes of the Christians one of the most striking commendations of the new religion. It cannot be stated too emphatically that at that time there was not the slightest suspicion that in the future a second sacred volume would come into being with authority equal to, indeed greater than, the first.' . . . It can be proved from testimony of the fourth century that certain writings of the Old Testament always stood in the foreground for private edification" (p. 40 n. 1). Also: "[Lessing] perceived that the New Testament as a book and as the recognised fundamental document of the Christian religion originated in the *Church.* But Lessing did not recognise that the Book from the moment of its origin freed itself from all conditions of its birth, and at once claimed to be an *entirely independent and unconditioned authority.* This was indeed only possible because the book at once took its place beside the Old Testament, which occupied a position of absolute and unquestionable independence because it was more ancient than the Church" (p. 145). This last quote is fighting on the main front of Lessing (the NT has authority only because the church gives it), but in so doing reveals a remarkable statement about why the authority of the NT took hold as it did, viz., because it followed and was paired with the authoritative scriptures of Israel, which already possessed this status.

28. See above all the work of Bockmuehl and Horbury cited herein. "The importance of the Jewish scriptures in Christian apologetic, therefore, was by no means confined to the argument with the synagogue. On the contrary . . . the scriptures were at the heart of the presentation of Christianity to the gentile world" (Horbury, p. 744). Compare Origen: "Come, sir, examine the poems of Linus, Musaeus, and Orpheus, and the writings of Pherecydes, side by side with the laws of Moses, comparing histories with histories, moral precepts with laws and commandments; and see which are more able to transform instantly those who hear them" (*Contra Celsum* 1.18).

29. See n. 12 above.

ments and lists of individual commandments in the New Testament can be explained according to principles known to us from within Jewish exegetical and halakic practice. It is wrong to attribute these to some freewheeling usage beginning with Jesus. Moreover, great caution appears to be exercised in the final form of the Gospel witness. Inappropriate combinations are an offense to the plain sense of the Old Testament, and demand a distinction between "tradition" and the Old Testament's literal sense, as in Mark 9.[30] The idea that one could combine a teaching from Leviticus ("you shall love your neighbor") with a loose interpretation of Deuteronomy's stern word concerning the Amalekite foe ("you shall hate your enemy") is opposed by Jesus, and equally, it could be said, by Leviticus 19 itself. There Israel is to love her neighbor within and outside the covenant, and nothing is said about hating an enemy as a codicil on that radical Levitical injunction.

5. Knowing and doing the law. Christians approach law through and in Christ. To know God's will and to do it requires the work of the Holy Spirit, which is God's gift in the obedient Son. Israel also reflected on the difference between knowing and doing. The generation which heard God speak his will in the "first legislation" immediately disobeyed and eventually died in the wilderness, not fully inheriting the promise or blessing God's law intended. Deuteronomy speaks of a generation who are humbled by this experience, and by God's merciful disciplining, and are so better empowered to do what they know to be his will. No adequate account of the Ten Commandments will avoid reference to empowerment to do God's will. It is not content alone which the commandments convey, but a living relationship. Only within that relationship can Israel expect to hear the final exhortations of Deuteronomy, which insist that the law is near and is good and can be done. That hearing comes on the other side of failure and divine mercy. It is the same access we outside the old covenant are given to the law of God, now through the obedient and empowering sacrifice of his Son. What we could not do by nature, in Christ, through whom all things were made, we are empowered to do by virtue of his own obedience and self-giving for us. We can know God's law and, in Christ, we can do it, through his obedience, to the glory of God the Father.

30. On this see Bockmuehl, *Jewish Law in Gentile Churches.*

II. FIRST TABLE OF THE LAW

No Other Gods

Thomas C. Oden

In 1520 Luther wrote in "A Brief Explanation of the Ten Commandments, the Creed, and the Lord's Prayer": "The ordinary Christian, who can not read the Scriptures, is required to learn and know the Ten Commandments, the Creed, and the Lord's Prayer; and this has not come to pass without God's special ordering. For these three contain fully and completely everything that is in the Scriptures, everything that ever should be preached, and everything that a Christian needs to know, all put so briefly and so plainly that no one can make complaint or excuse, saying that what he needs for his salvation is too long or too hard to remember."[1] There he will learn what he ought do, and "where to seek and find and get the strength he needs" when he finds that he cannot do the things he ought.

Introduction — Method: Listening to the Text through the History of Exegesis

My approach in this presentation follows directly from my special concern over the last thirty years: learning from the church fathers on pastoral care, theology, and history of exegesis. During the decade from 1973 to 1983 I focused primarily on learnings from the church fathers for pastoral

---

1. *Works of Martin Luther,* 6 vols. (Philadelphia: Muhlenberg, 1943), 2:354.

care. During the decade from 1983 to 1993 I focused primarily on learnings from the church fathers for systematic theology. During the last ten years, from 1993 to the present, I have been focusing primarily on learnings from the church fathers for Scripture exegesis and preaching.

The models for this way of thinking are found abundantly in the *Ancient Christian Commentary on Scripture*,[2] of which there are now twelve volumes available. This presentation, however, is patterned more specifically after the argument of the *Justification Reader*,[3] which takes one disputed doctrine, justification, and presents evidence from the history of exegesis to seek to establish a consensual view of classic Christian teaching, especially as correlated with the Reformers. For those who wish a short overview of this method, it is briefly set forth in two brief sections of my new book *The Rebirth of Orthodoxy*,[4] chapter 7, "Rediscovering the Earliest Biblical Interpreters," and chapter 11, "Rediscovering Classic Ecumenic Method." My only promise — constantly repeated since the seventies — is that I will say nothing new or personally creative, hoping to add nothing to the ever-new creativity of God the Spirit in speaking to us through the written Word, which does not come back void.

The Text: No Other Gods

Narrowing the range for my task today, I will take a single verse of Scripture, Exodus 20:3, and track its interpretation, first back through the consensus documents of the magisterial Reformation tradition, then comparing this to the Fathers, and then back to references to the "no other gods" text in the New Testament itself, letting its relevance for today speak for itself. This proceeds under three headings:

   I. The First Command of the Decalogue
  II. The First Command as Interpreted in the New Testament, Viewed through Ancient Consensual Exegesis
 III. Pastoral Applications

2. IVP, 1997-.
3. Grand Rapids: Eerdmans, 2002.
4. Harper San Francisco, 2003.

I. The First Command of the Decalogue

The text: The first commandment — "You shall have no other gods before me" (Exod. 20:3).

In the *Book of Concord* of Augsburg, you will find Luther's *Large
Catechism,* which stands as a normative teaching of Protestant faith,
quoted and extracted frequently in the Anglican and Reformed traditions. It begins by treating:

1. The Meaning of "Having a God." "What is it to have a god?"
asks Luther. "What is God? Answer: A god is that to which we look for
all good and in which we find refuge in every time of need. To have a
god is nothing else than to trust and believe him with our whole heart.
As I have often said, the trust and faith of the heart alone make both
God and an idol. If your faith and trust are right, then your God is the
true God. On the other hand, if your trust is false and wrong, then you
have not the true God. For these two belong together, faith and God.
That to which your heart clings and entrusts itself is, I say, really your
God."[5] Example: If someone has "great learning, wisdom, power, pres-
tige, family, and honor, and trusts in them, he also has a god, but not
the one, true God" (p. 366).

The true God is the one who incomparably is. Even his name
may be spoken only with awe, if at all, as a mystery: YHWH. A
"strange god" is any creature falsely elevated to claim this holiness of
itself. Anything in creation may be trusted as the center of value: social
status, money, education, and even children (whom we are to care for,
not worship) and parents (whom we are to honor but not worship). In
fact, it is the best in creation that is most tempting to pretend to make
into a god.

An idol is not just an object one can "stick away in one's purse"
(says Luther) or slip into one's chest of drawers. Idolatry "is primarily
in the heart, which pursues other things and seeks help and consolation from creatures" (p. 367). Idolatry "neither cares for God nor expects good things from him sufficiently to trust that he wants to help,

---

5. *Book of Concord* (1580), ed. T. G. Tappert (Philadelphia: Muhlenberg, 1959),
p. 365, quoting Luther's *Large Catechism* from the widely followed *Book of Concord*
so as to establish it as a document consensually received and followed, rather than
as an expression of individual opinion. Parenthetical references in the following
text are to the *Book of Concord.*

nor does it believe that whatever good it receives comes from God." The first commandment from the outset teaches how one shall meet God inwardly in the heart, so as to trust him as a child trusts his father.

Idolatry, according to Luther and the Reformers, is always in league with works righteousness. Finally, it seeks comfort and salvation in its own works and merits. It "presumes to wrest heaven from God. It keeps account how often it has made endowments, fasted, celebrated Mass, etc. On such things it relies and of them it boasts, unwilling to receive anything as a gift from God, but desiring by itself to earn or merit everything" (p. 367).

2. How Do I Know I Am Standing before the True God? Every believer every day is called to "examine your own heart thoroughly and you will find whether or not it clings to God alone. . . . Do you have the kind of heart that expects from him nothing but good, especially in distress and want, and renounces and forsakes all that is not God? Then you have the one true God. On the contrary, does your heart cling to something else, from which it hopes to receive more good and help than from God, and does it flee not to him but from him when things go wrong? Then you have an idol, another god" (p. 368).

3. Clear Warnings and Benevolent Promises Accompany the Command. "In order to show that this command is not to be taken lightly," YHWH attaches to it "first, a terrible threat, and then a beautiful, comforting promise" (p. 368). Here Luther adds an "Explanation of the Appendix to the First Commandment," which Calvin classifies as the second commandment, Exodus 20:4-5: "You shall not make for yourself a graven image, or any likeness of anything that is in heaven above, or that is in the earth beneath, or that is in the water under the earth" — that is, worship nothing in the created order. "For I the LORD your God am a jealous God, visiting the iniquity of the fathers upon the children to the third and the fourth generation of those who hate me." This is no laughing matter. Those who "hate me" are "those who persist in their stubbornness and pride. They refuse to hear what is preached. . . . We observe this every day in the case of bishops and princes" (p. 369).

By these warnings and promises, God "wishes to turn us away from everything else, and to draw us to himself, because he is the one, eternal good" (p. 366).

The classic exegetes asked:

4. Why Does the Lord God Describe Himself as a Jealous God? What is God teaching us when he announces himself as jealous, asks Origen. "Just as the bridegroom who wishes to make his bride live chastely so as to give her entirely to him and beware of any relationship whatever with any man other than her husband, pretends, though he be wise, to be jealous." In this way God is said to be provoked to jealousy whenever we worship other gods. Even more dramatically Calvin likens our idolatry to "a shameless woman who brings in an adulterer before her husband's very eyes only to vex his mind the more."[6]

5. Our Acts of Idolatry Are Always Obvious to God. God here makes it clear that "whatever we undertake, whatever we attempt, whatever we make, comes into his sight." Worshiping a strange god is an act that takes place blatantly "before my face" — God's own face and majesty. "For the Lord requires that the glory of his divinity remain whole and uncorrupted not only in our outward confession," says Calvin, "but in his own eyes, which gaze upon the most secret recesses of our hearts."[7] Origen calls us "to understand such words from the Scriptures in a reasonable manner, which were spoken metaphorically from the human viewpoint to set forth the fact that God wishes nothing alien to his will to be mingled with the soul."[8] There can be no third partner in this decisive I-Thou encounter. God will "vindicate his majesty and glory against any who may transfer it to creatures,"[9] and this too extends to the fourth generation when reinforced. My great-grandchildren may hear the echoes of my present idolatrous choices. These echoes can be studied psychoanalytically, or in intergenerational history, or sociologically.

6. The Promise to Subsequent Generations. But happily there is more: "Terrible as these threats are, much mightier is the comfort in

---

6. Calvin, *Institutes of the Christian Religion,* Library of Christian Classics 20-21, 26 vols. (Philadelphia: Westminster, 1953-61), 2.8.16. References are to book, chapter, and section numbers.

7. Calvin, *Institutes* 2.8.16.

8. Origen, *Commentary on the Gospel of John* 10.221, in Fathers of the Church, ed. R. J. Deferrari (Washington, D.C.: Catholic University of America Press, 1947-), 80:303; *Ancient Christian Commentary on Scripture,* ed. T. Oden (Downers Grove, Ill.: InterVarsity, 1998-), OT 3:103 (hereafter *ACCS*).

9. Calvin, *Institutes* 2.8.16.

the promise that assures mercy to those who cling to God alone," a blessing extending to "thousands of generations" if followed rightly,[10] "showing steadfast love to thousands of those who love me and keep my commandments" (Exod. 20:6). This "impels us to fix our hearts upon God with perfect confidence since the divine Majesty comes to us with so gracious an offer, so cordial an invitation, and so rich a promise."[11]

Here we learn how angry, so to speak, God is with those who rely on anything but his demonstrated self-giving grace once for all manifested on the cross, and yet "how kind and gracious he is to those who trust and believe him alone with their whole heart." We have the whole of experienced history to observe how these admonitions and promises in fact work themselves out concretely, where in God's own time, God indeed does root out "all false worship so that all who persist in it must ultimately perish."[12] The consequence of heeding this commandment brings "either eternal blessing, happiness, and salvation, or eternal wrath, misery, and woe."[13]

7. Why This Commandment Stands in the First Place before All the Others. These warnings and promises apply to all the commandments, but "are attached precisely to this one which stands at the head of the list because it is of the utmost importance for a man to have the right head. For where the head is right, the whole life must be right, and vice versa."[14] "Where the heart is right with God and this commandment is kept, fulfillment of all the others will follow of its own accord."[15] All the commands of the second table of law follow from the first, whose primary requirement is "no other gods." This is fitting since we had a Maker to love before we had a neighbor to love. It cannot be expected that one can be true to his neighbor who is false to God.[16]

8. Prayer Rightly Conceived Begins with the First Commandment. What we as supplicants owe to God under this command is

10. *Book of Concord*, p. 370.
11. *Book of Concord*, p. 370.
12. *Book of Concord*, p. 369.
13. *Book of Concord*, p. 370.
14. *Book of Concord*, p. 369.
15. *Book of Concord*, p. 370.
16. Matthew Henry, *Commentary*, vol. 1, on Exod. 20:3.

grouped in four points by Calvin: adoration, trust, invocation, and thanksgiving. The Lord does not permit any of these to be transferred to a creature. He commands that all worship be rendered wholly to himself.[17]

9. Who Is Speaking in This Command? The commandment is preceded by the personal disclosure and self-identification of the holy one who gives the command, who alone "shows himself to be the one who has the right to command."[18] Notice that he does not constrain us by his sheer might. Rather he attracts us by recollecting a historical memory of actual gracious events. "I am the LORD your God, who brought you out of the land of Egypt, out of the house of bondage" (Exod. 20:2), who promises: "I will be their God, and they shall be my people" (Jer. 31:33). He speaks with the unique authority of the one who has already shown in history his absolute trustworthiness.

Hence: "Our duty to God is, in one word, to worship him, that is, to give to him the glory due to his name" and very nature, extending from the inward worship of our affections to the outward attendance upon common worship and the ministries of Word and sacrament.[19]

The command draws a firm line between any "strange god" and the incomparable One who speaks the command. "And who is the strange god?" asks Gregory of Nyssa: "Surely, any who are alien from the nature of the true God."[20] Those who worship strange gods "apply to inanimate and senseless matter the name of the Lord God."[21]

II. The First Command as Interpreted in the New Testament, Viewed through Ancient Consensual Exegesis

There are many layers of the Gospels and Epistles that assume and work off of the command to have no other gods, but three particularly

17. Calvin, *Institutes* 2.8.16.
18. Calvin, *Institutes* 2.8.14.
19. Matthew Henry, vol. 1, on Exod. 20:3.
20. Gregory of Nyssa, *On the Faith,* in Nicene and Post-Nicene Fathers, ser. 2, 28 vols., ed. P. Schaff et al. (Grand Rapids: Eerdmans, 1952), 5:337 (quotation retranslated); *ACCS,* OT 3:102.
21. Origen, *Exhortation to Martyrdom* 6, in Ancient Christian Writers 19:146; *ACCS,* OT 3:102.

stand out (1 Cor. 10; 1 Cor. 8; Matt. 28). I will leave it to the earliest biblical interpreters, the ancient Christian writers, to set forth the consensual classic Christian interpretation of our text.

1. 1 Corinthians 10:14.

Shun the Worship of Idols. Paul writes that "We provoke the Lord to jealousy" (1 Cor. 10:22) when we try to partake of the table of demons and also of the table of the Lord. Hence the beloved are urgently warned by Paul to "shun the worship of idols" (10:14). "When the apostle says 'Flee from the worship of idols,' he means idolatry whole and entire. Look closely at a thicket and see how many thorns lie hidden beneath the leaves."[22] Those who are tempted and fascinated by idolatry will come to expect something from nothing, and this is what turns us away from full reliance upon God's grace.[23] In the struggle with our idolatries, we are called to pray for grace that we may not rely strictly upon our own wills to resist idolatrous temptations.[24] Better to do what lovers do, says Chrysostom — voluntarily "turn our eyes away from all other loves."[25] "The soul selects her own society" (Emily Dickinson).

2. In 1 Corinthians 8:4-7, Paul teaches that:

An Idol Has No Real Existence, but Only an Exaggerated Pretense of Being. Here Paul shows how precarious is the actual status of the gods within time and space, and how decisively they differ from the true God, who incomparably is. He points out the irony of the nonbeing of fantasized beings. In discussing food offered to idols, Paul writes that "we know that 'an idol has no real existence'" (8:4a). Origen explains: "An idol is nothing. One who makes an idol makes what is not. But what is that which is not? A form which the eye does not see but which the mind imagines for itself."[26] What are idols but

22. Tertullian, *The Chaplet* 10, in Fathers of the Church 40:254 (quotation retranslated); *ACCS*, NT 7:97.

23. Ambrosiaster, *Commentary on Paul's Epistles*, Corpus Scriptorum Ecclesiasticorum Latinorum 81:113; *ACCS*, NT 7:97.

24. Augustine, *Letter 179*, to Bishop John, in Fathers of the Church 30:113; *ACCS*, NT 7:96.

25. Chrysostom, *Homilies, Corinthians* 24.3, in Nicene and Post-Nicene Fathers, ser. 1, 12:139; *ACCS*, NT 7:97.

26. Origen, *Homilies on Exodus* 8.3, in Fathers of the Church 71:321; *ACCS*, NT 7:75.

things, as Scripture says, which "have eyes and see not"?[27] "Worship is proper only to the one who is God by nature."[28]

There Is No God but One. Paul continues: we know that "'there is no God but one.' For although there may be so-called gods in heaven or on earth — as indeed there are many 'gods' and many 'lords' . . ." Theodore of Mopsuestia notes further: "Paul says 'so-called' here because he is showing that they [these imagined gods] do not really exist," except in our idolatrous imagination destined for judgment.[29] Continuing: "yet for us there is one God" — "We say 'one' to stop anyone dreaming that there even could be another."[30]

What human imagination imagines as gods, though many, are utterly different from the one true God. "'There is no God but one' . . . — the Father, from whom are all things and for whom we exist" (8:4-6a). Here we see once again how the New Testament serves as a midrash on our Old Testament text in the light of what has happened in Jesus Christ. All of this is grounded in:

Triune Reasoning. 1 Corinthians 8:6b: There is no God but one, who is Father, "and one Lord, Jesus Christ, through whom are all things and in whom we exist," who ministers to us through his Holy Spirit. The consensual exegetes view this as a crucial text for unifying triune reasoning concerning the one God in three persons. In book 1, chapter 13 of his treatise on the Trinity, Augustine comments: "'From whom' means from the Father. 'Through whom' means through the Son. 'In whom' means in the Holy Spirit. It is self-evident that the Father, the Son and the Holy Spirit are one God."[31] Seen in the light of the fulfillment in the New Testament of the promises of the Old, this gift comes by one God the Father from whom all things exist, God the Son through whom all things are, and God the Spirit in whom we ourselves are brought to participate in God's holy love so as to trust him fully.

27. Augustine, *City of God* 8, in Fathers of the Church 14:68 (quotation retranslated); *ACCS*, NT 7:76.

28. Cyril of Alexandria, *Festal Letter* 8.6, in Sources chrétiennes 392:106; *ACCS*, NT 8:255.

29. Theodore of Mopsuestia, *Pauline Commentary from the Greek Church*, in NTA 15:182-84.

30. Cyril of Jerusalem, *Catechetical Lectures* 10.3, in Library of Christian Classics 4:311; *ACCS*, NT 7:76.

31. Fathers of the Church 45:16 (quotation retranslated); *ACCS*, 7:76.

This is what faith knows that unfaith does not grasp: despite the many so-called gods, "we know there is no God but one." "So all things are rightly ascribed to God since it is by him and in him and for him that all things exist, are co-ordered, remain, hold together, are completed and are returned."[32]

"However," notes Paul, "not all possess this knowledge" (1 Cor. 8:7a). "But some, through being hitherto accustomed to idols, eat food as really offered to an idol; and their conscience, being weak, is defiled. Food will not commend us to God. We are no worse off if we do not eat, and no better off if we do. Only take care lest the liberty of yours somehow become a stumbling block to the weak. For if any one sees you, a man of knowledge, at table in an idol's temple, might he not be encouraged, if his conscience is weak, to eat food offered to idols?" (8:7-10 RSV).

3. The Mystery of the True God Is Named in Baptism, Matthew 28:19.

Ambrose writes: "It is written (in Matthew's Gospel): 'Go baptize the nations in the name of the Father, and of the Son, and of the Holy Spirit.' 'In the name' [singular], he said, not 'in the names [plural].' . . . there is one God, not several names, because there are not two gods, not three gods."[33] Tritheists would have to baptize in the names of the gods, but from apostolic times Christians baptize in the name of the one God, Father, Son, and Spirit. Here *lex orandi, lex credendi* applies: we believe as we pray in baptism. The liturgical tradition shapes the doctrinal tradition.

4. What Do We Learn about the Old Testament from the New?

Through the eyes of the apostles we can now see that the one God to be worshiped as true God has met us in due course as Father, Son, and Spirit, so we can now trust him as a child trusts a caring, providing father. God the Father has taken up the cause of sinners on the cross through the Son, and this mission is now being completed in the Holy Spirit. Thus what the law requires, the gospel enables. The law teaches us what we ought to do. The gospel gives us the power to do it.

32. Pseudo-Dionysius, *The Divine Names* 980, CWS 129; *ACCS*, NT 7:76.
33. Ambrose, *The Holy Spirit* 13.132, in Fathers of the Church 44:83 (quotation retranslated); *ACCS*, NT 7:78.

III. Pastoral Applications

1. *Avoiding Temptation to Specific Offenses*

The most frequent and defining sin against the first commandment is "giving the glory and honor to any creature which are due to God only. Pride makes a god of self, covetousness makes a god of the belly; whatever is esteemed or loved, feared or served, delighted in or depended on, more than God, that (whatever it is) we do in effect make a god of."[34]

In and following late medieval scholasticism, as distinguished from the Fathers, a detailed study of particular cases of pastoral care was made on the first commandment, listing numerous specific offenses that are rooted in the neglect of the head command. Luther himself, despite his complaints against casuistry, goes fairly deeply into the specific ways we offend against the command. Here are some of them:

One worships a strange god, according to Luther, who "glories in his own piety, his wisdom, or other spiritual gifts . . . who does not trust in God at all times, and is not confident of God's mercy in all he does . . . who doubts concerning the faith or the grace of God." Among transgressions against the first commandment, Luther did not hesitate to point as illustrations not only to sorcery, witchcraft, following the zodiac, and fortune-telling, but also "He who blames his misfortunes and tribulations on the devil, or on wicked men, and does not accept them, with praise and love, as good and evil which come from God alone."[35]

The pastoral tradition often cites four notable, frequent cases of temptation to offend against the command to "have other gods":

2. *Superstition, Irreverence, Sacrilege, and Simony: Offenses against the Command*

In much traditional Christian moral reasoning, couched in the language of virtue, one may sin against the first commandment either by

---

34. Matthew Henry, *Commentary*, vol. 1.
35. Luther, "Brief Explanation," 2:358-59.

defect or excess, either by omission of some act God's holy love requires or by false worship of the one true God. Thus superstition, irreverence, sacrilege, and simony are typically discussed in pastoral handbooks under the rubric of offenses against the first commandment. All remain temptations in the contemporary church, insofar as false and idolatrous teaching seeks ways of mixing itself with classic Christian teaching.

Superstition consists of an excess of religion, where worship seizes upon false claims or exaggerated promises. This is especially characterized by a false worship of the true God or what may seem sincere worship of a false god. Whenever God is worshiped in a false way, mingling something false with that which is true in giving our adoration, we are worshiping a strange god.

Irreverence is the opposite of superstition, consisting in a deficit of the Spirit-led life, where worship is inattentive to God's warnings and promises. The excellence of holy living is violated by lack of due awe and reverence toward God. For example, it is irreverent to challenge God to produce signs and wonders on our mere whim. This is traditionally called tempting God, an offense against God's power, wisdom, and love.

Sacrilege occurs by dishonoring the sacred, violation of a person, place, or thing publicly dedicated to God and set aside for a sacred purpose. In a broad sense, every sin of every baptized believer is a sacrilege because "your members are the temple of the Holy Spirit." Sacrilege may be committed by unworthy reception of the means of grace; by unchastity committed by or with persons consecrated to God in Holy Orders; by unworthy treatment of a sacred place; by unbecoming treatment of holy things, such as use of chalices or sacred vessels at a drinking party; by improper or deceptive use of the words of Holy Scripture; by burning a church out of racial hatred; or by using money raised to help such a church for other purposes (as we saw happen when the National Council of Churches raised funds for the repair of burned Afro-American churches, but used them for pension funding).

Simony is the will to buy or sell a spiritual thing for temporal gain. This is viewed as an offense against the command to have no other gods.

Accordingly superstition, irreverence, sacrilege, and simony all are continuing obstacles to the life of having "no other gods" in our time: superstition, as seen in exaggerated and manipulative excesses of ministries of healing; irreverence, as seen in the desensitization of our society to acts of immodesty; sacrilege, as seen in the twisting of Scriptures to mean their opposite; and simony, as seen in the clergy's willingness to receive salaries for disseminating doctrines contrary to the Christian faith.

Conclusion: The Humble Status of "the Gods" on the Last Day.

Earlier we read in Exodus 20:4: "You shall not make for yourself a graven image, or any likeness of anything that is in heaven above, or that is in the earth beneath, or that is in the water under the earth" — that is, nothing in the created order is to be trusted as the source and center and end of all creaturely values. Philippians 2 looks precisely to that end of history when all the stories of all humans individually and collectively will be consummated. If the present time is rightly viewed from the vantage point of the end of time, there finally all creatures will properly worship the true God. Ultimately, in God's own time, God's glory will be brought to right recognition. In Philippians this appears in this form: on the last day it will occur that the true God will be truly worshiped, when "at the name of Jesus every knee should bow, in heaven and on earth and under the earth, and every tongue confess that Jesus Christ is Lord, to the glory of God the Father" (Phil. 2:10-11).

All the so-called gods will, so to speak, bend the knee to the only one due true worship, the only one worthy of the name God. But do not read this woodenly: "What spirit has knees?" asks Origen. "The bending of the knees indicates that all is in subjection and observes the worship of God."[36]

Athanasius summed it up: "The glory of the Father is that the human race not only was created but was re-created when lost, given life once again when dead, so as to become a renewed temple of God. For the powers in heaven also, the angels and the archangels, worship him and now worship the Lord in the name of Jesus. . . . The heavenly powers are not offended when they behold all of us being led into our heavenly abode as we share in his body. This could not have happened

---

36. Origen, *Commentary on Romans* 9.41, Patrologia Graeca 14:1243C; *ACCS*, NT 8:254.

in any other way. It happened only because, being in the form of God and taking the form of a slave, he humbled himself," dying for our sins on the cross.[37]

37. Athanasius, *Against the Arians* 1.42, in *Orations of Saint Athanasius* 43-44 (Oxford: Clarendon, 1871) (quotation retranslated); *ACCS*, NT 8:256.

God or Nothingness

David Bentley Hart

I

As modern men and women — to the degree that we are modern — we believe in nothing. This is not to say, I hasten to add, that we do not believe in anything; I mean, rather, that we hold an unshakable, if often unconscious, faith in *the* nothing, or in nothingness as such. It is this in which we place our trust, upon which we venture our souls, and onto which we project the values by which we measure the meaningfulness of our lives. Or, to phrase the matter more simply and starkly, our religion is one of very comfortable nihilism.

This may seem a somewhat apocalyptic note to sound, at least without any warning or emollient prelude, but I believe I am saying nothing not almost tediously obvious. We live in an age whose chief moral value has been determined, by overwhelming consensus, to be the absolute liberty of personal volition, the power of each of us to choose what he or she believes, wants, needs, or must possess; our culturally most persuasive models of human freedom are unambiguously voluntarist and, in a rather debased and degraded way, Promethean; the will, we believe, is sovereign because unpremised, free because spontaneous, and this is the highest good. And a society that believes this must, at least implicitly, embrace and subtly advocate a very particular moral metaphysics: the unreality of any "value" higher than choice, or of any transcendent Good ordering desire toward a higher

end. Desire is free to propose, seize, accept or reject, want or not want
— but not to obey. Thus society must be secured against the intrusions
of the Good, or of God, so that its citizens may determine their own
lives by the choices they make from a universe of morally indifferent
but variably desirable ends unencumbered by any prior grammar of
obligation or value (in America, we call this the "wall of separation").
Thus the liberties that permit one to purchase lavender bedclothes, to
gaze pensively at pornography, to become Unitarian, to market popular celebrations of brutal violence, or to destroy one's unborn child are
all equally intrinsically "good" because all are expressions of an in-
alienable freedom of choice. But, of course, if the will determines itself
only in and through such choices, free from any prevenient natural order, then it too is in itself nothing. And so, at the end of modernity each
of us who is true to the times stands thus, facing not God, or the gods,
or the Good beyond beings, but an abyss, over which presides the
empty, inviolable authority of the individual will, whose impulses and
decisions are their own moral index, and so in a sense precede the objects in which the will manifests its mysterious powers of election and
dereliction.

This is not to say that — sentimental barbarians that we are — we
do not still invite moral and religious constraints upon our actions;
none but the most demonic, demented, or adolescent among us genuinely desires to live in a world purged of visible boundaries and hospi-
table shelters. Thus this man may elect not to buy a particular vehicle
because he considers himself an environmentalist; or this woman may
choose not to have an abortion midway through her second trimester,
because the fetus, at that point in its gestation, seems to her too fully
formed, and she — personally — would feel wrong about terminating
"it." But this merely illustrates my point: we take as given the individual's right not merely to obey or defy the moral law, but to choose
which moral standards to adopt, which values to uphold, which fashion of piety to wear and with what accessories. Even our ethics are
achievements of will.[1] And the same is true of those custom-fitted

---

1. The fundamentally incoherent and even nonsensical use of the language
of ethics in the absence of the traditions of discourse that makes such language intelligible is compellingly described in the opening chapter of Alasdair MacIntyre's
After Virtue: A Study in Moral Theory, 2nd ed. (Notre Dame: University of Notre
Dame Press, 1984).

spiritualities — "New Age," occult, pantheist, "Wiccan," or what have you — by which many of us now divert ourselves from the quotidian dreariness of our lives. These gods of the boutique can come from anywhere — native North American religion, the Indian subcontinent, some Pre-Raphaelite grove shrouded in Celtic twilight, cunning purveyors of otherwise worthless quartz, pages drawn at random from Robert Graves, Aldous Huxley, Carl Jung, or that redoubtable old Aryan Joseph Campbell — but where such gods inevitably come to rest are not so much divine hierarchies as ornamental étagères, where their principal office is to provide symbolic representations of the dreamier sides of their votaries' personalities. The triviality of this sort of devotion, its want of dogma or discipline, its tendency to find its divinities not in glades and grottoes but in gift shops make it obvious that this is no reversion to pre-Christian polytheism. It is, rather, a thoroughly modern religion, whose burlesque gods command neither reverence, nor dread, nor love, nor belief; they are no more than the masks worn by that same spontaneity of will that is the one unrivaled demiurge who rules this age, and alone bids its spirits come and go.

Which brings me at last to my topic. "I am the Lord thy God," says the first commandment. "Thou shalt have no other gods before me." For Israel this was first and foremost a demand of fidelity, by which God bound his people to himself, even if in later years it became also a proclamation to the nations. To Christians, however, the commandment came through — and so was indissolubly bound to — Christ. As such, it was not simply a prohibition of foreign cults, but a call to arms, an assault upon the antique order of the heavens — a declaration of war upon the gods. All the world was to be evangelized and baptized, all idols torn down, all worship given over to the one God who, in these latter days, had sent his Son into the world for our salvation. It was a long and sometimes terrible conflict, occasionally exacting a fearful price in martyrs' blood, but it was, by any just estimate, a victory: the temples of Zeus and Isis alike were finally deserted, both the paean and the dithyramb ceased to be sung, altars were bereft of their sacrifices, the sibyls fell silent, and ultimately all the glory, nobility, and cruelty of the ancient world lay supine at the feet of Christ the conqueror. Nor, for early Christians, was this mere metaphor. When a Gentile convert stood in the baptistery on Easter's eve and, before descending naked into the waters, turned to the west to renounce the devil and devil's ministers, he was rejecting, and in fact reviling, the gods in bondage to whom he had languished all his life; and when he turned to the east to confess Christ, he was entrusting himself to the invincible hero who had plundered hell of its captives, overthrown death, subdued the powers of the air, and been raised the Lord of history. Life, for the early church, was spiritual warfare, and no baptized Christian could doubt how great a transformation — of the self and the world — it was to consent to serve no other god than him whom Christ revealed.

We are still at war, of course, but the situation of the church has materially altered, and I suspect that by comparison to the burden the first commandment lays upon us today, the defeat of the ancient pantheon, and the elemental spirits, and the demons lurking behind them will prove to have been sublimely easy. For, as I say, we moderns believe in nothing: the nothingness of the will miraculously giving itself form by mastering the nothingness of the world. The gods, at least, were real, if distorted, intimations of the *mysterium tremendum,* and so could inspire something like holy dread or, occasionally, holy love. They were brutes, obviously, but often also benign despots, and all of us, I think, in those secret corners of our souls where all of us are monarchists, can appreciate a good despot, if he is sufficiently dashing and mysterious, and able to strike an attractive balance between capricious wrath and serene benevolence. Certainly the Olympians had panache, and a terrible beauty whose disappearance from the world was a bereavement to obdurately devout pagans. Moreover, in their very objectivity and supremacy over their worshipers, the gods gave the church enemies with whom it could come to grips. Perhaps they were just so many gaudy veils and ornate brocades drawn across the abyss of night, death, and nature, but they had distinct shapes and established cults, and when their mysteries were abandoned so were they. How, though, to make war on nothingness, on the abyss itself, denuded of its mythic allure? It seems to me much easier to convince a man that he is in thrall to demons and offer him manumission than to convince him he is a slave to himself and prisoner to his own will. Here is a god more elusive, protean, and indomitable than either Apollo or Dionysus; and whether he manifests himself in some demonic titanism of the will, like the mass delirium of the Third Reich, or simply in the mesmeric banality of consumer culture, his throne has been set in the very hearts of those he enslaves. And it is this god, I think, against whom the first commandment calls us now to struggle.

There is, however, a complication even to this. As Christians, we are glad to assert that the commandment to have no other god, when allied to the gospel, liberated us from the divine ancien régime; or that this same commandment must be proclaimed again if modern persons are to be rescued from the superstitions of our age; but there is another, more uncomfortable assertion we should also be willing to make: that humanity could not have passed from the devotions of antiquity to those of modernity but for the force of Christianity in history, and so — as a matter of historical fact — Christianity, with its cry of "no other god," is in part responsible for the nihilism of our culture. The gospel shook the ancient world to its foundations, indeed tore down the heavens, and so helped to bring us to the ruin of the present moment.

II

Lest that last remark sound too impious, I had better dilate upon it. With the reader's indulgence, I shall therefore undertake something of an excursus.

The word "nihilism" has a complex history in modern philosophy, but I use it in a sense largely determined by Nietzsche and Heidegger,[2] both of whom not only diagnosed modernity as nihilism, but saw Christianity as complicit in its genesis; both, it seems to me, were penetratingly correct in some respects, if disastrously wrong in most, and both raised questions we Christians ignore at our peril.

2. In part, I am influenced also by Gianni Vattimo's recent reflections on the relation of Christian doctrine to nihilism; see, for instance, Vattimo, *Belief,* trans. Luca D'Isanto and David Webb (Stanford: Stanford University Press, 1999); and Vattimo, "The Trace of the Trace," in *Religion,* ed. Jacques Derrida and Gianni Vattimo (Stanford: Stanford University Press, 1998). Vattimo's interpretation of this relation is defective, simply because he is, by his own avowal, himself quite a cheerful and tenderhearted nihilist; as a result, he can make some sense of the Christian doctrine of *kenosis,* but has nothing to say of Christ's exaltation, and so ends up in a place perilously close to the comical banalities of the old "death of God" theologies. I should also mention the very interesting book by Marcel Gauchet, *The Disenchantment of the World: A Political History of Religion,* trans. Oscar Burge (Princeton: Princeton University Press, 1997).

Nietzsche's case is the cruder of the two, if in some ways the more perspicacious; for him modernity is simply the final phase of the disease called Christianity. Whereas the genius of the Greeks — so his story goes — was to gaze without illusion into the chaos and terror of the world, and respond not with fear or resignation but with affirmation and supreme artistry, they were able to do this only on account of their nobility, which means their ruthless willingness to discriminate between the "good" — that is, the strength, exuberance, bravery, generosity, and harshness of the aristocratic spirit — and the "bad" — the weakness, debility, timorousness, and vindictive resentfulness of the slavish mind. And this same standard — "noble wisdom," for want of a better term — was the foundation and mortar of Roman civilization. Christianity, however, was a slave-revolt in morality: the cunning of the weak triumphed over the nobility of the strong, the resentment of the many converted the pride of the few into self-torturing guilt, the higher man's distinction between the good and the bad was replaced by the lesser man's spiteful distinction between good and "evil," and the tragic wisdom of the Greeks sank beneath the flood of Christianity's pity and pusillanimity. This revolt, then, joined to an ascetic and sterile devotion to positive fact, would ultimately slay even God. And as a result we have now entered the age of the Last Men, whom Nietzsche depicts in terms too close for comfort to the banality, conformity, and self-indulgence of modern mass culture.

Heidegger's tale is not as catastrophist, and so emphasizes less Christianity's novelty than its continuity with a nihilism implicit in all Western thought, from at least the time of Plato (which Nietzsche, in his way, also acknowledged). Nihilism, says Heidegger, is born in a forgetfulness of the mystery of being, and in the attempt to capture and master being in artifacts of reason (the chief example — and indeed the prototype of every subsequent apostasy from true "ontology" — being Plato's ideas). Scandalously to oversimplify his argument, it is — says Heidegger — the history of this nihilistic impulse to reduce being to an object of the intellect, subject to the will, that has brought us at last to the age of technology, for which reality is just so many quanta of power, the world a representation of consciousness, and the earth a mere reserve awaiting exploitation; technological mastery has become our highest ideal, and our only real model of truth. Christianity, for its part, is not so much a new thing as a prolonged episode within the greater history of nihilism, notable chiefly for having brought part of this history's logic to its consummation by having invented the metaphysical God, the form of all forms, who grounds all of being in himself as absolute efficient cause, and who personifies that cause as total power and will. From this God, in the fullness of time, would be born the modern subject who has usurped God's place.

I hope I will be excused both for so cursory a précis and for the mild perversity that causes me to see some merit in both of these stories. Heidegger seems to me obviously correct in regarding modernity's nihilism as the fruition of seeds sown in pagan soil, and Nietzsche correct to call attention to Christianity's shocking — and, for the antique order of noble values, irreparably catastrophic — novelty, but neither grasped why he was correct. For indeed Christianity was complicit in the death of antiquity and birth of modernity, not because it was an accomplice of the latter but because it alone, in the history of the West, was a rejection of and alternative to nihilism's despair, violence, and idolatry of power; as such, Christianity shattered the imposing and enchanting facade behind which nihilism once hid, and thereby, inadvertently, called it forth into the open.

I am speaking (impressionistically, I grant) of something pervasive in the ethos of European antiquity, which I would call a kind of glorious sadness. The great Indo-European mythos, from which Western culture sprang, was chiefly one of sacrifice: it understood the cosmos as a closed system, a finite totality, within which gods and mortals alike occupied places determined by fate; and this totality was of necessity an economy, a cycle of creation and destruction, oscillating between order and chaos, form and indeterminacy: a great circle of feeding, preserving life through a system of transactions with death. This is the myth of "cosmos" — of the universe as a precarious equilibrium of contrary forces — which undergirded a sacral practice whose aim was to contain nature's promiscuous violence within religion's orderly violence. The terrible dynamism of nature had to be both resisted and controlled, by rites at once apotropaic — appeasing chaos and rationalizing it within the stability of cult — and economic — recuperating its sacrificial expenditures in the form of divine favor, a numinous power reinforcing the regime sacrifice served. And this regime was, naturally, a fixed hierarchy of social power, atop which stood the gods, a little lower kings and nobles, and at the bottom slaves; the order of society, both divine and natural in provenance, was a fixed and yet somehow fragile "hierarchy within totality" that had to be preserved against the forces that surrounded it, while yet drawing on those forces for its spiritual sustenance. Gods and mortals were bound together by necessity; we fed the gods, who required our sacrifices, and they preserved us from the forces they personified and granted us some measure of their power. There was, surely, an ineradicable nihilism in such an economy: a tragic resignation before fate, followed by a prudential act of cultic salvage, for the sake of social and cosmic stability.

As it happens, the word "tragic" is especially apt here. A sacrificial mythos need not always express itself in slaughter, after all. Attic tragedy, for instance, began as a sacrificial rite. It was performed during the festival of Dionysus, which was a fertility festival of course, but only because it was also an apotropaic celebration of delirium and death: the *Dionysia* was a sacred negotiation with the wild, antinomian cruelty of the god whose violent orgiastic cult had once, so it was believed, gravely imperiled the city; and the hope that prompted the feast was that if this devastating force could be contained within bright Apollonian forms and propitiated through a ritual carnival of controlled disorder, the polis could survive for another year, its precarious peace intact.[3] The religious vision from which Attic tragedy emerged was one of the human community as a kind of besieged citadel preserving itself through the tribute it paid to the powers that both threatened and enlivened it. I can think of no better example than the *Antigone,* in which the tragic crisis is the result of an insoluble moral conflict between familial piety (a sacred obligation) and the civil duties of kingship (a holy office): Antigone, as a woman, is bound to the chthonian gods (gods of the dead, so of family and household), and Creon, as king, is bound to Apollo (god of the city), and so both are adhering to sacred obligations. The conflict between them, then, far from involving a tension between the profane and the

3. I am not merely repeating the argument of Nietzsche's *Birth of Tragedy,* though I confess I find his dialectic between the Apollonian and Dionysian (which he would himself soon abandon) difficult to resist, at least as a kind of heuristic device. It is worth noting, in passing, that at least one ancient commentator on the myths and liturgies of the gods sees the "tension" between Apollo and Dionysus as disguising a secret identity between the two: Macrobius, *Saturnalia* 1.18.1ff. From a Christian perspective, this is almost obviously true; pagan myths of order or of chaos are, after all, simply the two sides of a single pagan myth, cosmic, religious, political, and moral.

holy, is a conflict within the divine itself, whose only possible resolution is the death — the sacrifice — of the protagonist. And other examples are legion. Necessity's cruel intransigence rules the gods no less than us; tragedy's great power is simply to reconcile us to this truth, to what must be, and to the violences of the city that keep at bay the greater violence of cosmic or social disorder.

Nor does one require extraordinarily penetrating insight to see how the shadow of this mythos falls across the philosophical schools of antiquity. To risk a generalization even more reckless than those I have already made: from the time of the pre-Socratics, all the great speculative and moral systems of the pagan world were in varying degrees confined to this totality, to either its innermost mechanisms or outermost boundaries; rarely did any of them catch even a glimpse of what might lie beyond such a world; and none could conceive of reality except as a kind of strife between order and disorder, within which a sacrificial economy held all forces in tension. This is true even of Platonism, with its inextirpable dualism, its dialectic of change and the changeless (or of limit and the infinite), and its equation of truth with eidetic abstraction; the world, for all its beauty, is the realm of fallen vision, separated by a great *chorismos* from the realm of immutable reality. It is true of Aristotle too: the dialectic of act and potency that — for sublunary beings — is inseparable from decay and death, or the scale of essences by which all things — especially various classes of persons — are assigned their places in the natural and social order. Stoicism offers an obvious example: a vision of the universe as a fated, eternally repeated divine and cosmic history, a world in which finite forms must constantly perish simply to make room for others, and which in its entirety is always consumed in a final *ecpyrosis* (which makes a sacrificial pyre, so to speak, of the whole universe). And Neoplatonism furnishes the most poignant example, inasmuch as its monism merely inverts earlier Platonism's dualism, and only magnifies the melancholy: not only is the mutable world separated from its divine principle — the One — by intervals of emanation that descend in ever greater alienation from their source, but because the highest truth is the secret identity between the human mind and the One, the labor of philosophy is one of escape: all multiplicity, change, particularity, every feature of the living world, is not only accidental to this formless identity but a kind of falsehood, and to recover the truth that dwells within, one must detach oneself from what lies without, including the sundry incidentals of one's individual existence; truth is oblivion of the flesh, a pure nothingness, to attain which one must sacrifice the world.

III

In any event, the purpose behind these indefensibly broad pronouncements — however elliptically pursued — is to aid in recalling how shatteringly subversive Christianity was of so many of the certitudes of the world it entered, and how profoundly its exclusive fidelity to the God of Christ transformed that world. This is, of course, no more than we should expect, if we take the New Testament's paschal triumphalism to heart: "Now is the judgment of this world, now will the prince of this world be cast out" (John 12:31); "I have overcome the world" (John 16:33); he is "far above all principality, and power, and might, and dominion," and all things are put "under his feet" (Eph. 1:21-22); "having spoiled principalities and powers, he made a show of them openly, triumphing over them in it" (Col. 2:15); "he led captivity captive" (Eph. 4:8); and so on. Still we can largely absorb Scripture's talk of the defeat of the devil, the angels of the nations, and the powers of the air, and yet fail to recognize how radically the Gospels reinterpreted (or, as Nietzsche would say, "transvalued") everything in the light of Easter.

The example of this I find most striking is the account John's Gospel gives of the dialogue between Christ and Pilate (18:28–19:12). Nietzsche, the quixotic champion of the old standards, thought jesting Pilate's "What is truth?" to be the only moment of genuine nobility in the New Testament, the wry taunt of an incisive ironist unimpressed by the pathetic fantasies of a deranged peasant. But one need not share Nietzsche's sympathies to take his point; one can certainly see what is at stake when Christ, scourged and mocked, is brought again before Pilate: the latter's "Whence art thou?" has about it something of a demand for a pedigree, which might at least lend some credibility to the claims Christ makes for himself; for want of which, Pilate can do little other than pronounce his truth: "I have power to crucify thee" (which would under most circumstances, to be fair, be an incontrovertible argument). It is worth asking ourselves what this tableau, viewed from

the vantage of pagan antiquity, would have meant? A man of noble
birth, representing the power of Rome, endowed with authority over
life and death, confronted by a barbarous colonial, of no name or estate,
a slave of the empire, beaten, robed in purple, crowned with thorns, in-
sanely invoking an otherworldly kingdom, and some esoteric truth,
unaware of either his absurdity or his judge's eminence. Who could
have doubted where, between these two, the truth of things was to be
found? But the Gospel is written in the light of the resurrection, which
reverses the meaning of this scene entirely. If God's truth is in fact to be
found where Christ stands, the mockery visited on him redounds instead upon the emperor, all of whose regal finery, when set beside the
majesty of the servile shape in which God reveals himself, shows itself
to be just so many rags and briers. This slave is the Father's eternal
Word, whom God has vindicated with victory, and so ten thousand im-
memorial certainties are unveiled as lies: the first become last, the
mighty are put down from their seats and the lowly exalted, the hungry
are filled with good things while the rich are sent empty away. Nietzsche was quite right to be appalled. Almost as striking, for me, is the
tale of Peter, at the cock's crow, going apart to weep.[4] Nowhere in the
literature of pagan antiquity, I assure you, had the tears of a rustic been
regarded as worthy of anything but ridicule; to treat them with reverence, as meaningful expressions of real human sorrow, would have
seemed grotesque from the perspective of all the classical canons of
good taste. Those wretchedly subversive tears, and the dangerous phil-
istinism of a narrator so incorrigibly vulgar as to treat them with anything but contempt, were most definitely signs of a slave revolt in morality, if not quite the one against which Nietzsche inveighed — a
revolt, moreover, that all the ancient powers proved impotent to resist.[5]

4. See Erich Auerbach, *Mimesis: The Representation of Reality in Western Literature,* trans. Willard R. Trask (Princeton: Princeton University Press, 1953), pp. 40-49.
   5. "Their ambition is laughable: people of *that* sort regurgitating their most
private affairs, their stupidities, sorrows, and petty worries, as if the Heart of Being
were obliged to concern itself with them; they never grow tired of involving God
himself in even the pettiest troubles they have got themselves into. And the appalling
taste of this perpetual familiarity with God" (Nietzsche, *The Anti-Christ,* trans. R. J.
Hollingdale [New York: Penguin Books, 1968], p. 144). I assume that this adolescent
tirade, so pregnant with that ultimate of bourgeois affectations — "patrician" disdain
— was prompted in part by the story of Peter's sorrow, though I cannot be certain.

In a narrow sense, then, one might say that the chief offense of the Gospels is their defiance of the insights of tragedy — and not only because Christ does not fit the model of the well-born tragic hero. More important is the incontestable truth that in the Gospels the destruction of the protagonist emphatically does not restore or affirm the order of city or cosmos. Were the Gospels to end with Christ's sepulture, in good tragic style, it would exculpate all parties, including Pilate and the Sanhedrin, whose judgments would be shown to be fated by the exigencies of the crisis and the burdens of their offices; the story would then reconcile us to the tragic necessity of all such judgments. But instead comes Easter, which rudely interrupts all the minatory and sententious moralisms of the tragic chorus, just as they are about to be uttered to full effect, and which cavalierly violates the central tenet of sound economics: rather than trading the sacrificial victim for some supernatural benefit, and so the particular for the universal, Easter restores the hero slain in his particularity again, as the only truth the Gospels have to offer. This is more than a dramatic peripety. The empty tomb overturns all the "responsible" and "necessary" verdicts of Christ's judges, and so grants them neither legitimacy nor pardon.

In a larger sense, then, the entire sacrificial logic of a culture was subverted in the Gospels. I cannot attempt here a treatment of the biblical language of sacrifice, but I think I can safely assert that Christ's death does not, in the logic of the New Testament sources, fit the pattern of sacrifice I have just described. The word "sacrifice" is almost inexhaustible in its polysemy, particularly in the Old Testament, but the only sacrificial model explicitly invoked in the New Testament is the atonement offering of Israel, which certainly belongs to no cosmic cycle of prudent expenditure and indemnity. It is, rather, a *qurban,* literally a "drawing nigh" into the life-giving presence of God's glory. Israel's God requires nothing, he creates, elects, and sanctifies without need; and so the atonement offering can in no way contribute to any sort of economy; it is instead a penitent approach to a God who gives life freely, and who not only does not profit from the holocaust of the particular, but who in fact fulfills the "sacrifice" simply by giving his gift again. This giving again is itself, in fact, a kind of "sacrificial" motif in Hebrew Scripture, achieving its most powerful early expression in the story of Isaac's *aqedah,* and arriving at its consummation, perhaps, in

Ezekiel's vision in the valley of dry bones. After all, a people overly burdened by the dolorous superstitions of tragic wisdom could never have come to embrace the doctrine of resurrection. I am tempted to say, then, that the cross of Christ is not simply *a* sacrifice, but the place where two opposed understandings of sacrifice clashed. Christ's whole life was a reconciling *qurban:* an approach to the Father, and a real indwelling of God's glory in the temple of Christ's body, and an atonement made for a people enslaved to death; in pouring himself out in the form of a servant, and in living his humanity as an offering up of everything to God in love, the shape of the eternal Son's life was already sacrificial in this special sense; and it was this absolute giving, as God and man, that was made complete on Golgotha. While from a pagan perspective (on the other hand) the crucifixion itself could be viewed as a sacrifice in the most proper sense — destruction of the agent of social instability for the sake of peace, which is always a profitable exchange — Christ's life of charity, service, forgiveness, and righteous judgment could not; indeed, it would have to seem the very opposite of sacrifice, an aneconomic and indiscriminate inversion of rank and order. Yet, at Easter, it is the latter that God accepts and the former that he rejects; what then of all the hard-won tragic wisdom of the ages?[6]

Naturally, with the death of the old mythos, metaphysics too was transformed. For one thing, while every antique system of philosophy had to presume an economy of necessity binding the world of becoming to its inmost or highest principles, Christian theology taught from the first that the world was God's creature in the most radically ontological sense: that it is called from nothingness, not out of any need on God's part, but by grace. The world adds nothing to the being of God, and so nothing need be sacrificed for his glory or sustenance. In a sense, God and world alike were liberated from the fetters of necessity; God

6. Much of what I say bears the mark of the thought of René Girard, though his overly narrow understanding of the variety of meanings to be found in the word "sacrifice," and his limited understanding of Hebrew Scripture, have sometimes led him to formulations verging on the Marcionite. His recent work, though, has improved on many of the failings in his earlier. See Girard, *The Scapegoat,* trans. Yvonne Freccero (Baltimore: Johns Hopkins University Press, 1986); Girard, *Things Hidden Since the Foundation of the World,* trans. Stephen Bann and Michael Metteer (Stanford: Stanford University Press, 1978); and Girard, *I See Satan Fall like Lightning,* trans. James G. Williams (Maryknoll, N.Y.: Orbis, 2001).

could be accorded his true transcendence and the world its true character as divine gift. The full implications of this probably became visible to Christian philosophers only with the resolution of the fourth-century trinitarian controversies, when the subordinationist schemes of Alexandrian trinitarianism were abandoned, and with them the last residue within theology of late Platonism's vision of a descending scale of divinity mediating between God and world — the both of them comprised in a single totality. That is a technical and disputable point, though; one more general, and uncontroversial, is that theology rejected nothing good in the metaphysics, ethics, or method of antique philosophy, but — with a kind of omnivorous glee — assimilated such elements as served its ends, and always improved them in the process. Stoic morality, Plato's language of the Good, Aristotle's metaphysics of act and potency — all became richer and more coherent when emancipated from the morbid myths of sacrificial economy and tragic necessity. In truth, Christian theology nowhere more wantonly celebrated its triumph over the old gods than in the use it made of the so-called *spolia Aegyptorum;* and by despoiling pagan philosophy of its most splendid achievements, and integrating them into a vision of reality more complete than philosophy could attain on its own, theology took to itself irrevocably all the intellectual glories of antiquity. The temples were stripped of their gold and precious ornaments, the sacred vessels were carried away into the precincts of the church and turned to better uses, and nothing was left behind but a few grim, gaunt ruins to lure back the disenchanted Christian or shelter a few atavistic ghosts.

IV

This last observation returns me to my earlier contention: that Christianity assisted in bringing the nihilism of modernity to pass. The command to have no other god but him whom Christ revealed was never for Christians simply an invitation to forsake an old cult for a new, but was an announcement that the shape of the world had changed, from the depths of hell to the heaven of heavens, and all nations were called to submit to Jesus as Lord. In the great "transvaluation" that followed, there was no sphere of social, religious, or intellectual life that the church did not claim for itself; much was abolished, and much of the grandeur and beauty of antiquity was preserved in a radically altered form, and Christian civilization — with its new synthesis and new creativity — was born. But what happens, then, when Christianity, as a living historical force, recedes? We have no need to speculate, as it happens; modernity speaks for itself: with the withdrawal of Christian culture, all the glories of the ancient world that it baptized and redeemed have perished with it in the general cataclysm. Christianity is the midwife of nihilism not because it is itself nihilistic, but because it is too powerful in its embrace of the world and all of the world's mystery and beauty; and so to reject Christianity now is, of necessity, to reject everything except the barren anonymity of spontaneous subjectivity. As Ivan Karamazov's Grand Inquisitor tells Christ, the freedom that the gospel brings is too terrible to be borne indefinitely. Our sin makes us feeble and craven, and we long to flee from the liberty of the sons of God; but where now can we go? Everything is Christ's.

This is illustrated with striking clarity by the history of modern philosophy, at least in its Continental (and, so to speak, proper) form. It is fashionable at present, among some theologians, to attempt precise genealogies of modernity, which in general I think it best to avoid doing; but it does seem clear to me that the special preoccupations and perversities of modern philosophy were incubated in the age of late scholasticism, with the rise of nominalism and voluntarism: whereas earlier theology spoke of God as Goodness as such, whose every act (by virtue of divine simplicity) expresses his nature, the specter that haunts late scholastic thought is a God whose will precedes his nature, and whose acts then are feats of pure spontaneity. It is a logically incoherent way of conceiving of God, as it happens,[7] but a powerful idea, elevating as it does will over all else and redefining freedom — for God and, by extension, for us — not as the unhindered realization of a nature (the liberty to "become what you are"), but as the absolute liberty of the will in determining even what its nature is.[8] Thus when modern philosophy

7. This is not the place to argue the point, and I have addressed it in other places: for example, Hart, "No Shadow of Turning: On Divine Impassibility," *Pro Ecclesia* 11 (spring 2002): 184-206.

8. This is not a genealogy of nihilism without precedent; something quite similar is argued by Michael Allen Gillespie in his *Nihilism before Nietzsche* (Chicago: University of Chicago Press, 1995). The great flaw of this book, however, is that the author is not sufficiently familiar with scholastic theology and so, in vari-

established itself anew as a discipline autonomous from theology, it did so naturally by falling back upon an ever more abyssal subjectivity. Real autonomy could not be gained by turning back to the wonder of being or to the transcendental perfections of the world, for to do so would be to slip again into a sphere long colonized by theology. And so the new point of departure for reason had to be the perceiving subject rather than the world perceived. Descartes, for instance, explicitly forbade himself any recourse to the world's testimony of itself; in his third meditation he seals all his senses against nature, so that he can undertake his rational reconstruction of reality from a position pure of any certitude save that of the ego's own existence. The world is recovered thereafter only insofar as it is "posited," as an act of will. And while God appears in that reconstruction, he does so only as a logical postulate following from the idea of the infinite. From there it is a short step to Kant's transcendental ego, for whom the world is the representation of its own irreducible "I think," and which (inasmuch as it is its own infinity) requires God as a postulate only in the realm of ethics, and merely as a regulative idea in the realm of epistemology. And the passage from transcendental idealism to absolute idealism, however much it involved an attempt to escape egoistic subjectivity, had no world to which to return; even Hegel's system, for all that it sought to have done with petty subjectivism, could do so only by way of a massive metaphysical myth of the self-positing of the Concept, and of a more terrible economy of necessity than any pagan antiquity had imagined. This project was in every sense incredible, and its collapse inevitably brought philosophy, by way of Heidegger, to its "postmodern condition" — a "heap of broken images." If Heidegger was right — and he was — in saying that there was always a nihilistic core to the Western philosophical tradition, the withdrawal of Christianity leaves nothing but that core behind, for the gospel long ago stripped away both the deceits and the glories that had concealed it; and so philosophy becomes, almost by force of habit, explicit nihilism.

Modern philosophy, however, merely reflects the state of modern culture and modern cult; and to this sphere I should turn now, as this is where spiritual warfare is principally to be waged.

---

ous places, badly misrepresents aspects of the tradition. On the whole, though, the argument is persuasive and powerful.

I should admit that I, for one, feel considerable sympathy for Nietzsche's plaint, "Nearly two-thousand years and no new god"; and also for Heidegger, decrepit and despairing in the deepening twilight, intoning his mournful oracle: "Only a god can save us." But of course none will come. The Christian God has taken up everything into himself; all the treasures of ancient wisdom, all the splendor of creation, every good thing has been assumed into the story of the incarnate God, and every stirring toward transcendence is soon recognized by the modern mind — weary of God — as leading back toward faith. Antique pieties cannot be restored, for we moderns know that the hungers they excite can be sated only by the gospel of Christ and him crucified. To be a Stoic today, for instance, is simply to be a soul *in via* to the church; a Platonist, most of us understand, is only a Christian manqué; and a polytheist is merely a truant from the one God he hates and loves. The only cult that can truly thrive in the aftermath of Christianity is a sordid service of the self, of the impulses of the will, of the nothingness that is all that the withdrawal of Christianity leaves behind.[9] The only

9. At the conference at which this paper was delivered, two respected theologians in attendance — themselves conference lecturers — rose at the end and raised certain objections to this remark that made me aware that I had perhaps failed entirely to explain my meaning. One of my interrogators protested that he had seen quite a lot of selflessness on September 11, from firemen and police in particular, and that in his experience many of his students, for all the cultural privations they suffer, are decent and admirable lads and lasses. To elucidate my position, then: it is not my intention to suggest that because modernity has lost the organic integrity of Christianity's moral grammar, every person living in modern society must therefore become heartless, violent, or unprincipled. My observations are directed at the dominant language and ethos of a culture, not at the souls of contemporary Westerners. Many among us retain some loyalty to ancient principles, most of us are in some degree premodern, and in America in particular Christianity maintains some real hold on persons' hearts and imaginations; moreover, there are always and everywhere to be found examples of natural virtue, innate nobility, congenital charity, and so on, for the light of God is ubiquitous and the image of God is impressed upon our nature. The issue for me is whether, within the moral grammar of modernity, any of these good souls could give an account of his or her virtue. Here I advert again to Alasdair MacIntyre's point concerning the odd bricolage that ethics has become in the wake of a morality of the Good. As far as I can tell, *homo nihilisticus* may often be in several notable respects a far more amiable rogue than *homo religiosus*, exhibiting a far smaller propensity for breaking the crockery or slaying the nearest available infidel. But ah, love, let us be true to one another: even when all of this is granted, it would be a willful and culpable blindness for us to refuse to recognize how brutal, depraved, aes-

futures open to post-Christian culture are conscious nihilism, with its inevitable devotion to death, or the narcotic banality of the Last Men, which may be little better than death. Surveying the desert of modernity, we would be, I think, morally derelict not to acknowledge that

---

thetically arid, culturally worthless, and spiritually empty modern Western society has become. One need only look at some of the hideously violent video games that so many of our young are permitted to play again and again and again; or read the lyrics of much of today's popular "music"; or survey the wreckage of our institutions of public education; or visit the cinema; or consider the frequency of school shootings, though — per capita — guns were far more prevalent in American society seventy years ago, when such events were unheard of; or reflect upon the fact that, in America alone, more than 40 million babies have been aborted since the Supreme Court invented the "right" that allows for this, and that there are many for whom this is viewed not even as a tragic "necessity," but as a triumph of moral truth. When the Carthaginians were prevailed upon to cease sacrificing their babies, at least the place vacated by their god reminded them that they should seek the divine above themselves; we offer up our babies to "my" freedom of choice, to "me." No society's moral vision has ever, surely, been *more* degenerate than that. This is no time to moderate our polemic; the night draws on, the shadows deepen, and the watch fires are few and far between. As for my second interrogator, he expressed his fear that the starkly stated alternative of "Christianity or nihilism" amounted to a denial of the goodness of natural wisdom and virtue, and seemed to suggest that *gratia non perficit, sed destruit naturam.* Three responses to this should be made. First, my analysis here does not concern the entirety of human experience, nature, or culture; it is a historical observation only, strictly hermeneutical, and concerns one particular location in time and space: late Western modernity; I have nothing here to say about cultures or peoples who have not suffered the history of faith and disenchantment we have, or who do not share our particular relation to European antiquity or the heritage of ancient Christendom; "nihilism" is simply a name for post-Christian sensibility and conviction (and not even an especially opprobrious one, to judge from the willingness of some Continental philosophers to adopt the term for their philosophies). Second, the alternative between Christianity and nihilism is never, in actual practice, a kind of Kierkegaardian either/or posed between two absolute antinomies, incapable of alloy, ambiguity, or medium; it is an antagonism that occurs along a continuum, whose extremes are rarely perfectly expressed in any single life (else the world would be all saints and satanists). Third, and most important, my observations do not concern nature at all, which is inextinguishable and which, at some level, always longs for God; they concern culture, which has the power to purge itself of the natural in some considerable degree; that is why so much of the discourse of late modernity — speculative, critical, moral, and political — consists in an attempt to deny the authority or even the reality of any general order of nature or natures; nature is good, but modernity is unnatural, is indeed antinature, or even anti-Christ, and so goeth about as a roaring lion, seeking whom it may devour.

Nietzsche was right in holding Christianity responsible (even if he misunderstood why) for the catastrophe around us; we should confess that the failure of Christian culture to live up to its victory over the old gods has allowed the dark power that once hid behind them to step forward in propria persona; and we should certainly dread whatever rough beast it is that is being bred in our ever coarser, crueler, more inarticulate, more vacuous popular culture; because cloaked in anodyne insipience lies a world increasingly devoid of merit, wit, kindness, imagination, or charity.

Which is why I repeat that our age is not one in danger of reverting to paganism (would that we were so fortunate). If we turn from Christ today, we turn only toward the god of absolute will, and embrace him under either his most monstrous or his most vapid aspect. A somewhat more ennobling retreat to the old gods is not possible for us; we can find no shelter there, nor can we sink away gently into those old illusions and tragic consolations that Christ has exposed as falsehoods. To love or be nourished by the gods, we would have to fear them; but the ruin of their glory is so complete that they have been reduced — like everything else — to commodities. Nor will the ululations and lugubrious platitudes and pious fatalism of the tragic chorus ever again have the power to recall us to sobriety. The gospel of a God found in broken flesh, humility, and measureless charity has defeated all the old lies, rendered the ancient order visibly insufficient and even slightly absurd, and instilled in us a longing for transcendent love so deep that — if once yielded to — it will never grant us rest anywhere but in Christ. And there is a real sadness in this, because the consequences of so great a joy rejected are a sorrow, bewilderment, and anxiety for which there is no precedent. If the nonsensical religious fascinations of today are not in any classical or Christian sense genuine pieties, they are nevertheless genuine — if deluded — expressions of grief, encomia for a forsaken and half-forgotten home, the prisoner's lament over a lost freedom. For Christians, then, to recover and understand the meaning of the command to have "no other god," it is necessary first to recognize that the victory of the church in history was not only incomplete, but indeed set free a force that the old sacral order had at least been able to contain; and it is against this more formless and invincible enemy that we take up the standard of the commandment today.

Moreover, we need to recognize, in the light of this history, that this commandment is a hard discipline: it destroys, it breaks in order to bind; like a cautery, it wounds in order to heal; and now, in order to heal the damage it has in part inflicted, it must be applied again. In practical terms, I suspect that this means that Christians must make an ever more concerted effort to recall and recover the wisdom and centrality of the ascetic tradition. It takes formidable faith and devotion to resist the evils of one's age, and it is to the history of Christian asceticism — especially, perhaps, the apothegms of the Desert Fathers — that all Christians, whether married or not, should turn for guidance. To have no god but the God of Christ, after all, means today that we must endure the Lenten privations of what is most certainly a dark age, and strive to resist the bland solace, inane charms, brute viciousness, and brute passivity of post-Christian culture — all of which are so tempting precisely because they enjoin us to believe in and adore ourselves. It means also to remain aloof from many of the moral grammars of our time, which are — even at their most sentimental, tender, and tolerant — usually as decadent and egoistic as the currently most fashionable vices. It means, in short, self-abnegation, contrarianism, a willingness not only to welcome but to condemn, and a refusal of secularization as fierce as the refusal of our Christian ancestors to burn incense to the genius of the emperor. This is not an especially grim prescription, I should add: Christian asceticism is not, after all, a cruel disfigurement of the will, contaminated by the world-weariness or malice toward creation that one can justly ascribe to many other varieties of religious detachment; it is, rather, the cultivation of the pure heart and pure eye, which allow one to receive the world, and rejoice in it, not as a possession of the will or an occasion for the exercise of power, but as the good gift of God. This is why it has the power to heal us of our modern derangements: because, paradoxical as it may seem to modern temperaments, Christian asceticism is the practice of love, what Maximus the Confessor calls learning to see the logos of each thing within the Logos of God,[10] and it eventuates most properly in the

---

10. For the metaphysics of such a claim, see especially *Ambiguum* 7; for the relevant spiritual discipline, see especially *The Centuries on Charity*.

grateful reverence of a Bonaventure or the lyrical ecstasy of a Thomas Traherne.[11]

Still, it is a discipline for all that; and for us today it must involve the painful acknowledgment that neither we nor our distant progeny will live to see a new Christian culture in the Western world; we must accept this with both charity and faith. We must, after all, grant that in the mystery of God's providence, all of this has followed from the work of the Holy Spirit in time. Modern persons will never find rest for their restless hearts without Christ, for modern culture is nothing but the wasteland from which the gods have departed, and so this restlessness has become its own deity; and, deprived of the shelter of the sacred and the consoling myths of sacrifice, the modern person must wander or drift, vainly attempting one or another accommodation with death, never escaping anxiety or ennui, and driven as a result to a ceaseless labor of distraction, or acquisition, or willful idiocy. And, where it works its sublimest magic, our culture of empty spectacle can so stupefy the intellect as to blind it to its own disquiet, and induce a spiritual torpor more deplorable than mere despair. But we Christians — while not ignoring how appalling such a condition is — should yet rejoice that modernity offers no religious comforts to those who would seek them. In this time of waiting, in this age marked only by the absence of faith in Christ, it is well that the modern soul should lack repose, piety, peace, or nobility, and should find the world outside the church barren of spiritual rapture or mystery, and should discover no beautiful or terrible or merciful gods upon which to cast itself. With Christ came judgment into the world, a light of discrimination from which there is neither retreat nor sanctuary. And this means that, as a quite concrete historical condition, the only choice that remains for the children of post-Christian culture is not whom to serve, but whether to serve him whom Christ has revealed or to serve nothing — *the* nothing; no third way lies open for us now, because — as all of us now

---

11. I might also call it the cultivation of a "Marian" spirituality, one that has learned to wait upon and yield everything up to the love of God, and so to become fruitful with the beauty of his Word. For this reason (and here I suppose I show my confessional colors), it occurs to me that while it may be possible to live a life of imitation of Christ without the aid of a strong devotion to the Mother of God, it is certainly much harder to do so.

know, whether we acknowledge it consciously or not — all things have been made subject to him, all the thrones and dominions of the high places have been put beneath his feet, until the very end of the world, and — simply said — there *is* no other god.

Taking the Lord's Name in Vain

Ephraim Radner

Whoever opens his or her mouth to speak publicly about the desecration of God's name must do so under a terrible judgment. If such a one is not simply driven to silence, then at least he or she must be pressed into some deathly humility. "I will lay mine hand upon my mouth. . . . I abhor myself and repent in dust and ashes" (Job 40:4; 42:6). That is, the third commandment is *not* about how to manipulate our speech in order to avoid moral missteps. It is about who we are before God. In the end, this fact is my main point, made in the context of the gospel of Jesus Christ — my only point really. And I will proceed with it by moving backward, as it were, from the present, skipping through the early modern period and landing squarely in the Scriptures. In so doing I will secretly ask us questions such as this: What is it we really want from the commandment regarding God's name? What are we looking for? What guidance, what help, what hope, what plan for life? Where shall *this* commandment set us down? And with whom?

I. Blasphemy and the World's Order

Allow me to begin, then, in the present, with a long, digressive introduction, a vignette from a part of the world I once worked in. You can read it in a recent article by Samantha Power, who over the past few years has been sternly reporting to us on the horror and aftermath of the 1992 genocide in Rwanda, Africa. You recall, at least in general, those three months only ten years ago in which 800,000 Tutsi men, women, and children were slaughtered, and thousands of others mutilated and raped. What, 6 persons killed each minute, 60 minutes an hour, 24 hours a day, for 90 days?

In a 2003 article, Power writes about the attempt to deal with the thousands of prisoners now held for their role in the episode, deal with them through a messy system of public accusation and confession, held in local villages and hills, known as *gacaca,* named after leaves upon which traditional judges would sit while hearing cases. Surviving victims, witnesses, the accused stand and speak or listen or shout and scream. Who saw what? Is anyone left alive who could have seen or known? Is the man in prison these past ten years falsely charged by greedy neighbors or shamefaced lovers? And then someone tries to discern the truth in all this, the truth about the unspeakable, through the midst of whose sad fog innocence and guilt float like whispering specters.

Power describes one such preparatory gathering among the thousands that have already taken place:

> When presented to the crowd, "TM" [as we shall call him], a suspected killer with an incomplete file, said he had no part in the death of a young Tutsi boy, whom he happened to find murdered. Witnesses leaped up to contradict him, including one who said he saw TM commit the crime. TM was asked if he would like to rethink his plea of innocence, and he said, "I insist I found the boy when he was already dead, but, just to make sure, it is true, I hit him on the head. That I confess to." The crowd whistled and jeered at TM's feeble and belated admission. His file would now include the witnesses' murder charges as well as his response. Still, if TM can learn to master the art of confession before the actual *gacaca* hearings begin in his district next year, he may go free. [Another inmate] Stilaton Siborurema, forty-five, stood with his arms folded at the center of the circle. He was accused of taking part in the killing of three Tutsi children. As witnesses stepped into the circle to testify, he looked as if he was napping standing up. But he was fortunate. The dozen or so villagers who spoke argued that he had been framed. By the time Siborurema was asked to sit down, charges against two new men had been lodged, and the consensus

in the audience was that, for nearly seven years, Siborurema had been unjustly imprisoned, and he was provisionally released.[1]

Reading this, I think, "What a sorry mess." No different perhaps than the cacophony of our muted marriages, our politics, our convoluted friendships, our churches; but of an even starker, emptier resonance, don't you think? Would it help, I wonder, if *God* could sort this out? "In the name of God," if only someone said, "in the name of God, *this* is the truth, this is light!" Not my words, nor yours, but *God's* word, God's word about himself, God's self-named word hitched to the wagon of our driven ignorances, and of our grotesquely fabricated nightfalls.

You see the motive of my question, don't you? It is the same, in a basic way, as that which fueled John Locke's exclusion of atheists from his famous seventeenth-century scheme of civic toleration: "Lastly, those are not at all to be tolerated who deny the being of a God. Promises, covenants, and oaths, which are the bonds of human society, can have no hold upon an atheist. The taking away of God, though but even in thought, dissolves all."[2] A society can bear every and any sect, Locke insisted, every form of belief in God, however bizarre, except that which denies God's existence altogether. For how, Locke asked, could you ever trust the word of an atheist, for whom the name of God could not certify an oath? The order of a commonwealth would crumble, would it not? Whom could you believe? What witness, what commitment, what character could ever pin our doubts to some clear truth without the name of God to swear by, if only silently?

Two things I would say, then, in broaching the topic of God's holiness profaned — a topic I shall approach primarily through a consideration of the third commandment. First, we tend to forget our own need for such ordering of truth within our common lives, such as Locke demanded. Not only do we forget the chaos that lies at the root of our lives and hovers continually over its fragile limping, but we forget our lives' essential accountability for such order, its ever lying before the judge of its being.

---

1. Samantha Power, "Rwanda: The Two Faces of Justice," *New York Review of Books,* January 16, 2003, pp. 49-50.

2. John Locke, *A Letter Concerning Toleration* (1689), in *Treatise of Civil Government and a Letter Concerning Toleration,* ed. Charles L. Sherman (New York: Appleton-Century-Crofts, 1937), p. 212.

Yet even more perhaps than this, and secondly, and in our role as so-called religious people (among whom Locke himself was proud to be numbered), we forget the *sheer impossibility* of ever founding such an order, certain in the eyes of God, upon the name or word of any. *Gacaca* may be necessary, but they don't add up to truth or peace. It is odd, in a way, that Locke could ever have believed that even the *thought* of God might form a plausible basis upon which to stabilize society, when in fact he formed many of his political ideas in direct response to the carnage articulate Christians had enacted against one another. Much like Christian Rwanda on a smaller scale. To say that "our help is in the name of the Lord" is both true and also, given who we are, a kind of invitation to blasphemy itself: For who calls upon the "name of the Lord" with the purity of heart and desire and act that could do anything *other* than profane the very thing it seeks to touch? Our *Book of Common Prayer* Compline service has as one of its appointed readings Jeremiah 14:9, "Lord, you are in the midst of us, and we are called by your Name." That's very comforting at the end of a long day. But the reading stops short of the next verse, where God replies, "They have not restrained their feet, therefore the Lord does not accept them, and now will remember their iniquity and punish their sins" (14:10; cf. v. 14). The name, in its utterance, judges the utterer. "Not everyone who says to me, 'Lord, Lord' shall enter the Kingdom of heaven" (Matt. 7:21). Oh, no; just the opposite. *Most* of those who use God's name, do so vainly. Can we understand this?

There is a sense, a real sense, then, in which blasphemy is the universal character of human life, nay of religious life itself. As several commentators on the third commandment have long noted,[3] without drawing any conclusions, alas, the prohibition against taking the Lord's name "in vain" easily takes aim at the very center of *every act* we do and at its motivation in the human heart, even and especially as these motivations clothe themselves with religious goals. Are our most spiritual desires at all ever governed by ambition, or by pride, or by base fear and the like? If so, then the prayer, "O Lord, make speed to save us; O God, make haste to help us!" turns into a curse. And whose prayers are not so governed by such a heart and such a life as this?

3. So Calvin, Lancelot Andrewes, Henry Hammond *(Practical Catechism),* and others.

Yet this is the very life that God would save from itself — the life that blasphemes even as it speaks of God. In this sense there is a double character to the "name" of God: much like the Law, God's name stands as a refracting articulation of human sin; unlike the Law, the name of God enacts a supreme and resolving sovereignty over sinful creation itself. In the name of God, judgment and mercy meet together. "The LORD, the LORD, a God merciful and gracious, slow to anger and abounding in steadfast love and faithfulness, keeping steadfast love for thousands, forgiving iniquity and transgression and sin, but who will by no means clear the guilty, visiting the iniquity of the fathers upon the children and the children's children, to the third and the fourth generation" (Exod. 34:6ff.). The Lord, the Lord, the refusal of whose voice shakes earth and heaven without escape, yet whose very blood is sprinkled upon the earth in love (Heb. 12:24-29). "You shall not take the name of the LORD your God in vain; for the LORD will not hold him guiltless who takes his name in vain" (Exod. 20:7). Yet "Thus says the LORD who made the earth, the LORD who formed it to establish it — the LORD is his name: Call to me and I will answer you" (Jer. 33:2f.).

It is this double character I wish now to trace, as it emerges into the glaring light of Christ Jesus; and almost blinded, as it were, the onlooking church, I will suggest, has bit by bit turned its head away and lapsed into a miasma of interpretive avoidance. Locke's appeal to the need for right oath taking, solid oath taking, as forming the only essential — yet still fundamental! — religious basis for society, represents but a politically aware form of the curious limitation by the church herself of the third commandment as referring primarily to modes of "swearing." Thereby has she herself obscured the vast cloud of blasphemy encircling even the civil sphere in its search for peace.

Obviously there was some basis to this way of restricting the commandment, perhaps even within Scripture itself, and I shall return to this question in a moment. But it remains something of a historical curiosity that the elaborated interpretive focus on oath taking as the commandment's core was, in general, a late development within the church, appearing, as far as I can see, only in the High Middle Ages, and taking the field in the early modern era.

We see it emerge, for instance, with Peter Lombard in the twelfth century, in an age when canon law comes into its own as an articulated discipline for the first time in conjunction with the initial descent into chaos of a papal system dismembered by competing parties.[4] The matter of what kind of oaths are to be respected and how they are to be made begins to take up growing space within the commentary on this part of the Decalogue just in this realm of desired institutional reordering. Thomas Aquinas, in the midst of his extraordinarily rich discussion of the Old Testament Law, explicitly prefers the reading of the commandment as it pertains to oath taking (as opposed to broader referents), given that it appears, he says, to focus on "words" in particular as they are used in relationship with God.[5] But Thomas mentions, only to reject as crucial, an earlier and common interpretation in the *Glossa* — the standard medieval scriptural commentary — that applied the commandment to the broad sweep of doctrinal exposition itself, as if wondering how such a vast swath of thought and speech could ever be usefully held up under the scrutiny of so harsh a criterion as the commandment represents. I suppose most theologians would prefer to leave this aspect to the side! In his small treatise *On the Ten Commandments,* at any rate, Thomas enshrines the interest of the commandment in oath taking as primary, and the whole of it is explicated in terms of what an oath is and how an oath is justly or unjustly taken. Summing up the threefold evil of a false oath, Thomas turns to the social aspect: "He [who swears falsely], finally, does an injury to other men. For there can be no lasting society unless men believe one another. Matters that are doubtful may be confirmed by oaths," he writes, and then adds, citing Hebrews 6:16: "'An oath in confirmation puts an end to all controversy.' Therefore, he who violates this precept does injury to God, is cruel to himself, and is harmful to other men."[6] The pull of the *gacaca!*

We may wonder at the reasons for this delimitation, and I would tend to give weight to sociological explanations that examined the on-

---

4. Cf. Peter Lombard's *De perjurio* and *De voto,* in Migne, *Patrologia Latina,* 192, cols. 831ff., 932. On some of the history behind the evolution of canon law during this period, cf. the work of Stephen Kuttner, esp. *Harmony from Dissonance: An Interpretation of Medieval Canon Law* (Latrobe, Pa.: Archabbey Press, 1960).

5. *Summa theologiae* 1a2ae 100 a.5.

6. A translation of the *opusculum* on the Decalogue can be found in *The Catechetical Instructions of St. Thomas Aquinas,* trans. J. B. Collins (New York: Joseph F. Wagner, 1939).

going and useful force of an approach to the Decalogue, and this commandment in particular, that could apply its authority to the parsing of an increasingly complex society. Certainly, Thomas's attachment of the Decalogue as a whole to the obligatory character of a universal "natural law," however much dependent on some aspect of divine revelation, represented an extraordinarily useful way of organizing the sanctions that might uphold an expanding and increasingly sophisticated cultural nexus. Distinguishing the Decalogue from the bulk of the Old Testament's cultic or ceremonial precepts, and locating its power within the extended social realm that captured all human decision making regardless of religious self-awareness, represented both an inflation of the commandments' referents and a thinning out of their theological reach.

The fact that the Reformers themselves latched on to this use — with or without the natural law framework (and Anglicans often had no problem with the latter) — seems congruent with this larger tendency. For both Luther and Calvin, the third commandment's main pertinence, as with Thomas, lay in its discussion of oath taking, and the arguments with Anabaptists and others on this matter conspired to maintain this topic as fundamental.[7] By the seventeenth century the question of proper oath taking focuses more and more on its function as a part of civil society's glue, an element whose reach simply overtakes the theological currents otherwise exposed in the commandment. One might note, for instance, the strange migration of Lancelot Andrewes's argument on the third commandment in his *Pattern of Catechistical Doctrine*, which contains one of the fullest Anglican discussions of the Decalogue.[8] From stating that "the end of this commandment is the praise of God," Andrewes moves rapidly into the main discussion of oath taking. The principle of the precept, then, he explains thus: "therefore an oath is taken necessarily to end strife, which cannot be done before there be a stronger confirmation on the one side than the other." The use of God's name, then, is to be done in a way that shows its power to provide social order. This includes the

---

7. I have in mind Luther's discussions in the *Large Catechism,* and Calvin's in the *Institutes.*

8. Andrewes, *Pattern of Catechistical Doctrine* (Oxford: John Henry Parker, 1846), pp. 143ff.

use of oaths in fostering "trust" among citizens, and thereby further-
ing "blessing" upon society. All of this is a particular concern for early
modern Europe. Indeed, it is a renewed matter of anxiety for the
American society of today. Locke's appeal to the "natural law" in this
regard, as the container of the Decalogue and in its republished evangelical form as the aim of Jesus' coming, can be seen therefore as the
expression of a very modern yearning for a graspable civil order which
Christianity might simply comprehend instrumentally.[9] I have no
doubt, furthermore, that much interest in the Decalogue today, including the press for its publication in courthouses and the rest, is governed by the same desire.

But is the desire theologically sound, at least in its appropriation
of the commandment itself and of the Scriptures that provide it? For
there is a sense in which the modern church's gradual disengagement
of the Decalogue from the Scripture's particular historical and contex-
tual referents, and its relocation within a sociologically distracting and
religiously inert civil context, have been part of an ironically subversive movement vis-à-vis the Christian gospel. It is "ironic," that is, for
those contemporary proponents of the Decalogue's civic value whose
explicit Christian commitments would seem to fuel their advocacy for
the Ten Commandments' reentry into the public square, even while
the basis for doing so may well contradict the evangelical meaning of
the texts themselves. For the modern church's constriction of their
meaning — in this case, the third commandment's in particular — has
had the effect of turning the whole of Pauline theology about the Law
on its head: no longer Christ, no longer freedom, no longer communion with God; but nature, the obedience of works, and in the face of
the wolves within, no longer the cross but civic order.

II. The Blasphemed Redemption of Vanity

This, then, is where we are. But what should we be about? I move now
to the commandment itself; and here I will concentrate on the question
of the character of the prohibited sin — "vanity" — rather than on its
object, the name of God. So how shall we understand the using of

---

9. This is the general argument of his *Reasonableness of Christianity.*

God's name *"in vain"?* At the time of Jesus there seem to have been two directions of interpretive application, tied ostensibly and respectively to the semantic determinations of the Hebrew or Greek renditions of the word we translate as "vanity." In Hebrew the word *shav* in the commandment signals more literally a "lie," while in the Greek translation of the Septuagint the term *mataios* properly points to something "futile" and "empty." Thus a perhaps subtle difference: in the Hebrew, "do not make the Lord's name a lie" or "associate it with a lie" as opposed to a Greek sense of "do not render the Lord's name empty or useless." Jewish interpretation in Jesus' time (including a Hellenist thinker like Philo) seems to move in the direction of hearing the commandment as prohibiting the application of God's name to something false, and hence the concern among commentators of the time and of later rabbinic tradition with the whole question of "swearing" and taking oaths.[10] Jewish and Christian tradition eventually meet here. And it is possible, after all, that this use of the third commandment to focus on oaths was already embedded within the Mosaic law itself, as in Leviticus 19:12: "And you shall not swear by my name falsely, and so profane the name of your God: I am the LORD." Do Jesus' own sensibilities move in this direction? This is what many later Christians have supposed, reading his remarks and Levitical citations in the Sermon on the Mount (Matt. 5:33ff.) in this light: "Again you have heard that it was said to the men of old, 'You shall not swear falsely, but shall perform to the Lord what you have sworn.' But I say to you, Do not swear at all, either by heaven. . . ."

I am not myself convinced of this intentional or certainly direct linkage between Jesus' exhortation to plain speech or his prohibition of oaths and the third commandment. In any case, the New Testament as a whole moves in the direction of the Greek rendition's theological reach: "vanity," that is, as "emptiness" rather than as "deceit" (though the two are obviously related). The use by the LXX of the word *mataios* in the third commandment fills itself out through its application to a spectrum of commentary on the world as a whole, including Ecclesiastes' famous refrain of lament over human life, "Vanity of vanities, all is

---

10. Cf. Brevard Childs, *The Book of Exodus: A Critical, Theological Commentary* (Philadelphia: Westminster, 1974), pp. 409ff., within the larger context of his discussion of the Decalogue, pp. 385-439.

vanity." The word is the same. Thus, the potential drawing of God himself into this regretful observation hovers, if only linguistically, as a shadow of desecration over human weariness and cynicism as a whole.[11]

As it is, Saint Paul places the created world itself within the realm of this dark dynamic of human worthlessness and divine denial, when he writes of sin's disease and God's permissive punishment. In Romans 1:20f. he writes: "So they are without excuse; for although they [i.e., human beings] knew God they did not honor him as God or give thanks to him, but they became *futile* — literally 'vain' — in their thinking and their senseless minds were darkened." Consigned to this "futility," human society and its shaping of the world's surrounding form stands, it seems, as the embodiment of the very act God warns against in the third commandment — society becomes "vanity" itself, and we ourselves become the image of our own willful reconstruction of God.

Paul, as we know, unfolds a history of the entire human race here. For instance, as he and Acts (cf. 14:15) emphasize elsewhere, "vanity" describes the character of Gentile behavior and marks quite literally the face of human idolatry as it seeks to deny the first and second commandments. "We know that idols are nothing" — are "vain" — Paul writes, simply applying in the course of another kind of argument the basic reality of human worship exposed in Scriptures like Psalm 115: "Not to us, O Lord, not to us, *but to thy Name give glory. . . .* Why should the nations say, 'where is their God'? . . . Their idols are the works of men's hands. They have mouths, but do not speak; eyes, but they do not see . . . those who make them *are like them.*" The world's own visage, you see, comes to resemble over time its own inner wishes for God's disappearance.

Hence, the term "vanity" comes to have as a synonym in the New Testament the word "empty" *(kenos),* which in its turn describes the human spirit and claim, the human faith even, that has behind it little except the nothingness of purposeless passion. Without the actual resurrection of Christ, Paul insists, the Christian faith is "futile,"

---

11. For a rich exploration of some of this semantic area of Scripture, cf. Jean-Luc Marion, *God without Being* (Chicago: University of Chicago Press, 1991), chap. 4, "The Reverse of Vanity," pp. 108-38.

even as God's grace in calling him would have been "empty"; and the only proper response to such foolishness would be the refrain of Isaiah's wanton sinners, "let us eat and drink, for tomorrow we die," whose invitation so mirrors the Preacher's positive call in the face of the vanity of all things: "there is nothing better for man than that he should eat and drink . . . this also is a striving after wind" (cf. 1 Cor. 15:17, 10, 32; cf. Isa. 22:13; Eccles. 2:24). Here we look at the mirror of a human life left to its own honest reasoning.

Now the moral link that connects the "vanity" of the third commandment with the emptiness of human spiritual vagary seems to lie here: that is, in treating God — summoned through his name — as a literal "nonentity," equivalent to the pagan idols in their brute and numbing powerlessness and to the behavior of the world tied to them. "We know that an idol has no existence," writes Paul, favorably quoting the knowledgeable Corinthians (1 Cor. 8:4; cf. 10:19). And to treat God as a kind of "nothing," analogous to the uselessness of human pride's self-assertion into the void, to yoke God to such vacuous projections, appears in general to be the contradiction of the command itself. But it also opens up a vast arena of blasphemy, simply through the referring character of our lives, a character whose embodiment constitutes in every aspect a "breaking of the law" in its vast and comprehensive detail. If "the fool says in his heart 'there is no God'" (Ps. 14:1), we are *all* fools, sad fools indeed. Every act of faithlessness, of despair, of contempt, of calculated willfulness, of self-asserting strategy, of disdain . . . sad fools we are.

Paul's description in Romans 1 of humanity's lapse into "depravity of mind . . . filled with every kind of wickedness" (Rom. 1:28ff.) moves deliberately in the direction of this equation between blasphemy and human life itself, outlined in terms of the Law's particular boundaries particularly and exhaustively broken down. So he concludes, "You who boast in the law, do you dishonor God by breaking the law? For, as it is written, 'The name of God is blasphemed among the Gentiles because of you'" (Rom. 2:23f.). This is the New Testament's clearest explicit reference to the third commandment (citing Ezek. 36:20ff.). Coming as the summary transgression for all Israelite transgressions, themselves mirrors of human transgression heightened by the fuel of twisted religious self-righteousness, the commandment's reference by Paul opens up a vista on the stark wastes of existence that Paul's gospel is then articulated in order to address (though not in the context of Ezekiel's original prophecy).

And he addresses it through displaying the infinite weight of the human and divine historical contrast: in Romans, for instance, Paul exposes the human side, concluding his argument regarding the shape of the blasphemed life of Adam's kin by placing "all under the power of sin" (Rom. 3:9ff.): "We have already charged that all men, both Jews and Greeks, are under the power of sin, as it is written: 'None is righteous, no, not one; no one understands, no one seeks for God. All have turned aside, together they have gone wrong; no one does good, not even one . . . their mouth is full of curses and bitterness,'" and so on. Note what Paul is quoting from here: psalms that detail the blasphemy of men (5; 10; 16), Ecclesiastes itself, and Psalm 14, which begins how? "The fool says in his heart, 'there is no God.'" "All are under the power of sin," that is, "vanity." And all this Paul expresses in Romans in order to unveil the revelation of him, by contrast, who "at the right time, died for the ungodly" (Rom. 5:6). Vanity, yes; but vanity now unveiled as the object of divine sacrifice. The God *called* "nothing" — whose name is taken "in vain" — becomes nothing, and so overcomes the power of nothingness's name.

The famous hymn in Philippians 2 gives voice to this astonishing act, using the very semantic tools of the third commandment's concerns: "Have this mind among yourselves, which is yours in Christ Jesus, who, though he was in the form of God, did not count equality with God a thing to be grasped, but emptied himself, taking the form of a servant, being born in the likeness of men . . . becoming obedient to death, even death on a cross. Therefore God has highly exalted him and bestowed on him the name which is above every name, that at the name of Jesus every knee should bow, in heaven and on earth and under the earth, and every tongue confess that Jesus Christ is Lord, to the glory of God the Father" (Phil. 2:5-11). Note carefully: God becomes "empty" — vain — for the sake of his name! The literal "formulation" of Jesus Christ in time becomes the divine fulfillment of the third commandment itself, indeed of all Scripture in its role as explicator of a way or law and the prophecy of its fate (in this case taking up Isaiah's promise for the divine name's resonating vindication; cf. Isa. 45:23). The "envainment" of the cross — "he emptied himself" — becomes the filling-up of God's life in the world: for the gospel of Christ is now preached so that the power of the cross be not "emptied" (1 Cor. 1:17), a power, a sacrifice, a death, given for the "glorification" of God's name through God's self-emptying, as John writes in his Gospel (John 12:28): "'Father, glorify thy name!' Then a voice came from heaven, 'I have glorified it, and I will glorify it again.'" When? "'When I am lifted up from the earth,' which he said to show by what death he was to die."

I am deliberately pressing the paradoxical character of this use of the language of vanity and emptiness as applied to Christ. For Paul's gospel of Jesus is, in part, a response to the implications of the third commandment, whose historical consequences are absolutely devastating to human existence and being. The profanation of God's name consigns the "fools" that men and women are to the vanity, the emptiness, and the futility of their own wishes — "I will not hold guiltless those who take my name in vain"; "he makes a pit, digging it out, and falls into the hole which he has made" (Ps. 7:15). The fool disappears upon himself. And only, as it were, from *beyond* this failed human struggle between reality and nothingness does God's truth come to bear within the world of time. From "beyond" the quandaries that oaths are meant to fix. "Would it help if God could sort this out?" Indeed, from beyond blasphemy the blasphemed God is sanctified by choosing to become the form of blasphemy itself: he becomes a "curse" for us (Gal. 3:13), he becomes "sin" for us (2 Cor. 5:21), he becomes "vain" for the "vainsayers."

And why? So that, in the place of our being and nothingness, in place of justice solitary and intolerant, there should now be only love itself — justice joined to mercy — who is God himself. And yes, the command then finds its practical fulfillment in *this* revelation, who is Christ incarnate, seen and touched (1 John 1:1); and it finds its "obedience," even "unto death," in the form of the follower of *this* Christ. "I am speaking the truth in Christ, I am not lying; my conscience bears me witness in the Holy Spirit, that I have great sorrow and unceasing anguish in my heart. For *I could wish that I myself were accursed and cut off* from Christ for the sake of my brethren, my kinsmen by race" (Rom. 9:1-3). Cursed, cut off, rendered empty and vain, "for the sake of" my own brethren. It is the answer to every blasphemy, and every quandary of the truth that blasphemy provokes, from the Rwandan hills to the church's spoiled precincts.

The only profanity, then, that crumbles hope before God is that which rejects the cross of God — the cursedness of those who reject the cursedness of Christ, "enemies of the Cross of Christ" (cf. Phil. 3:17f.). And holiness, the holiness of God, is given by contrast in the cross-takers, whose sanctity is proven in his own death for our sin, embodied in the suffering of its own assaulted purity. Here, at last, the whole Levitical system is given weight and form for the whole of time and space. And this is why, as well, the Law, every "jot and tittle" of it (Matt. 5:17-20), remains in force, is still to be read, is still to be noted and digested, is still our own law, reburnished in the glow of divine vanity whose self-stripping uncovers glory. For shame on a church that no longer reads Leviticus with wonderment and joy!

III. The Church's Redeemer

Let me now offer a summary conclusion to this contrast of contemporary searching and scriptural exposition, retracing quickly once again the church's own history of relationship with this text. For it seems to be the disengagement of the Decalogue from this scriptural habitation I have just outlined that has so undermined its revelatory matter. The manner in which this happened remains to be traced by the scholarly community, and I can hardly attempt it here, except to say that as Scripture and cross became conceptually detached and often opposed, and more particularly as the cross itself has achieved some kind of categorical self-explanatory religious power outside of its press back into the Scriptures, so too the Decalogue has drifted free into legal realms undetermined by the reality of God's self-revealed character in Christ.

It is curious, for instance, that the earliest church did not appear to interest itself in the Decalogue at all as some separate or distinctive element of God's law. When not simply equating the "superstition" of pagans and Jews together as a form of faithless idolatry (cf. Diognetus),[12] early Christian writers made an effort to contrast the form of God's covenants between the Mosaic dispensation for "hard hearts" and the New "Testament" given "within" the heart, by which right ac-

---

12. *Letter to Diognetus* 3-4; *Epistle of Barnabas* 1-4, 13.

tion was made possible through the work of Christ (Justin).[13] Here the "laws" of Christ were described simply according to the catena of various Gospel texts, including those of the Sermon on the Mount (cf. *Didache*),[14] which may or may not have included references to common moral demands appearing in the Decalogue, like thievery and, on our topic perhaps, perjury (cf. Justin).[15] "Commandment" in this context indicated the general demand of God for righteousness, now simply understood as tied to the figure of Christ. In particular, the "way" of the Christian was usually tied to the "way" of Christ himself, and to the degree that scriptural — that is, Old Testament — commands were discussed at all, they were seen in the light of this specific form of life, often tied to the witness of the early Christian martyrs themselves.

The peculiarity of the Decalogue was of course eventually recognized, and the question of the continuity, substantively and historically, of Jesus' commands with the rest of Scripture was then raised as well. If anything, however, these developing theological topics pressed the Decalogue into a firmer connection with the evangelical doctrines concerning Christ, and not away from them. Even Irenaeus,[16] who is seen as the first to link the Decalogue specially with some "natural law" common to all people, actually read "nature" in this case in a thoroughly christocentric (and thus, for him, resolutely scriptural) fashion, as the image of God's purpose in salvation. And this purpose is, according to Irenaeus, "friendship" or "communion" with God, given in Christ the Word, who "shares" the glory of the Father. In Christ this "natural" law is taken up — it was always his, after all — and following the disciplined life of Israel, repromulgated through him, and "expanded" and deepened, as in the Sermon on the Mount, a series of teachings that reflects the form of Christ's own inclusive life. And thus our life "in" Christ becomes the locus of the Law's own power and form.[17]

13. Justin Martyr, *Dialogue with Trypho* 11, 46.
14. *Didache* 1-3.
15. Justin Martyr, *Dialogue with Trypho* 12.
16. Irenaeus, *Against Heresies* 4.12-14. Irenaeus is a central figure in the *Catechism of the Catholic Church*'s discussion of the Decalogue and its connection with "natural" moral law (cf. 2063 and 2070), although the use to which he is put is arguably somewhat deforming of his own vision.
17. Cf. the Cappadocians, who take the lead in this area in their own way, through reading the entire account of the giving of the Law figuratively as pertain-

The later argument between Protestants and Catholics over whether or not Christ was "in" the Decalogue (or for that matter, whether the Decalogue is part of the "old" or the "new" covenant) shows how very far the matter had drifted from this early Christian vision over the centuries.[18] Though Augustine, for instance, was adamant that the Decalogue pertained, as much as the cultic statutes, to the "letter that kills," his point was not to reject the Decalogue's value to Christians[19] but to bring the *whole* law, and not the Decalogue only, into connection with Christ and his Spirit.[20] It was a move that went firmly against the hierarchicalizing schemas of later Christian attempts to distinguish "moral," "ceremonial," and "civil" aspects of the Old Testament revelation, and instead attempted to place the Decalogue's substance within the overall work of Christ's Spirit and its work of "charity" and self-sacrifice. By the early Middle Ages it was still that case that, for example, Rabanus Maurus and the *Glossa Ordinaria,* which, as I noted above, Thomas later cited in order to question, continued to argue that the "vanity" referred to by the third commandment touched upon a relationship with Christ himself, with his divinity and thus with the fact and character of his sacrifice upon the cross: to deny *this* is to take the name of God "in vain."[21] "Blasphemy"

---

ing to an opening up of the human soul to the life of God, via the Spirit of Christ, all of which is figured in the "tables" of Moses given in the heart (the "stone" ones being "broken"); cf. Gregory of Nyssa, *The Life of Moses* 202ff. Here is a key theological area where the question of God's "name" arises: the "name" of the third commandment is shown to be "bigger" than the "Jewish" identification. Cf. Ps.-Dionysius, e.g., *The Divine Names,* where God's name takes in the whole of his person and character (as Origen would say), even within created matter, leading to the incarnation. The "hallowing" of God's name itself embraces the full spiritual appropriation of this "named" reality, which is possible only "in Christ," as joined to his incarnation and form. (This reading of Christian Neoplatonism stands in contrast to, e.g., Derrida and much postmodern negative theology; cf. Derrida's *On the Name* [Stanford: Stanford University Press, 1995], "Sauf le nom," pp. 35ff.)

18. Cf. Andrewes, p. 62.

19. Augustine's famous sermons on the Decalogue make this clear; cf. *Sermons* 8 and 9, in the English edition of his *Works* put out by New City Press (Brooklyn, N.Y., 1990), pt. 3, vol. 1.

20. Augustine, *On the Spirit and the Letter* 14.23.

21. Cf. Rabanus Maurus's *Commentary on Exodus,* which became the basis for many subsequent medieval discussions, including the *Glossa,* in Migne, *Patrologia Latina,* 108, col. 99.

in this context was understood globally, as a denial of God's reality in Christ, in word and deed. It is a sin in which we are obviously all lodged mysteriously, and to which Christian practice had long sought some response before the modern era.

Yet even as movements like Saint Francis's were seeking to bring believers into some conformity with the emptied self of blasphemy's divine absolution, with the true "sorting out of God," canonists of the twelfth century were rediscovering Roman jurisprudence for the sake of stabilizing the body politic. Instead of such a death as Christ Jesus' standing over the commandment as its light, the church turned to the question of swearing. Instead of martyrdom, oaths. Instead of the awful apprehension of redemption dragging a penitent soul, or church, or world into the lake of a self-emptying mercy — instead of this, civil order. In this sense the developing modern question is not John Locke's concern over "how — in an ordered society — can you trust an atheist?" In the modern world — as in any — it is not enough to found our common lives on the good will of some basic religiosity, take whatever form you will, as if the trustworthiness of such spiritual decency could protect our fragile diversities. More practically we should be asking "how do we live in a world in which, on some basic level, we are *all* atheists?" where all of us in different ways set "at naught" God's name, where all of us "empty" it of power and reality, consigning it to the vanities of our own construction, where churches and Christians themselves evacuate God's name over and over again through the vanitizing of the cross, even as God himself secretly enacts the force of such a self-willed offering?

How? How in Rwanda, how in the United States, how on a globe set against itself as it is today? We have two options, as I suggested in my opening remarks: we are either silent altogether, or we turn toward another "way" wherein our lives are taken up not by order at all, but by the disorder of a ravenous world undone by its own voraciousness into which we willingly fall in faith. "You shall not take the name of the Lord your God in vain." You cannot read these words therefore, and their cognates, upon a courthouse door, a school pavilion, a church's chancel, without shuddering at the very trivialization of Christ that has thereby been effected in our midst. As if such miming of the Decalogue could hold back the forces of our chaos. Far from thrusting our Savior into the public square, for the sake of keeping our tidiness running on time — a square where he himself knows too well the fleshly consequences of his display — the third commandment secretly uncovers the deep loneliness and love of Jesus taken to the edges and far corners of our profaning lives. It says to us, "Beware: you cannot trust a single oath, except the oath — the Testament — that God has made for you; if you would grasp it, drink his cup. Are you willing?" (cf. Mark 10:38).

Only God can swear. Only God keeps promises. And only on that basis can we live at all. This is how the commandment directs us. Here is where the commandment sets us down. It is not a place without morals, or a place without directions, a place where nothing is done because it is all too hard. It is a place, rather, of "fear and trembling" (Phil. 2:12) given over, with the whole of our life's possessions, to Christ Jesus, who himself has given over all. One hundred fifty years ago Isaac Williams, the Oxford poet who wrote Tract 87 shortly before Newman shattered the hopes of a catholic reform for the Church of England, bemoaned the contemporary banalization of the cross of Christ, bandied in the "marketplace" by gospel scalpers, summoned up by religious devotees, distributed as a social medicine for the deserving poor. So that even from the profligate use of such gracious names as this — "sacrifice" and "atonement" — "we almost shrink at feeling that [these words] have been used in an unreal manner, and 'taken in vain'; for these holiest of words may be constantly used by us, when we are not at all affected and influenced by so concerning a doctrine, which may be seen by the whole of our character in daily life, and tone of our teaching; by self-confidence, and an absence of that fear and trembling, which ever follows the consciousness, that it is GOD that worketh in us both to will and to do." The truth of God, Williams insists, is a "dangerous" truth, the "knowledge of God an occasion of fear, the more so, because not now considered so," and the holiness to which we are called the very thing we cannot have, except if we finally ourselves enter the danger of our Master's path.[22] Put another way, there is the old spiritual, from Williams's era but voiced across the Atlantic from within our own midst. Sorting out the vain blasphemies of life, in silence or in deathly humility, or both together, it sings: ". . . they crucified my Lord . . . an' He never said a mumblin' word."

22. [Isaac Williams], Tract 87, V:3; VI:10.

"Keeping It Holy": Old Testament Commandment and New Testament Faith

Markus Bockmuehl

> holy adj. *(holier, holiest) 1 belonging to, devoted to, or empowered by, God (obs.)*

> *"Very true," said the Duchess: "flamingoes and mustard both bite. And the moral of that is — 'Birds of a feather flock together.'" "Only mustard isn't a bird," Alice remarked. "Right, as usual," said the Duchess: "what a clear way you have of putting things!"*

"Curiouser and curiouser!" That is how Alice in Wonderland responds to the unfamiliar experience of observing her feet take leave of her head. It is also our late modern culture's instinctive response as we watch the Bible's strange preoccupation with ideas like holiness and purity receding into the distance. We simply cannot relate to something so remote, so bizarre, so alien to our brave new and virtual

---

An earlier version of this paper was presented to a conference of the Society for Ecumenical Anglican Doctrine, Charleston, S.C., January 2003 (under the assigned title "Profaning the Holy?"). I am grateful for valuable comments received from members of the audience as well as from Stephen C. Barton, Michael B. Thompson, and my students David J. Rudolph and Clinton E. Wahlen.

world. As one recent book on Old Testament ethics puts it, these writings now offer us little more than "glimpses of a strange land."[1] They simply do not fit our communities of discourse.

Judging from recent developments in many "oldline" Protestant churches, this present obsolescence of holiness in the church's teaching has been greeted by many of our contemporaries with considerable delight: what a relief to find that a cocktail of late modern and inherited Christian assumptions allows us to get by without taking that "strange Old Testament land" too seriously! A culture of holiness and purity that worried about menstrual uncleanness and mixed fibers in clothing can have nothing more to say to us about practical Christian ethics. Some of us may still concede that the Old Testament narrative envisaged God personally giving the Torah to Israel. But fortunately, "we now know that we all have knowledge." And at least since Origen we know that Jesus abolished the Law, and even serious-minded Christians are free to take it only in its "spiritual" sense.[2]

Then again, perhaps some of us like our religion a little more conventional and Calvinist in flavor, or indeed more Anglican and in keeping with the Thirty-nine Articles (cf. Art. VII). We are temperamentally conservative, and prefer evolution to revolution. We prefer to mind our p's and q's more carefully, and so to distinguish between moral, civil, and ceremonial laws of Moses. Strictly speaking, Jesus

---

1. Rodd 2001.

2. For Origen see, e.g., Diestel 1869: 45-46 on passages like *C. Cels.* 5.48; 7.26. This is despite Origen's otherwise strictly biblical theology (cf. Harnack 1931: 144-45; Campenhausen 1959: 46-48), which on occasion even allowed him to reapply Levitical legislation to the Christian priesthood (see, e.g., Horbury 1990: 746 n. 88 on Origen, *In Lev. hom.* 5.4). Passages like Matt. 5:17 nevertheless restrained most of the Fathers from an explicit affirmation of this discontinuity in terms of "abolition." For them, Christ "fulfilled" rather than "destroyed" the law — and yet put a new one in place of the old. One of the clearest affirmations of this is in Eusebius, *Praep. evang.* 1.6-7, where the destruction of the temple is said to have destroyed the Law and turned the Jews into lawbreakers: at that point "the whole of the Mosaic covenant was abolished (*eluto*, cf. Matt 5.17, 19!), and what pertained to the old covenant was destroyed *(periēreto)*"; the curse was now transferred to the new lawbreakers who continued to obey Moses' law when its time had passed and it had been replaced by the perfect new Law. This is in contrast to the alternative position (e.g., in the Gnostic *Letter of Ptolemy to Flora; Ps-Clem. Hom.* 3.47; etc.) that the Law was flawed from the start because it was either given by an inferior deity or humanly corrupted by false pericopae.

abolished only the third of these; the civil laws applied only to the polity of ancient Israel in the first place, while the moral laws are permanent and apply in some sense to Christians too. And of course, the Ten Commandments are the moral law par excellence. Either way, much of the Old Testament legislation is preoccupied with ritual — and therefore its talk of distinguishing holy and profane need not overly concern us.[3]

But then suddenly our peace may be disturbed when we return to the text and read words like these: "Remember the Sabbath day, *to keep it holy* . . . the LORD blessed the Sabbath day and *made it holy*."[4] Or even, "Do not lift up the name of the Lord for uselessness." Why not? Because, the Septuagint continues, "the Lord will not *purify* the one who seizes his name for uselessness" (cf. also Deut. 5:11).

"Holiness"? "Purity"? Here are these dreaded words of ancient ritual and myth right in the middle of the Ten Commandments! Surely there must be a mistake in this awkward intrusion of ceremonial law into what was supposed to be the pure milk of universal reason and morality. . . .

Enter the Anthropologists

Anthropologists and philosophers of religion have not been slow in coming to our aid. Standard critical approaches to this matter eliminate holiness and purity from practical consideration in Christian ethics. They do this in a number of ways.

Whether directly or indirectly, the dominant approach for most

---

3. Modern scholarship sometimes contrasts "sacred" (rather than "holy") with "profane," due in part to the influence of Eliade 1987. NRSV reflects this trend in using "sacred" twice as often as RSV, although it does so very unsystematically and in many cases where "holy" or "sanctified" represents the sense. Biblically, it is difficult to sustain a distinction between "holy" and "sacred." Exod. 30:25 and Lev. 10:17 RSV/NRSV are interesting examples of the Hebrew's clear synonymity being compromised in favor of such a supposed distinction.

4. In Moses' reiteration of the commandment in Exod. 35, this awkward intrusion of ritual is even stronger: "Six days shall work be done, but on the seventh day you shall have a holy Sabbath of solemn rest to the LORD; whoever does any work on it shall be put to death" (35:2).

of the twentieth century was that of Rudolf Otto, who in turn was indebted to Friedrich Schleiermacher.[5] Otto's 1917 book *Das Heilige* de-
constructed the holy from a fundamentally psychological perspective,
stressing the emotive response that holiness evokes: feelings of the numinous, the fascinating and awesome mysteriousness that is summoned up by the "wholly other."

There can be no doubt about Otto's enormous influence even to
the present day, or about the important contribution he made to the
study of holiness at the anthropological and psychological level. He
also rightly drew attention to the nonrational side of religion. At the
same time, however, two distinctive features of Otto's contribution
have arguably hampered rather than helped Western understanding
of the biblical view of holiness. First, he reinforced a tendency to treat
holiness as an abstraction in search of an ontology, assuming that we
can meaningfully speak about holiness without ever confronting its divine source.[6] He downplayed the fact that in Scripture, as in many
other faiths, holiness is first and foremost a quality of God.

Equally apropos to our present ecclesiastical and cultural climate
is a second feature of Otto's program. He believed that the numinous
must be understood as devoid of moral content. His theory of experience allowed for no ethical dimension — thereby ignoring the extent
to which all the Abrahamic faiths closely link awe of the divine realm
with practical reverence for the divine will.[7] The fact that criticisms
were soon raised both by philosophers of religion and by dialectical
theologians[8] did not prevent the continued influence of Otto's mode of
thought. This influence is evident not only in academic theologians
like Tillich, but also in the book's enduring readership. *Das Heilige*
went through more than thirty German editions, and Oxford University Press keeps the second English edition of his work in print to this
day (under the oddly misleading title *The Idea of the Holy*).

An analogous but slightly different phenomenological approach
was taken by scholars like Nathan Söderblom[9] and, later, Mircea

5. Schleiermacher 1958: 19-82.
6. Cf. also Lanczkowski 1985.
7. This is a point rightly stressed by Lanczkowski 1985: 696-97.
8. Note, e.g., Oxtoby 1987: 437, contrasting Otto's *Das Heilige* with Barth's
Römerbrief.
9. Söderblom 1913.

Eliade,[10] who recognized that what is holy must always be read in opposition to what is profane — whether in the realm of space, of time, of
nature, or of humanity itself. But both authors were led by this
phenomenological insight to abstract holiness fundamentally from the
biblical particularity of the holy Lord God of Israel. Holiness, indeed,
was explicitly viewed by Söderblom as the more fundamental concept,
more basic even than divinity.

Other anthropologists following the school of Émile Durkheim
took a more sociological approach and suggested that holiness is primarily an attribute of inviolability or power that societies convey upon
certain persons, objects, times, or places; the profane, by contrast, is
whatever attempts to violate or weaken the holy.[11]

Turning to the Old Testament, scholars of ritual have developed
such anthropological accounts of holiness and purity more specifically
in a structuralist direction.[12] We find that these notions function as instruments of taxonomy, enabling the ancient Semites to impose order
on a confusing world of disorder. On this view, the seemingly arbitrary
taxonomy of clean and unclean derives from an attempt to order the
world on the basis of primeval taboos and magical practices.

The End of Purity? The Rise and Rise
of L. William Countryman

From a Christian perspective, however, the precise nature of that taxonomy, like the mechanisms of de-sanctification and resanctification,
remains specific to Israel, and highly marginal in the New Testament's
address to Gentiles. Purity and impurity, the creaturely states that
qualify or disqualify a person from participation in God's holiness, appear similarly decentered from the overall New Testament scheme of
things — though not (as we shall see) moved off the map altogether. In

10. E.g., Eliade 1987.

11. For the history of scholarship about the holy, see further Idinopulos and
Yonan 1996; Paden 2003; also Rogerson 2003: 5-16; Crowder 2003.

12. Stimulated by the anthropologists Douglas (1966) and Turner (1969).
Among the more important works they influenced have been Neusner 1973 (cf.
Eilberg-Schwartz 1987) and Gammie 1989, but also numerous New Testament
scholars including Malina (1986) and Neyrey (1990).

dealing with the Decalogue, therefore, we obviously face the pressing question: What further role can holiness, let alone purity, possibly play in *Christian* practice?

To acknowledge and illustrate the extent of our confusion on this point, I would like to comment briefly on one of the most widely influential books on purity in the last twenty years, L. William Countryman's *Dirt, Greed, and Sex.*[13] First published in 1985 and frequently reprinted (but never revised), this book is a rhetorically masterful exposé of the new orthodoxy in sexual ethics in many mainline Protestant churches. In some ways it is characteristic of the contemporary heritage of Otto's emotive-experiential account of purity and holiness — although with a curious twist, as we shall see.

Countryman's argument begins by introducing the reader to ancient Old and New Testament notions of purity and of property, drawing selectively on the work of the anthropologist Mary Douglas.[14] He argues that biblical laws about purity and impurity are essentially a codification of taboos, intensely emotive reactions of revulsion that are specific to a given culture — its "yuk factor," one might say.[15] Hence his preferred reference to "dirt" rather than "impurity." The purity system, on Countryman's reading, is used in the Old Testament to provide "emotional reinforcement" for other kinds of moral or ethical concerns, especially in the area of sex.[16] First-century Judaism picked up this theme and ran with it, with Essenes and Pharisees in particular zeroing in on certain distinctive sexual practices of the purity code and turning them into defining characteristics of Jewishness (p. 55).

The New Testament, however, shows no further interest in an ethic of sexual or any other kind of physical purity (pp. 66, 74). Jesus and the Gospels set aside the whole notion of pure and impure (pp. 75,

13. Countryman 2001; parenthetical page references in the following text are to this work.

14. Like many other NT scholars, Countryman draws only on her early and more general work (Douglas 1966), which underwent considerable refinement in her subsequent studies of Leviticus (Douglas 1999b; cf. also Douglas 1999a) and Numbers (Douglas 2001).

15. Countryman 2001: 17-20 and passim.

16. So for example the Torah's treatment of cross-dressing and male homosexual acts is reinforced by calling them "abominations," which Countryman somewhat questionably translates "disgusting things" (Countryman 2001: 26).

85, 124-25) and henceforth consider sexual ethics *solely* under the heading of sexual property: it becomes a matter not of purity but of greed, the respect for what rightfully belongs to another. Paul likewise agrees that purity is solely of metaphorical or spiritual interest, making "sexual satisfaction a legitimate and sufficient reason for marriage" (p. 213); the Johannine school, meanwhile, is "rejoicing in the power of unclean rites to convey salvation" (p. 125). What this means for sexual ethics is obvious: private sexual property may be affirmed, but membership in the church is no longer subject to purity considerations. As a result, *no* sexual act can now be wrong in and of itself (pp. 221-27). Chastity ceases to be an issue, while "nonmarital liaisons" may well "serve to meet legitimate needs in the absence of genuine alternatives" (p. 244).

The success of Professor Countryman's book has been so comprehensive that it continues to be remarkably difficult to find any thoroughgoing criticism of it — indeed, the very suggestion that a critique might be needed can meet with blank incomprehension. To this day the book graces parish book tables as well as college and seminary reading lists in ever new editions. It manages the rare achievement of engaging difficult Old and New Testament topics in ways that are both accessible and immediately relevant to contemporary concerns. Clearly Professor Countryman's arguments are particularly topical and congenial to the spirit of our age.

One could discuss this phenomenon from a number of perspectives. One would be to address Countryman's development of sexual ethics in relation to our topic of holiness — especially given the remarkable fact that "holiness" is virtually absent as a point of reference by campaigners on either side of the recent sex wars in the Anglican and other churches.[17] Revisionists and traditionalists alike owe us a theologically credible account of Christian holiness in sexual ethics. But it is not my brief to address Countryman's sexual ethics here; and who knows, perhaps in the current climate a heavenly "half hour of silence" (Rev. 8:1) on this matter could turn out to concentrate the mind — and to offer a theologically fruitful moment of respite to all concerned.

A further, and in some ways more interesting, angle of discus-

17. On the marginalization of holiness, cf. similarly Barton 2003: 193.

sion might be to examine the tools of Professor Countryman's cultural analysis of ancient Israel — by applying them to the analyst himself, and to his cultural context in late modern biblical scholarship. What would it mean to shine on this *contemporary* culture's defining myths the critical floodlight provided by a starting point in more deliberate sympathy with the biblical texts and the living communities of faith they continue to generate and sustain? One example may help to illustrate this. From the vantage point of catholic and apostolic Christian faith, how meaningful is it to presuppose that the scriptural authors belong to a social world that is *categorically* alien to ours, and that they are therefore enlightening at best for their cultural curiosity rather than for any inhabitable norms or propositions? That sort of analysis might well shed light on what Robert Jenson has called biblical scholarship's sectarian ecclesiology[18] — in other words, its assumption that orthodox Christian doctrine represents a fundamentally mistaken understanding of New Testament texts. Is it really the case that Christian readers encounter Scripture's implied authors and audiences (in the words of one famous scholar) like "a group of foreigners somehow dropped in our midst"[19] — rather than as part of a continuous diachronic communion of faith and interpretation? Professor Countryman belongs to a long-standing tradition of NT scholarship that privileges aims and methods incompatible with the reception and praxis of Scripture in the ecclesial contexts in which it has in fact lived and prospered. Although often very interesting intellectually, ecclesiologically this vantage point is indeed "sectarian." Once again, however, while this discussion of Countryman seems promising, it would detract from our present concern with the issue of holiness.

Here, therefore, we can confine our critique to a very simple observation. And that is this: Professor Countryman manages to dispatch the subject of *purity* down the theological kitchen sink without ever touching on how this might bear on the subject of *holiness* — a subject that merits *no* discussion at all in his three-hundred-page book, let alone an entry in its otherwise helpful index. At first sight, such an

18. R. Jenson 1999: 98; cf. Green 2002: 10.
19. Thus explicitly Malina 2001: 24 and passim, followed by many other scholars, including, e.g., Philip F. Esler in Countryman 2001: x-xii.

omission may seem hardly worth fussing about. An ounce or two of further reflection, however, shows that silence to be both deafening and devastating. Both Old and New Testament theology make it impossible to discuss the idea of purity or impurity without recourse to the distinction between holy and unholy. These terms certainly have quite different nuances for Jewish and Gentile audiences, but they remain part of an indispensable moral and theological whole, as the following discussion demonstrates.

So What Makes "Old Testament" Holiness Tick?

On one level, much in the anthropological analysis of writers like Otto and Douglas and even Countryman can be useful and defensible as an account of the structural dimensions of purity and holiness, especially in the Old Testament. The problem arises in the attempt to flay or pare these issues off from Christian faith, like the husk from the kernel.

Within the Old Testament itself, the issue may appear relatively straightforward. Holiness pertains first of all to God, and by derivation to his entourage in heaven and to the people, places, times, and objects associated with him on earth. The application of this belief certainly helps to reinforce and manage a multitude of sociological, legal, hygienic, psychological, and gender-related norms. Concentric shades of graduated holiness apply to all creatures as they approach the divine absolute.

But before asking what Christian significance this can possibly have, it is worth noting four further features of the Old Testament's own account of holiness, and of purity, that are not always recognized or understood.[20]

1. Biblical talk of purity and impurity makes sense only within the context of holiness or its absence. Pollution (whether moral, ritual, or physical) precludes entry into the presence of the holy God of Israel.

20. See also Milgrom 2000: 1530; cf. more generally P. Jenson 1992: 44-53 and P. Jenson 2003; Harrington 2001: 11-44 (esp. 38-43); Olyan 2000: 17 and passim.

2. What is ritually pure may be either holy or profane, but what is impure can never be holy.[21]

3. Both holiness and impurity can be "contagiously" transferred to people or objects that are not holy or impure. The unholy and the pure, by contrast, are both static, "default" conditions. Their status derives solely from the absence of the opposite.

4. Between both polarities (pure-impure, holy-unholy), human beings can move in either direction. But the call of the people of God is to participate in his exclusively one-way mission: to push the boundaries of holiness further and further into the realm of the profane, and to eliminate pollution in order to expand the realm of purity. To sanctify times or places or people or objects means to transfer things from the profane to the holy.

What might that divine calling look like? For the people of God, holiness is a divine gift, constituted by their relationship to God, who is its only source. De-sanctification can occur through defilement by unholy actions or entities, especially relating to the desecration of the holiness of life, sex, and worship. Resanctification can be achieved by ritual means or in some cases through appropriate actions. These are actions that God prescribes not to prevent but to enable fellowship with God, just as the holiness with which these actions are concerned is invariably God's own. Thus it is foundational to Old Testament and Jewish belief that God's name is quintessentially holy, as Philo of Alexandria expounds in his treatise on Moses.[22] And unless the impurities polluting God's people in the sanctuary are removed, God cannot abide there and will abandon it.[23]

In the context of the Ten Commandments, this plays out very clearly in the preparations for the revelation at Sinai: a holy God elects and constitutes a holy people. God says to Moses, "You shall be for me a priestly kingdom and a holy nation. These are the words that you shall speak to the Israelites" (Exod. 19:6). Every one of the command-

21. Wright 1992: 246-47 seems mistaken in his claim that objects can be holy and impure at the same time: his examples are less than persuasive. Cf. the more nuanced treatment in Wright 1999.

22. Cf. *to hagiotaton kai theion onoma:* Philo, *Mos.* 2.208.

23. This is the implication of Lev. 4–16, graphically spelled out in Ezek. 8–11. Cf., e.g., Wright 1999: 358; Milgrom 1991 passim.

ments needs to be mentally prefaced with that preamble: "I am the LORD your God, who brought you out of the land of Egypt, out of the house of slavery — you shall be for me a holy nation." By that election you are holy, and that is why you are to keep holy your worship, your language, your time, your relationships, your property.

This theme of Israel constituted as a holy people through the exodus has also been highlighted in recent canonical criticism.[24] In an important essay, Stephen Barton has articulated the link between liturgy and ethics in the narrative logic of Exodus 19–20: "The experience of the holiness of God is an invitation to become a priestly kingdom who celebrate God's holiness in worship. But the liturgical or cultic community has to be also the moral community which celebrates God's holiness in lives devoted to doing God's will."[25]

In Scripture, to be a holy people as God is holy entails a necessary *imitatio Dei:* it is at once a call to sanctify, to make holy as God makes holy, i.e., make fit for fellowship with God. This indeed is the proper interpretation of every single commandment of the Decalogue: it is about participating in God's own sanctification in time and space of the divine name and image. This *imitatio Dei* in setting apart the sacred from the profane is perhaps most obvious in relation to the Sabbath, which Israel is to sanctify as God sanctified it: for God himself "makes holy the Sabbath and Israel and the seasons," as the synagogue's festival prayer puts it.[26]

The eschatological vibrancy of the scriptural witness to the Sabbath is well captured by the Jewish philosopher Abraham Heschel:

> He who wants to enter the holiness of the day must first lay down the profanity of clattering commerce, of being yoked to toil. He must go away from the screech of dissonant days, from the nervousness and fury of acquisitiveness and the betrayal in embezzling his own life. He must say farewell to manual work and learn to understand that the world has already been created and will survive without the help of man. . . . The Sabbath is a day for the sake of life. . . . The Sabbath is not for the sake of the weekdays; the

24. See Wells 2000.
25. Barton 2002: 26; cf. further Barton 2003.
26. *Meqaddesh ha-shabbat we-yisra'el we-ha-zemanim,* Singer 1962: 312. Also cited in Hayward 2003: 167 to conclude a study of the sanctification of time in *Jubilees.*

weekdays are for the sake of the Sabbath. It is not an interlude but the climax of living.[27]

The polarity of holy versus profane pervades the Law, Prophets, and Writings as a theologically indispensable building block of Israel's faith. Just as in the Decalogue, it recurs throughout in relation both to the Sabbath (and the festal calendar) as God's time (e.g., Exod. 20:8; 31:14; Ezek. 22:8; cf. Lev. 23:2-44; etc.) and also to God's holy name (e.g., Lev. 21:6; Ezek. 36:22; 39:7).

But this polarity is also inextricably bound up with the much wider issue of righteousness and sin. And so we find that elsewhere in the Pentateuch several of the Ten Commandments resurface with the preamble "You shall be holy, for I the Lord your God am holy." This partnership in God's holiness is the reason for honoring father and mother; this is why God's people are to keep the Sabbaths and to turn from idolatry (note, e.g., Lev. 19:1-4).

The Prophets and Writings, especially Isaiah, Ezekiel, and Zechariah, spell out a vision of purity and holiness appropriate to Israel's life in the land that has Jerusalem's holy place as its center. Here too, this vision always maintains a profoundly moral dimension. Ezekiel (36:17, 19), like Leviticus (18:25, 28), sees moral profanity as defiling the land; while Amos speaks of God's holy name being profaned when people "trample the head of the poor into the dust of the earth, and push the afflicted out of the way" and when "father and son go in to the same girl" (2:7). The impurity of immorality in the Old Testament and ancient Judaism has received close attention in some recent studies.[28] In the Old Testament, sin is not understood as defilement in *ritual* terms, but it is no less devastating as a result. Second Temple Judaism further intensified that connection between sin and impurity, so that it becomes one of the key links between how purity works in the Old Testament and how it works in the New.[29]

---

27. Heschel 1998: 9, 13-14, as quoted in Barton 2002: 31-32.

28. See Klawans 2000, whose dissertation is also cited approvingly by McKnight 1999b: 84-89.

29. Cf., e.g., Klawans 2000; McKnight 1999b: 88-89.

The Old Replaced in the New — or Is It?

How then does all this work in the New Testament? Surely Jesus and Paul take holiness for granted, and consider the Old Testament purity laws abolished?

It is indeed possible to argue this by pressing into service supersessionist readings of Mark (7:19), Galatians (e.g., 3:23-26), and Hebrews (e.g., 8:13; 13:9-10). And even respected Christian interpreters have admittedly done this from time to time, thereby directly or (more often) indirectly fueling the assumption that Old Testament concerns about holiness are entirely passé.

In this vein, Christians have often argued that in the New Testament these notions are swept aside as obsolete relics of an ethnic particularism. They are best universalized on the basis that in Christ all foods are equally clean, all days and seasons are equally special; and no time or place, land or person can now be holier than any other. Christ is above all and in all; no human endeavor is outside his grace, and therefore outside the realm of God's holiness. One leading theological reference work concludes its article on the question by saying, "The mediation of holiness through Christ and the Spirit makes obsolete the traditional distinction between holy and profane, as indeed that between pure and impure."[30]

But is this all that can be said on the subject? Perhaps not. The word *hagios* and cognate terms for holiness occur in the New Testament 275 times — more than a great many other words that are regarded as unquestionably central to Christian theology. Of these, 50 passages are in the Gospels and another 55 in Acts. That still leaves the Pauline corpus with 96, most of them in the undisputed letters, and 73 in the Catholic Epistles and Revelation. The semantic field defining purity is rather more diffuse, but similar statistics could be compiled here too; the relevant number of references is certainly in excess of 150.[31]

The stress on God's transcendent holiness cannot be dismissed as

---

30. So Taeger 2000: 1533 (my trans.). See also P. Jenson 2003: 118-20 on the impact of revisionist ideological criticism on scholars' ability to perceive sympathetically what the Priestly texts are saying.

31. This figure includes the roots *hagn-, (a)kathar-, (a)mia(i)n-, molun-*, as well as *askoinoō* (but no other *koin-* words).

the obsolete expression of a primitive mythology. It is instead the very starting point for any human encounter with Israel's God in the Old Testament — and indeed in the New. "Holy, Holy, Holy is the Lord God of hosts," say the seraphs to Isaiah in the temple, and thereby reduce him to a stammering confession of his own people's moral guilt and impurity (Isa. 6:3-5) — leaving the possibility of Israel's purification as God's people entirely in God's gift and initiative.[32] And "Holy, Holy, Holy is the Lord God Almighty who was and is and is to come," sing the four creatures in the book of Revelation to the One who sits on the heavenly throne, and whose scroll no one in heaven or on earth is worthy to open except the Lamb (Rev. 4:8–5:6). The message has not changed: God is holy, and no one can stand in God's presence to worship him "with all the company of heaven" — except by God's own gift of holiness.[33] That true holiness is at the same time the only possible context of worship which cannot degenerate into idolatry and which enjoys the promise of an eschatological future.[34]

Paul, Holiness, and Purity

It is worth focusing on the Apostle to the Gentiles for a moment, as a key example of what this entails. Paul speaks of holiness twice as much as the four Gospels put together. If one bears in mind the largely Gentile address, the meaning of this language has not undergone the sort of drastically discontinuous de-Judaization that the popular Protestant narrative supposes. Strange as it sounds to Greek ears,[35] the God of Israel remains for Paul the source of all holiness. This is now fo-

---

32. On this reading of Isa. 6, cf. recently Moberly 2003: 136-39 and passim.

33. Cf. similarly Hawthorne 1997: 486. This is why the words of Isa. 6:3 reappear in the Sanctus of the Christian Eucharist since at least the fourth century (cf. perhaps already *1 Clem.* 34.6f.). As the 1662 *Book of Common Prayer* puts it, "Therefore with Angels and Archangels, and with all the company of heaven, we laud and magnify thy glorious Name; evermore praising thee, and saying, Holy, holy, holy, Lord God of hosts, heaven and earth are full of thy glory."

34. Cf. Barton 2003: 212-13. That the primary context of Rev. 4 lies in worship rather than in the critique of political power is not fully acknowledged in the otherwise stimulating and valuable study of Söding 1999.

35. So, e.g., Schlatter 1929: 12, also cited by Procksch and Kuhn 1964.

cused in the fact that by his death Jesus has "become our sanctification" once for all (1 Cor. 1:30; cf. Heb. 10:10, 14, 29; 13:12), and by his resurrection he has been "declared to be Son of God with power according to the *Spirit of Holiness*" — the classic Jewish designation of the Holy Spirit (Rom. 1:3-4).[36] And it is the "holy ones" in whose company Christ will return and who will judge the world (1 Thess. 3:13; 2 Thess. 1:10; 1 Cor. 6:2). All believers, indeed, are called "holy ones," although the Jerusalem church is assigned a special status in this regard: the collection "for the saints" is specifically for them, and Paul prays that the offering of the Gentiles may be sanctified by the Holy Spirit (Rom. 15:16).

But is this perhaps merely the kind of theological mood music that might inevitably accompany Alice's experience that "all must have prizes"? After all, Christ has already "become our sanctification" — distinctions between holy and profane can presumably make no further sense in a Christian view of the world. And surely purity concerns have become wholly irrelevant?

To be sure, Paul's language does presuppose that all who belong to Christ are indeed "cleansed" from whatever defilement of sin they might once have had (e.g., 1 Cor. 6:11; Eph. 5:26; cf. 2 Cor. 7:1). They and even their children are now seen within the sphere of holiness and purity (1 Cor. 7:14). It is clear that holiness is a gift that belongs freely and constitutionally to all the people of God, including both Jews and Gentiles: the church is holy by definition, by its incorporation in Christ (e.g., Rom. 11:16; 1 Cor. 3:17; Eph. 2:21).[37]

Contrary to the heirs of Rudolf Otto, however, holiness is not for Paul morally indifferent. Those who are baptized into Christ are called to "present your members as slaves to righteousness *for holiness*" (Rom. 6:19), just as the new man is created "in the likeness of God in the righteousness and holiness of truth" (Eph. 4:24). Christians are called to a life without blemish (Phil. 2:15; Col. 1:22; Eph. 1:4). Indeed, the pursuit of moral "holiness" rather than "impurity" is explicitly said to be "God's will" for Gentile Christians: the will of God is noth-

36. Barton 2003: 201 rightly notes the pervasiveness of holiness terminology in the opening of Romans.

37. Cf. also Rosner 1995 on the continuing importance of holiness terminology in 1 Corinthians for the definition of God's people.

ing less than their constitution and progression in holiness — and Paul quite deliberately singles out holiness as concerned with matters of sexual purity (1 Thess. 4:4-7).

Regardless of authorship, the Pastoral Epistles offer a splendid précis of this Pauline logic (Titus 2:11-14): "For the grace of God has appeared, bringing salvation to all, training us to renounce impiety and worldly passions, and in the present age to live lives that are self-controlled, upright, and godly, while we wait for the blessed hope and the manifestation of the glory of our great God and Saviour, Jesus Christ. He it is who gave himself for us that he might redeem us from all iniquity and *purify* for himself a people of his own who are zealous for good deeds." The holiness of God's people is thus both soteriologically and morally charged — and retains a vital connection with concerns of "purity," however different these may at first sight appear from those of Leviticus. There continues to be a categorical difference between what is holy and what is not, between the sphere of sin and uncleanness on the one hand and the sphere of righteousness and holiness on the other. As E. P. Sanders puts it, Paul tends to prefer the language of righteousness to describe entry into the elect community, but the language of holiness for maintenance of that membership.[38]

As in the Old Testament, removal of defilement is the necessary corollary for participation in holiness. The church is for Paul a holy realm to which nothing unclean can belong and from which all that is not holy must be removed, as 1 Corinthians 5–6 shows patently. Holiness forms the only possible context of true worship (Rom. 12:1-2), both in liturgy and in its "extension and re-appropriation" to our whole existence.[39] Far from profaning the sacred or approaching it through divination, Paul seeks the hallowing of all of life (and in this respect stands much nearer Jewish than Greco-Roman views of holiness).[40]

In the midst of their day-to-day life stands the believers' fellow-

38. Sanders 1983: 45, 63 n. 138. At the same time, Peterson 1995: 23 and passim is right to stress that holiness and sanctification for Paul have their source invariably in God's gift and initiative (rather than in human achievement).

39. On this point see Barton 2002: 26-27, and cf. more generally Thompson 1997.

40. Cf., e.g., Harrington 2001: 72-86 and passim.

ship in the body and blood of Christ, which requires them to "discern" the social reality of "the body" (1 Cor. 10:16; 11:27-29). That discernment, however, is achievable only in the bright light of a categorical separation between the cup of the Lord and the cup of demons (10:21). In order to celebrate the feast of our holy Passover lamb, one must first cleanse out all old "yeast of malice and wickedness," replacing it with pure "sincerity and truth" (5:7-8) — the latter part of the paschal metaphor is invariably omitted in contemporary eucharistic shorthand. In that sense, too, the bread and wine offer not merely the liturgical "gifts of God for the people of God," but "sanctified gifts to sanctified people," to borrow from the Orthodox Liturgy of Saint Chrysostom.[41] The holiness and the purity of that people are constituted in baptism (cf. 1 Cor. 6:11; Eph. 5:26; also Acts 22:16; John 3:25-26; Heb. 10:22).

In other words, Paul's theological toolbox has no concept of new holy being that does not issue forth in the pursuit of holy and morally pure doing, "cleansing ourselves from every defilement of body and of spirit, making holiness perfect in the fear of God" (2 Cor. 7:1). Being and doing are each necessary to constitute the other. As those who are made alive by the Spirit who is holy, Christians will also keep in step with that same Spirit who is and makes holy (Gal. 5:25).[42] That notion of the Spirit's holiness, incidentally, is by no means a leftover of Old Testament stereotypes: of over ninety biblical references to the *Holy Spirit*," only three appear in the Old Testament, but fully 75 percent are in Luke-Acts and Paul.

A holy people called to a holy life in fellowship with a holy God — this same priority is clearly evident in the anonymous Letter to the Hebrews, where we hear that without the practical pursuit of holiness "no one will see the Lord" and "many will be defiled" (10:10, 14; 12:10, 14-15). The whole purpose of Christ's self-giving sacrificial death was to purify and "make holy" the people of God (9:14, 23; 13:12) — and he is able to do so as the high priest who alone enters the heavenly Holy of Holies (9:11-14). So too in the Catholic Epistles, especially 1 Peter

41. *ta hagia tou hagiois.* Note also the important study of Klawans 2002 on the Last Supper as emphatically an *extension,* rather than a replacement or "spiritualization," of temple holiness and temple service.

42. So rightly Schnelle 2000: 1573.

with its explicit reappropriation of Exodus in the call to be holy in our conduct as he who called us as a holy people is himself the source of that holiness (1:15-16; 1:2; 2:9; cf. 2 Pet. 3:11). Purity is part of the eschatological vision of the Johannine writings, where all who hope in his appearing are said to "purify themselves just as he is pure" (1 John 3:2-3). That same vision is finally encapsulated in Revelation, where the holiness of the Lamb is conveyed to his bride, the holy heavenly city of Jerusalem, which nothing and no one unclean can enter — and where those who are invited to the marriage of the Lamb have washed their robes (21:26-27; 22:14-15). This suggests a continuing affirmation of a distinctively holy people, made so by God in Christ, and even of times and places associated with that holiness.[43]

Profaning the Sacred or Hallowing the Profane?
The Case of Jesus

We could spend the remainder of our inquiry exploring this New Testament evidence in greater detail. To a somewhat less explicit extent the same issues can be traced in the Synoptic Gospels and in John. We would discover that the biblical theology of holiness is far from abolished in the ecclesiology of a people of God elected out of Jews and Gentiles. Although clearly universalized in its application to Gentiles,

43. Note, e.g., the "holy mountain" of the transfiguration (2 Pet. 1:18), the "holy city" of Jerusalem (Rev. 11:2; 21:2, 10; 22:19; also Matt. 4:5; 5:35; 24:15; 27:53), not to mention the Scriptures (Rom. 1:2; 7:12) and the Eucharist (e.g., 1 Cor. 11:27; *Did.* 9.5): see the discussion in Hawthorne 1997: 487, following Procksch and Kuhn 1964. To be sure, the church of the second and subsequent centuries was deeply confused about the extent to which this ongoing Christian concern for holiness meant an ongoing role for Old Testament Law, let alone of purity law. And this confusion cuts right across the commandments about the Sabbath and about images in the otherwise highly valued Decalogue. But it is important to note, again contra Countryman et al., that the early church's sometimes haphazardly Platonizing readiness to allegorize the Levitical purity laws never extended to the sphere of sexual morality: as in Philo and contemporary Hellenistic Judaism, sexual purity was taken literally and interpreted ascetically (see, e.g., Wendebourg 1984: 157-59 and passim). And the authority of the Old Testament for theology and ethics remained a matter of core conviction, as, e.g., the masterful treatment of Horbury 1990 amply demonstrates (e.g., pp. 737, 760-61).

the polarity of sacred and profane remains foundational, and linked in significant ways to a moral framework of purity.

At one level this might seem to be nothing other than what one would expect, if the Old Testament were taken seriously as Christian Scripture. But in the current Gnosticizing hermeneutical climate it certainly is a point well worth reiterating. There is no such thing as "the Old Testament God" who is somehow in a different category from the New Testament version.

What is more, for Christian doctrine it is highly pertinent that the New Testament's theology of holiness emerges within a fundamentally trinitarian frame. As is the case throughout Christian Scripture, God continues in the New Testament to be "the Holy One" par excellence (John 17:11; 1 John 2:20; 1 Pet. 1:15-16; Rev. 4:8). But his Son Jesus Christ, raised from the dead by God's Spirit of holiness (Rom. 1:4), has been revealed to all as the Holy One of God (Mark 1:24; Luke 4:34; John 6:69) who is able through his death and resurrection to invite his disciples into the holy fellowship of love that the Son shares with the Father (John 17:17-21).

But rather than provide an exhaustive dot-to-dot New Testament theology of holiness, I would like instead to highlight the striking importance of holiness and purity in the ministry of Jesus. Amidst all the hullabaloo of recent years over the self-styled Jesus Seminar and various conspiracy theories about the Dead Sea Scrolls, it would have been easy to miss the fact that scholars quietly engaged in the so-called third quest for the historical Jesus have witnessed a striking sea change in our understanding of his inalienably Jewish context and message.

One of the key themes to emerge in this discussion is the realization that holiness matters very profoundly to the shape of Jesus' teaching. His approach to the issue is admittedly radical and in significant respects differs strikingly from the mainstream of contemporary Pharisaic and later rabbinic views. Explicit mentions of the issue are relatively few in number, even if those few occasions leave no doubt that he endorses the Torah's distinction between holy and profane, and even between pure and impure. "Do not give what is holy to dogs; and do not throw your pearls before swine"[44] pretty neatly encapsulates those twin polarities.

44. Matt. 7:6; *Did.* 9.5; *Gos. Thom.* 93.

But it is now coming increasingly to be understood that we cannot hope to engage with the story of Jesus without taking much more seriously his passionate concern for the sanctity both of the temple and of the restored twelve tribes of Israel.[45] At the most basic level, Jesus endorses sacrifices and gifts to the temple (e.g., Mark 12:41-44 par.; Matt. 5:23; 23:19) and participates in the festal pilgrimage calendar.[46] In his dramatic action in the temple during the last week of his life, Jesus stakes his whole ministry on his belief that the house of prayer for all nations had been turned into a den of thieves. Corruption and commercialism desecrate "the holy place," as do false vows.[47] What Jesus seeks is instead to inaugurate Zechariah's vision of a day when a spring for sin and uncleanness will flow from Mount Zion into all the land: then there will no longer be any traders in the house of the Lord, but instead the holiness of the temple reaches out to encompass every cooking pot in Jerusalem and Judea.[48] And far from undermining this prophetic vision of holiness, the Last Supper's interpretation of Jesus' own death in sacrificial terms appropriates and universalizes it as the new covenant with all Israel in his blood.[49]

Aside from participating in the great festivals, Jesus shows by the very shape of his debate with the Pharisees (e.g., Mark 3:4 par.) that he affirmed the sanctity of the Sabbath.[50] And despite the frequently overinterpreted dispute of Mark 7:1-23 par., Jesus also continues to take

45. E.g., McKnight 1999a.

46. In addition to his final Passover, attested in all four Gospels, note the references to other pilgrimages at Passover, the Feast of Booths, and Hanukkah in John 2:23; 5:1; 6:4; 7:2, 10, 14, 37; 10:22.

47. Matt. 24:15. Note also that the temple's holiness sanctifies both the offerings and the offerer: "What then is greater, the gold or the Temple which sanctified the gold?" (Matt. 23:17, 16-22). Cf. Mark 11:16 on secular traffic through the temple.

48. Zech. 13:1; 14:8, 20-21. The cooking pots may in turn point to the inclusive holiness of Israel's food and table fellowship, as Clinton Wahlen has suggested to me.

49. Klawans 2002 and Dunn 2002: 466 rightly criticize the widespread notion that the Last Supper is somehow antisacrificial or at least anti-temple in orientation, pace Chilton 1992: 150-54; Chilton 2000: 253-55; Ådna 2000: 419-30. Dunn himself, on the other hand, significantly underestimates the continuing importance of holiness and purity concerns in Jesus' ministry; see n. 50 below.

50. See further Mark 2:27; Matt. 24:20; and note Luke 23:56. Cf. *Gos. Thom.* 27.

for granted the biblical purity laws.[51] He even tends to avoid contact with Gentiles (Matt. 10:6; cf. Mark 7:27 par.) to such an extent that the exceptions are rare enough to be specially highlighted in the Gospels.

All through his ministry Jesus followed John's washing of repentance for the forgiveness of sins by his own "baptism" with none other than the Spirit of holiness. This does not mean that Jesus either abolishes purity or ignores it, as we just saw. Rather, in his teaching, exorcism, and table fellowship he both *presumes* the holiness and purity of Israel and at the same time *brings it about* "by the finger of God" (Luke 11:20). In the act of exorcism, this extension of God's holiness to displace the profanity of demons makes Jesus stand out as "the holy one of God" par excellence (Mark 1:24 par.).[52] Ever since the infancy stories, the Gospels link Jesus with Jewish messianic hopes to celebrate in his coming the holiness of God's name (in the Magnificat, Luke 1:49) and the birth of the messianic child who "will be called holy" (Luke 1:35).

That said, it is of course true that Jesus' hallowing of table and of time, including the Sabbath and the festal calendar, does not sit easily with strict Pharisaic or rabbinic views.[53] This would soon become grist to the mill of Gentile Christians like Ignatius, who found it "monstrous to talk of Jesus Christ and to practise Judaism."[54] But apart from a famously enigmatic and perhaps ironic aside in John (5:16-18),[55] no Gos-

---

51. See, e.g., Mark 1:44 par.; Luke 11:44; Matt. 7:6; 23:27; also Mark 5:11-13 par. On Jesus' differentiated affirmation of purity, cf. further Bockmuehl 2000: 3-15, 23-33; McKnight 1999b; Tomson 2001. Note also Chilton 1992, 1996, 2000, among others; while Dunn 2002: 464 is rightly critical of certain overstatements in Chilton's position (e.g., "purity was Jesus' fundamental commitment, the lens through which he viewed the world," Chilton 2000: 90), his own view skates over the evidence for purity concerns rather too nonchalantly. See, e.g., Dunn 2002: 461; Dunn 2003: 180-91 (and cf. studies like Kazen 2002), where Jesus is said to be "indifferent" to purity.

52. Israel's presumed purity, therefore, derives from the Lord. Drawing on Mark 7:15, Dunn 2002: 464 rightly rejects Chilton's claim (cf. Chilton 2000: 87 and passim) that purity is "from within": in this context it is in fact *impurity* that comes from within, while purity is from God.

53. For rabbinic views of holiness, see the important treatment of Harrington 2001.

54. So Ignatius, *Magn.* 10.3, following his observation that the apostolic generation of "divine prophets," who "once walked in ancient customs, came to a new hope, no longer practising the Sabbath but living life according to the Lord's Day" (*mēketi sabbatizontes, alla kata kuriakēn zontēs*), 9.1.

55. Cf. also 7:22-24, with which compare Matt. 12:5.

pel text accepts that Jesus willfully or even inadvertently breaks the Sabbath. Indeed, on several occasions in the Synoptics he cites established views about the Sabbath that appear to meet with the tacit agreement of his Pharisaic opponents;[56] and on several issues Jesus' position is evidently in dialogue with the range of attested rabbinic interpretation, sometimes well within and sometimes just outside it.

The Sabbath as such is a given, and what is at stake is not the holiness of the Sabbath but how it should be understood. For Jesus it means to set free sons and daughters of Abraham who are under the bondage of Satan (Luke 13:16; cf. John 7:23). It is to *this* end that "the Son of Man is Lord even of the Sabbath." To sanctify the Sabbath means to save life and do good, not just to rest but to *give rest* to others — an adaptation of a good rabbinic principle, anticipated in Deuteronomy's vision of the Sabbath (Deut. 5:14).

The Pharisees and the Dead Sea sect shared with Jesus a desire for the purity and holiness of temple, land, and nation — a desire nourished by numerous prophetic texts of the Old Testament.[57] Their default vision of that true and holy Israel, however, was sectarian and centripetal, requiring ordinary Israelites to "opt in" or be excluded.[58] For Jesus, God's holiness moves out from the center to embrace the whole nation. His mission is explicitly to all the lost sheep of the house of Israel (Matt. 10:6; 15:24), which ultimately includes all those who will return from the east and the west to sit at the messianic banquet with Abraham (Matt. 8:11), and even "sheep who are not of this fold" (John 10:16).

Once again this has important antecedents in Zechariah, Ezekiel, and other prophetic texts that presuppose that in the eschaton God's holiness reaches out from the sanctuary to encompass all of Jerusalem, indeed all of the Promised Land. For Jesus the land of Israel, like the people, is holy in its entirety. Where the Pharisees and Essenes shun the contagious impurity of the nonobservant *Am Ha-Aretz*,[59] Jesus pre-

56. So rightly Tomson 2001: 33 with reference to Luke 6:6-11; 13:10-17; 14:1-6; Mark 2:27.
57. For the eschatological purification of the temple, see, e.g., Isa. 4:4; Mal. 3:1-3; *Pss. Sol.* 17.30; etc., and cf. also Dunn 2002: 466.
58. For Qumran this means that the sectarian *Yaḥad* is the eschatological core of Israel. Cf. further Bockmuehl 2001.
59. Cf. the classic study of Büchler 1968: 41-46 on early rabbinic attitudes; Newton 1985 on Qumran (also Dunn 1997 on this implication in 4QMMT).

sumes to dispel profanity by the Lord's contagious holiness — extending it to all the house of Israel. By what one might call the imperialism of the holy "finger of God," he expels the profanity of unclean spirits to perish in a herd of unclean swine. In his meal fellowship and healing ministry Jesus reaches out to the lost sheep of the house of Israel, whose holiness and purity he affirms — and effects — as an eschatological a priori.[60] That explains why he refuses to reach out directly to Gentiles, but visits Gentile and Samaritan areas within the larger biblical boundaries of the land.[61]

Conclusion: Hallowing God's Time and Name

This brief tour of Exodus, Paul, and Jesus may well have raised more questions than answers. If so, it will have scored a success. On the subject of holiness, the pastoral task of theology in the West may now be to goad the comfortable more than to comfort them. I hope to have shown lines of continuity between the Old and New Testaments in the categorical distinction between holy and profane, pure and impure — a distinction that moreover enjoys eschatological significance.

As ancient Jewish writers well understood, Old Testament law was inevitably and necessarily modified in being applied to Gentiles, since the Torah addressed only a handful of commandments to a wider audience.[62] Those few, however, form the basis for a kind of Jewish canon of universal ethics, on which the New Testament and early Christian ethics draw extensively. In this connection, the distinction between holy and profane remains intrinsic to Jewish as well as Gentile faith in the God of Israel — indeed, it is significant that Gentiles in Christ are now newly adopted into God's "holy people." For any reve-

---

60. This may also explain why there is a presumption of purity in the case of doubtful foods: if *koinos* (as distinct from *akathartos*) could be seen as whatever has not been certified holy or pure (cf. also Dunn 2002: 451), then it may be significant that Jesus (Mark 7:15), Peter (Acts 10:14-15), and Paul (Rom. 14:14; cf. 1 Cor. 10:27-29) reject the presumption of impurity in what is uncertified. This has obvious application to the question of meal fellowship, both of Jewish Christians with Gentiles and of Christians with pagans.

61. See, e.g., Bockmuehl 2000: 61-70, 75-79.

62. See Bockmuehl 2000: 87-173 and passim.

lation or worship of Israel's God, therefore, the embrace of holiness and repudiation of its opposite remain both a vital prerequisite and also its indispensable *telos,* its manifest outcome in the communion of saints.[63]

Purity, to be sure, carries no palpable "ritual" function for Gentiles, and yet the inherited Jewish view of immorality as pollution ensures that New Testament Christianity retains a vital concern for the *moral* purity of believers — i.e., above all in the cardinal areas of idolatry, sex, and bloodshed.[64] Faced with the stress on discontinuity in the early anti-Jewish Christian rhetoric of identity, one must always interpret this in view of the remarkable continuity — not just of Scripture and monotheism, but of moral praxis at least in these three crucial areas.

In this respect it is unsurprising that Irenaeus and Ezekiel were at one in condemning religious teachers who abandon the distinction between holy and profane and thereby profane God's very presence among them.[65] Invariably this created a clash between Judeo-Christian and pagan understandings of God, as it seems to do today.[66]

Smooth operators in every generation revel in their seemingly unprecedented discovery that holy and profane are all much of a muchness — or else that everything is holy, nothing is profane. "Flamingoes and mustard both bite," says the Duchess to Alice in Wonderland. "And the moral of that is — 'Birds of a feather flock together.'" To which Alice retorts, "Only mustard isn't a bird." Would that our theological debates displayed similar clarity of insight!

We conclude by returning once more to the text at hand. "I am the LORD your God, who brought you out of the land of Egypt, out of the house of slavery. . . . You shall not take the name of the LORD your God in vain; for the LORD will not hold him guiltless who takes his

---

63. Cf. on this point Fergusson 1999, citing Wesley and Hauerwas.
64. Cf. Bockmuehl 2000: 145-73, 230-38.
65. Ezek. 22:26; Irenaeus, e.g., *Adv. haer.* 1.6.2, "For even as gold, when submersed in filth, loses not on that account its beauty, but retains its own native qualities, the filth having no power to injure the gold, so they affirm that they cannot in any measure suffer hurt, or lose their spiritual substance, whatever the material actions in which they may be involved. Wherefore also it comes to pass, that the 'most perfect' among them addict themselves without fear to all those kinds of forbidden deeds of which the Scriptures assure us that 'they who do such things shall not inherit the kingdom of God.'"
66. Cf. further Harrington 2001.

name in vain. Remember the Sabbath day, to keep it holy" (Exod. 20:2, 7-8). The holiness of God's name and the holiness of God's time: Jesus brings both these concerns to a point in his teaching and practice of prayer. The Gospels show him orienting his own life around separated times of prayer, not least at moments of initiative, crisis, decision, temptation. Prayer is the hallowing of time, whether it happens to be externally placid or overwhelming. Perhaps that is why in Matthew and Luke he prefaces his teaching on the subject with the words *"Whenever* you pray. . . ." Such hallowing of our time is not erratic but habitual, as it were the punctuation of a life with God.

And this hallowing of time centers on the hallowing of God's name. As in the great *Qaddish* of the synagogue,[67] this is the first and overarching petition of the prayer Jesus teaches his disciples, governing all that follows: "Our Father in heaven, may your name be *sanctified.*" The content of this petition is the positive equivalent of the third commandment: for Jesus, "do not take the name of the Lord in vain" entails the prayer that this holy name should be hallowed, made and kept holy — with the little phrase "on earth as it is in heaven" qualifying all three of the opening petitions. This prayer, in the very act of praying, initiates its own fulfillment.[68] And for ancient Jews and Christians alike, the supreme human sanctification of the name consisted in the act of laying one's life in testimony to it: so Jews died for *qiddush ha-Shem,* the "sanctification of the Name," while Christians died for the confession "I belong to Christ," *Christianus sum.*[69] For Christian life, in fact, it has always been the confession or denial of that holy name, in deed as in creed, which most deeply determines our identity and destiny.[70]

---

67. *Yitgaddal we yiqaddash shemeh rabba be-'alma' di-bera' ki-r'uteh,* "Magnified and sanctified be his great name in the world which he created according to his will" (Singer 1962: 80).

68. Cf. Cullmann 1995: 45.

69. Cf. further Bockmuehl 2000: 238-40.

70. Matt. 10:32-33; 1 John 2:23; Rev. 3:7-8. Cf. also the second-century Christian redactor of 4 Ezra 2.45-47: "'These . . . have confessed the name of God; now they are being crowned, and receive palms.' Then I said to the angel, 'Who is that young man who places crowns on them and puts palms in their hands?' He answered and said to me, 'He is the Son of God, whom they confessed in the world.' So I began to praise those who had stood valiantly for the name of the Lord."

Just as God's holiness dwelt with Israel "in the midst of their uncleannesses" and sins (Lev. 16:16), "tabernacled among us" in his Son who bears God's name (John 1:14; 17:12; Phil. 2:9-11), and empowers the church by the Spirit of holiness who raised him from the dead (Rom. 1:3-4; 8:11), so the prayer of Jesus seeks the sanctification of God's name right here in the profane times and places of our existence.

WORKS CITED

Ådna, Jostein. 2000. *Jesu Stellung zum Tempel: Die Tempelaktion und das Tempelwort als Ausdruck seiner messianischen Sendung.* Wissenschaftliche Untersuchungen zum Neuen Testament 2:119. Tübingen: Mohr Siebeck.

Barton, Stephen C. 2002. "'Mercy and Not Sacrifice'? Biblical Perspectives on Liturgy and Ethics." *Studies in Christian Ethics* 15: 25-39.

———. 2003. "Dislocating and Relocating Holiness: A New Testament Study." In *Holiness Past and Present,* edited by S. C. Barton, pp. 193-213. London: T. & T. Clark; New York: Continuum.

Bockmuehl, Markus. 2000. *Jewish Law in Gentile Churches: Halakhah and the Beginning of Christian Public Ethics.* Edinburgh: T. & T. Clark.

———. 2001. "1QS and Salvation at Qumran." In *Justification and Variegated Nomism.* Vol. 1, *The Complexities of Second Temple Judaism,* edited by D. A. Carson et al., pp. 381-414. Wissenschaftliche Untersuchungen zum Neuen Testament 2:140. Tübingen: Mohr Siebeck; Grand Rapids: Baker.

Büchler, Adolf. 1968. *Der galiläische 'Am-ha'ares des zweiten Jahrhunderts: Beiträge zur inneren Geschichte des palästinischen Judentums in den ersten zwei Jahrhunderten.* Vienna, 1906. Reprint, Hildesheim: G. Olms.

Campenhausen, Hans von. 1959. *The Fathers of the Greek Church.* New York: Pantheon Books.

Chilton, Bruce. 1992. *The Temple of Jesus: His Sacrificial Program within a Cultural History of Sacrifice.* University Park: Pennsylvania State University Press.

———. 1996. *Pure Kingdom: Jesus' Vision of God.* Studying the Historical Jesus. Grand Rapids: Eerdmans; London: SPCK.

———. 2000. *Rabbi Jesus: An Intimate Biography.* New York: Doubleday.

Countryman, L. William. 2001. *Dirt, Greed, and Sex: Sexual Ethics in the New Testament and Their Implications for Today.* 2nd ed. SCM Classics. London: SCM Press.

Crowder, Colin. 2003. "Rudolf Otto's *The Idea of the Holy* Revisited." In *Holiness Past and Present,* edited by S. C. Barton, pp. 22-47. London: T. & T. Clark; New York: Continuum.

Cullmann, Oscar. 1995. *Prayer in the New Testament.* London: SCM Press.

Diestel, Ludwig. 1869. *Geschichte des Alten Testamentes in der Christlichen Kirche.* Jena: Mauke.

Douglas, Mary. 1966. *Purity and Danger: An Analysis of Concepts of Pollution and Taboo.* London: Routledge and Kegan Paul.

———. 1999a. "Justice as the Cornerstone: An Interpretation of Leviticus 18–20." *Interpretation* 53: 341-50.

———. 1999b. *Leviticus as Literature.* Oxford: Oxford University Press.

———. 2001. *In the Wilderness: The Doctrine of Defilement in the Book of Numbers.* Rev. ed. Oxford: Oxford University Press.

Dunn, James D. G. 1997. "4QMMT and Galatians." *New Testament Studies* 43: 147-53.

———. 2002. "Jesus and Purity: An Ongoing Debate." *New Testament Studies* 48: 449-67.

———. 2003. "Jesus and Holiness: The Challenge of Purity." In *Holiness Past and Present,* edited by S. C. Barton, pp. 168-92. London: T. & T. Clark; New York: Continuum.

Eilberg-Schwartz, Howard. 1987. "Creation and Classification in Judaism: From Priestly to Rabbinic Conceptions." *History of Religions* 26: 357-81.

Eliade, Mircea. 1987. *The Sacred and the Profane: The Nature of Religion.* San Diego: Harcourt Brace Jovanovich.

Fergusson, D. 1999. "Reclaiming the Doctrine of Sanctification." *Interpretation* 53: 380-90.

Gammie, John G. 1989. *Holiness in Israel: Overtures to Biblical Theology.* Minneapolis: Fortress.

Green, Joel B. 2002. "Scripture and Theology: Failed Experiments, Fresh Perspectives." *Interpretation* 56: 5-20.

Harnack, Adolf von. 1931. *Dogmengeschichte.* 7th ed. Tübingen: J. C. B. Mohr.

Harrington, Hannah K. 2001. *Holiness: Rabbinic Judaism and the Graeco-Roman World. Religion in the First Christian Centuries.* London and New York: Routledge.

Hawthorne, Gerald F. 1997. "Holy, Holiness." *Dictionary of the Later New Testament and Its Developments,* pp. 485-89.

Hayward, Robert. 2003. "The Sanctification of Time in the Second Temple Period: Case Studies in the Septuagint and Jubilees." In *Holiness Past and Present,* edited by S. C. Barton, pp. 141-67. London: T. & T. Clark; New York: Continuum.

Heschel, Abraham Joshua. 1998. *The Sabbath: Its Meaning for Modern Man.* New York: Farrar, Straus and Giroux.

Horbury, William. 1990. "Old Testament Interpretation in the Writings of the Church Fathers." In *Mikra: Text, Translation, Reading, and Interpretation of the Hebrew Bible in Ancient Judaism and Early Christianity,* edited by M. J.

Mulder and H. Sysling, pp. 727-87. Compendia Rerum Iudaicarum ad Novum Testamentum 2:1. Assen: Van Gorcum; Minneapolis: Fortress.

Idinopulos, Thomas A., and Edward A. Yonan. 1996. *The Sacred and Its Scholars: Comparative Methodologies for the Study of Primary Religions Data.* Leiden and New York: Brill.

Jenson, Philip Peter. 1992. *Graded Holiness: A Key to the Priestly Conception of the World.* Journal for the Study of the Old Testament — Supplement Series 106. Sheffield: JSOT Press.

——. 2003. "Holiness in the Priestly Writings of the Old Testament." In *Holiness Past and Present,* edited by S. C. Barton, pp. 93-121. London: T. & T. Clark; New York: Continuum.

Jenson, Robert W. 1999. "The Religious Power of Scripture." *Scottish Journal of Theology* 52: 89-105.

Kazen, Thomas. 2002. *Jesus and Purity Halakhah: Was Jesus Indifferent to Impurity? Coniectanea Biblica: New Testament Series* 38. Stockholm: Almqvist & Wiksell.

Klawans, Jonathan. 2000. *Impurity and Sin in Ancient Judaism.* Oxford and New York: Oxford University Press.

——. 2002. "Interpreting the Last Supper: Sacrifice, Spiritualization, and Anti-Sacrifice." *New Testament Studies* 48: 1-17.

Lanczkowski, Günter. 1985. "Heiligkeit I: Religionsgeschichtlich." In *Theologische Realenzyklopädie,* 14:695-97.

Malina, Bruce J. 1986. *Christian Origins and Cultural Anthropology: Practical Models for Biblical Interpretation.* Atlanta: John Knox.

——. 2001. *The New Testament World: Insights from Cultural Anthropology.* 3rd ed. Louisville: Westminster John Knox.

McKnight, Scot. 1999a. *A New Vision for Israel: The Teachings of Jesus in National Context.* Grand Rapids: Eerdmans.

——. 1999b. "A Parting within the Way: Jesus and James on Israel and Purity." In *James the Just and Christian Origins,* edited by B. Chilton and C. A. Evans, pp. 83-132. Novum Testamentum, Supplements 98. Leiden: Brill.

Milgrom, Jacob. 1991. *Leviticus 1–16: A New Translation with Introduction and Commentary.* New York: Doubleday.

——. 2000. "Heilig und profan: II. Altes Testament." *Religion in Geschichte und Gegenwart* 3: 1530-32.

Moberly, R. W. L. 2003. "'Holy, Holy, Holy': Isaiah's Vision of God." In *Holiness Past and Present,* edited by S. C. Barton, pp. 122-40. London: T. & T. Clark; New York: Continuum.

Neusner, Jacob. 1973. *The Idea of Purity in Ancient Judaism.* Studies in Judaism in Late Antiquity 1. Leiden: Brill.

Newton, Michael. 1985. *The Concept of Purity at Qumran and in the Letters of Paul.* Society for New Testament Studies Monograph Series. Cambridge: Cambridge University Press.

Neyrey, Jerome H. 1990. *Paul, in Other Words: A Cultural Reading of His Letters.* 1st ed. Louisville: Westminster John Knox.

Olyan, Saul M. 2000. *Rites and Rank: Hierarchy in Biblical Representations of Cult.* Princeton: Princeton University Press.

Oxtoby, Willard G. 1987. "Holy, the Idea of the." *Encyclopedia of Religion* 6: 431-38.

Paden, William E. 2003. *Interpreting the Sacred: Ways of Viewing Religion.* Rev. ed. Boston: Beacon Press.

Peterson, David. 1995. *Possessed by God: A New Testament Theology of Sanctification and Holiness.* New Studies in Biblical Theology. Grand Rapids: Eerdmans.

Procksch, O., and K. G. Kuhn. 1964. *"Hagios Ktl."* In *Theological Dictionary of the New Testament,* edited by Kittel and Friedrich, 1:88-115.

Rodd, Cyril S. 2001. *Glimpses of a Strange Land: Studies in Old Testament Ethics.* Edinburgh: T. & T. Clark.

Rogerson, John. 2003. "What Is Holiness?" In *Holiness Past and Present,* edited by S. C. Barton, pp. 3-21. London: T. & T. Clark; New York: Continuum.

Rosner, Brian S. 1995. "Temple and Holiness in 1 Corinthians 5." *Tyndale Bulletin* 42: 137-45.

Sanders, E. P. 1983. *Paul, the Law, and the Jewish People.* Philadelphia: Fortress.

Schlatter, Adolf. 1929. *Der Evangelist Matthäus: Seine Sprache, sein Ziel, seine Selbständigkeit.* Stuttgart: Calwer.

Schleiermacher, Friedrich. 1958. *On Religion: Speeches to Its Cultured Despisers.* New York: Harper and Row.

Schnelle, Udo. 2000. "Heiligung: II. Neues Testament." *Die Religion in Geschichte und Gegenwart* 3: 1572-73.

Singer, Simeon. 1962. *The Authorised Daily Prayer Book of the United Hebrew Congregations of the British Commonwealth of Nations.* 2nd ed. London: Eyre and Spottiswoode.

Söderblom, Nathan. 1913. "Holiness (General and Primitive)." *Encyclopedia of Religion and Ethics* 6: 731-41.

Söding, Thomas. 1999. "Heilig, heilig, heilig: Zur politischen Theologie der Johannesapokalypse." *Zeitschrift für Theologie und Kirche* 96: 49-76.

Taeger, Jens-Wilhelm. 2000. "Heilig und profan: III. Neues Testament." *Religion in Geschichte und Gegenwart* 3: 1532-33.

Thompson, Michael B. 1997. "Romans 12.1-2 and Paul's Vision for Worship." In *A Vision for the Church,* edited by M. Bockmuehl and M. B. Thompson, pp. 121-32. Edinburgh: T. & T. Clark.

Tomson, Peter J. 2001. "Jesus and His Judaism." In *The Cambridge Companion to Jesus*, edited by M. Bockmuehl, pp. 25-40. Cambridge: Cambridge University Press.

Turner, Victor Witter. 1969. *The Ritual Process: Structure and Anti-Structure.* Lewis Henry Morgan Lectures, 1966. Chicago: Aldine.

Wells, Jo Bailey. 2000. *God's Holy People: A Theme in Biblical Theology.* Journal for the Study of the Old Testament — Supplement Series 305. Sheffield: Sheffield Academic Press.

Wendebourg, Dorothea. 1984. "Die alttestamentlichen Reinheitsgesetze in der frühen Kirche." *Zeitschrift für Kirchengeschichte* 95: 149-70.

Wright, David P. 1992. "Holiness: Old Testament." *Anchor Bible Dictionary*, 3:237-49.

———. 1999. "Holiness in Leviticus and Beyond: Differing Perspectives." *Interpretation* 53: 351-64.

III. SECOND TABLE OF THE LAW

Killing in the Name of God

William T. Cavanaugh

The Lord God said, "You shall not kill," and yet those who profess to be bound by these words do a lot of killing. Indeed, we are told, one of the most fundamental contemporary threats to world peace is the conviction of some that God not only does not forbid them to kill, but positively commands them to do so. Commentary on the war in Iraq and the ongoing "war on terrorism" often implies that a major source of the violence is religion, specifically the fanatical conviction that God commands acts of violence against the unfaithful. In common opinion in the West, killing in the name of God is subject to the most thoroughgoing distaste and reproach. In the "clash of civilizations" worldview,[1] a dichotomy is established between religious violence and secular tolerance. Secular societies still must resort to violence, but it is the kind of controlled and rational violence necessary to contain essentially irrational religious violence. In this view, killing in the name of God is always an outrage; killing in the name of the secular nation-state can be necessary and praiseworthy.

In this essay I will argue precisely the opposite: killing in the name of God is the only type of killing that could be legitimate. I will arrive at this conclusion by examining the commandment against kill-

---

1. This view was popularized by Samuel Huntington's widely influential book, *The Clash of Civilizations and the Remaking of World Order* (New York: Touchstone Books, 1998).

ing in the context of the rest of the Decalogue and the biblical treatment of violence. I will consider the biblical conviction that life is God's alone to give and to take. We are perhaps accustomed to applying this conviction to other of the "life" issues: abortion, euthanasia, capital punishment, genetic engineering, and so on. I think we are less accustomed to applying the conviction that God alone is the Lord of life and death to the issue of war. I will focus on war because it is so timely and because too much of Christian reflection on war is based on applying just-war criteria in abstraction from the crucial theological question of God's command.

I will begin with an example of the common opinion that killing in the name of God is taboo. I will then show that, in the biblical view, killing in the name of God is the only kind of killing that can possibly be justified. I will then examine arguments that religion exacerbates the problem of violence, and how the arguments themselves serve to legitimate the transfer of loyalties to false gods. Finally, I will examine what God actually commands of us with regard to killing, and argue that Jesus Christ takes the commandment against killing to its broadest and most complete extent.

I. Religious Violence versus Secular Tolerance

A piece by Andrew Sullivan in the *New York Times Magazine* will serve as one example out of countless possible of the logic I seek to question. Sullivan justifies the overall war against terrorism — and the subsidiary wars of which it is composed — in terms of an "epic battle" as momentous and grave as the ones against Nazism and Communism.[2] He labels it a "religious war," but not in the sense of Islam versus Christianity and Judaism. It is rather radical Islam versus Western-style "individual faith and pluralism" (p. 44), or "a war of fundamentalism against faiths of all kinds that are at peace with freedom and modernity" (p. 45). Sullivan operates with the same slippery and expansive definition of "fundamentalism" that is so common in public commen-

2. Andrew Sullivan, "This *Is* a Religious War," *New York Times Magazine,* October 7, 2001, p. 53. Parenthetical page references in the following text are to this article.

tary on matters of faith. Fundamentalism need have no connection to those American Christians who trace their lineage to the early-twentieth-century movement to identify five fundamental doctrines of the Christian faith.[3] For Sullivan, fundamentalism refers to the "blind recourse to texts embraced as literal truth, the injunction to follow the commandments of God before anything else, the subjugation of reason and judgment and even conscience to the dictates of dogma" (p. 46). Absent the word "blind" and the stark opposition of dogma to reason, I suspect many Christians, myself included, would be happy to identify ourselves in this characterization, even though we do not consider ourselves fundamentalists.

If a fundamentalist is anyone who takes the command of God seriously, a fundamentalist, furthermore, is someone who refuses to accept that religion is an individual thing. Sullivan quotes Dostoyevsky's Grand Inquisitor as saying of humans, "These pitiful creatures are concerned not only to find what one or the other can worship, but to find something that all would believe in and worship; what is essential is that *all* may be together in it. This craving for *community* of worship is the chief misery of every man individually and of all humanity since the beginning of time." Sullivan completely misses the fact that this craving for community was a cornerstone of Dostoyevsky's own worldview. Instead, Sullivan comments, "This is the voice of fundamentalism. Faith cannot exist alone in a single person. Indeed, faith needs others for it to survive — and the more complete the culture of faith, the wider it is, and the more total its infiltration of the world, the better." Because it needs others, fundamentalism will seek to coerce others violently into its own camp.

A fundamentalist, then, in Sullivan's view, is someone who puts the commandments of God before anything else and also refuses to confine faith to an individual and private realm. Given that most Christians, Muslims, and Jews throughout history would therefore qualify as "fundamentalists," Sullivan does not hesitate to cast his net as widely as possible, claiming, "It seems almost as if there is something inherent in religious monotheism that lends itself to this

---

3. For an analysis of the media misuse of the term "fundamentalism," see Robert Jenson, "The God Wars," in *Either/Or: The Gospel or Neopaganism*, ed. Carl E. Braaten and Robert W. Jenson (Grand Rapids: Eerdmans, 1995), pp. 27-30.

kind of terrorist temptation" (p. 46). Killing in the name of the one God has been a curse on history; Sullivan cites the usual litany of crusades, inquisitions, and religious wars. The problem seems to be too much faith, a loyalty to one God that excludes accommodation to other realities. "If faith is that strong, and it dictates a choice between action or eternal damnation, then violence can easily be justified" (p. 47).

At root, the problem is epistemological. According to Sullivan, it took Western Christians centuries of bloody "religious wars" to realize "the futility of fighting to the death over something beyond human understanding and so immune to any definitive resolution" (pp. 46-47). The problem with obedience to the commands of God is that God's commands are simply not available to us mortals in any form that will produce consensus rather than division. Locke, therefore, emerges as Sullivan's hero, for it was Locke who recognized the limits of human understanding of revelation and enshrined those limits in a political theory. Locke and the founding fathers saved us from the curse of killing in the name of God. "What the founders and Locke were saying was that the ultimate claims of religion should simply not be allowed to interfere with political and religious freedom" (p. 53). In theory, we have the opposition of a cruel fanaticism with a modest and peace-loving tolerance. However, Sullivan's epistemological modesty applies only to the command of God and not to the absolute superiority of our political system over theirs. According to Sullivan, "We are fighting for the universal principles of our Constitution." *Universal* knowledge is available to us after all, and it underwrites the "epic battle" we are currently waging against fundamentalisms of all kinds. Sullivan is willing to gird himself with the language of a warrior and underwrite U.S. military adventures in the Middle East in the name of his secular faith. Sullivan entitles his piece "This *Is* a Religious War," though the irony seems to elude him entirely. The underlying message, crudely put, is this: "Lighten up, you Muslims! Taking God's command too seriously causes violence. Learn to privatize your faith. If you don't, we might just have to bomb the hell out of you."

II. Killing for God

A Christian who takes the Bible seriously as God's revelation must of course refuse such false epistemological modesty. The precise interpretation of God's Word is seldom a simple matter, but we undertake it in community with the whole church in the firm conviction and hope that God speaks to us in the Scriptures. The Ten Commandments are received as God's authoritative word to us. Taking God's commandments too seriously is not the root cause of violence; the problem is not taking them seriously enough. Killing in the name of God is not a peculiar problem to be dealt with by quarantining the will of God from the routine use of force. The reverse is the case: if any killing is ever justified, it can only be because God wills it.

The commandment against killing in the Decalogue is brief enough that its precise meaning is not simply obvious. The two Hebrew words — *lo tirtsach* — that constitute the whole commandment in both Exodus 20:13 and Deuteronomy 5:17 evade simple translation. "You shall not murder" is the favored translation of some English versions of the texts, but the root verb *ratsach* is used elsewhere in the Old Testament (Deut. 4:41-43 and 19:1-13; Num. 35; Josh. 20 and 21) to refer to unintentional killing. The more traditional rendering, "You shall not kill," is not unproblematic either, because there are clearly instances in which killing is not only accepted but commanded of the Israelites. Deuteronomy 24:16 limits capital punishment to putting people to death for their own crimes, but the Law has no difficulty finding crimes for which death is the proper and required punishment. Slaughter in war is also mandated and congratulated. Samuel reports the following words of YHWH to Saul: "I will punish the Amalekites for what they did in opposing the Israelites when they came up out of Egypt. Now go and attack Amalek, and utterly destroy all that they have; do not spare them, but kill both man and woman, child and infant, ox and sheep, camel and donkey" (1 Sam. 15:2-3). Similar examples abound in the book of Judges and elsewhere. It seems, then, that the commandment cannot cover all kinds of killing, for there are clearly some kinds upon which YHWH looks favorably, or at least some circumstances under which killing is allowed or demanded.

The use of the verb *ratsach* in the Old Testament is relatively rare.

It appears 46 times, as opposed to 165 for *harag* and 201 for *hemit*, both of which are used to express killing. The latter terms have multiple uses, including murder, killing the enemy in battle, and putting someone to death according to the Law. *Ratsach*, on the other hand, is used only once for killing someone guilty according to the Law (Num. 35:30), and never for killing someone in battle. As opposed to *harag* and *hemit*, the use of *ratsach* is restricted, according to Johann Stamm, to "illegal killing inimical to the community."[4] This is not much help, however, for it amounts to saying that *ratsach* is the kind of killing you shall not do. We know that already from the Decalogue.

If we are looking to unlock the meaning of the commandment, we might do better to concentrate not on the verb but on the subject of the verb. The subject of the verb "to kill" is you, the human members of the Israelite community. The speaker is God. What the commandment establishes is an absolute divide between God and humans in the issue of killing. If we humans must not kill, it is not because killing as such is always an evil deed. It is because killing belongs to God, and not to us. We know that killing as such is not evil because elsewhere God commands it. What the Decalogue establishes is the difference in authority over life and death between us and God. Our task is not to try to supply a detailed list of types of killing that are and are not permitted, a list that the Decalogue somehow forgot to include. Instead we are called to see that life is not ours to take, but belongs to God alone.

The structure of the Decalogue as a whole supports paying more attention to the subject than to the verb. In both versions, the Decalogue begins not with the law but with the Lawgiver: "I am the LORD your God, who brought you out of the land of Egypt, out of the house of slavery; you shall have no other gods before me" (Exod. 20:2-3; Deut. 5:6-7). The first table of the Ten Commandments is about the subject of the Law, its giver, and what human subjects owe to God. Only after this is established can the second table begin to spell out what humans owe to each other. The first table is not simply supplemented in the second by a more or less arbitrary list of some important things that people ought not do. All the commandments of the

---

4. Johann Jakob Stamm, with Maurice Edward Andrew, *The Ten Commandments in Recent Research* (London: SCM Press, 1967), pp. 98-99.

second table, and most especially the commandment against killing, take their significance from the self-proclamation of a "jealous God" in the first table. You shall not kill for just the same reason that you shall not worship other gods: because there is only one God who is sovereign over life and death. The prohibition against idols especially establishes the absolute divide between the Creator and the created. All the things of the heavens, the earth, or the waters below the earth are mere creatures and can in no way represent the God whose power gave them life.

Karl Barth, Patrick Miller, and Walter Brueggemann have drawn attention to the centrality of the Sabbath commandment to the vision of the Decalogue.[5] In Exodus the Sabbath is commanded as a way of remembering the creation account of Genesis 1 and God's rest on the seventh day. For Barth the Sabbath is a concrete way that humans remember their status as creatures that depend utterly on God. According to Barth, "The Sabbath commandment explains all the other commandments."[6] It does so because it points us away from everything we can achieve and toward what God has done and is doing for us in creation and in redemption in Jesus Christ. The Sabbath is a recognition that we are here not because of our work but because of God's work. However, the Sabbath commandment does not merely point backward to Genesis but also forward to the Yes that God says to creatures in the redemptive work of Jesus Christ. The absolute divide that the commandments reinforce between the Creator and creatures does not therefore negate creatures but rather invites us to affirm life as a gift of God's grace. Life is affirmed precisely in the Son's relinquishing of control over life and death to the Father on our behalf.[7]

The key point of reference for the commandment against killing in the Decalogue is in God's words to Noah in Genesis 9:1-7. In the postfall world, provision is made for the shedding of animal blood where none had been made in the pristine condition of the original creation. Nevertheless, YHWH tells Noah, "For your own lifeblood I will surely require a reckoning: from every animal I will require it and

5. Patrick D. Miller, "The Human Sabbath: A Study in Deuteronomic Theology," *Princeton Seminary Bulletin* 6 (1985): 81-97; Walter Brueggemann, *Deuteronomy* (Nashville: Abingdon, 2001), pp. 72-81.

6. Karl Barth, *Church Dogmatics* III/4 (Edinburgh: T. & T. Clark, 1961), p. 53.

7. Barth, pp. 53-54.

from human beings, each one for the blood of another, I will require a reckoning for human life. Whoever sheds the blood of a human, / by a human shall that person's blood be shed; / for in his own image / God made humankind" (9:5-6). Though it is here established that humans may shed the blood of other humans, they may do so only and precisely in obedience to God.[8] The shedding of human blood by another human is strictly prohibited, unless it is in punishment for killing another, a punishment mandated by God. Here God proclaims ownership over the lifeblood of humans. It is because humans are made in the image of God that lifeblood belongs to God, and may not be taken by a mere human acting on his or her own initiative. Because the killer was understood as taking possession of the victim's blood, the killer had to be executed to compensate the true owner, God.[9]

The basic conviction that life is God's alone to give and take is found not only in Israelite law regarding capital punishment but also in the way war is presented in the Old Testament. The Ten Commandments are set within the remembrance of how YHWH has single-handedly delivered the Israelites from Pharaoh and his army. In Deuteronomy's version of the Decalogue, even the Sabbath command is explained with reference not to the Genesis account of God's rest on the seventh day, but to the mighty hand and outstretched arm that delivered the Israelites from Egypt.[10] No credit is due to the Israelites for fighting their way to freedom. The entire account in Exodus is based on the conviction that vanquishing the Israelites' foes was entirely the work of YHWH. Thus Exodus 14:13-14: "Moses said to the people, 'Do not be afraid, stand firm, and see the deliverance that the LORD will accomplish for you today; for the Egyptians whom you see today you

8. On this point see Walter Harrelson, "Karl Barth on the Decalogue," *Studies in Religion* 6, no. 3 (winter 1976-77): 236.

9. Anthony C. J. Phillips, "Respect for Life in the Old Testament," *King's Theological Review* 6 (fall 1983): 32-35.

10. Although the reference to the seventh day in Genesis seems more logical, Deuteronomy may be commemorating the fact that the liberation from Egypt allowed the Israelites once again to keep the Sabbath, a practice denied them in Egypt. YHWH was motivated to liberate the Israelites not only by a general opposition to oppression, but so that the Sabbath could once again be observed; see Calum M. Carmichael, *Law and Narrative in the Bible: The Evidence of the Deuteronomic Laws and the Decalogue* (Ithaca, N.Y.: Cornell University Press, 1985), pp. 325-26.

shall never see again. The Lᴏʀᴅ will fight for you, and you have only to keep still.'" The conviction that it is God who fights, and not the Israelites, is essentially the same even when the Israelites take up the sword. When the Israelites defeat the Amalekites in Exodus 17, their victory is not attributed to the skill of the Israelite warriors but to the intervention of YHWH. Israel prevails only when Moses holds the "staff of God" aloft; Amalek prevails when the staff is lowered. The account ends with YHWH telling Moses, "I will utterly blot out the remembrance of Amalek from under heaven" (17:14), and Moses' declaration that "The Lᴏʀᴅ will have war with Amalek from generation to generation" (17:16). It is YHWH who makes war; the Israelites do so legitimately only as proxies for YHWH.

This conviction holds firm through the many accounts of Israelite battles to take and keep possession of the Promised Land. As John Howard Yoder points out, pious Jewish readers of the conquest narratives would not have read them in terms of a general justification of war or reflection on the morality of different types of killing. The pious reader would instead have been struck by the promise that the occupants of the land would be driven out not by military might but by the hand of God.[11] The battle of Jericho was won by trumpet, not sword, for the Lord said, "See, I have handed Jericho over to you" (Josh. 6:2). The narratives of the historical books place little emphasis on military might and preparation. In fact, the emphasis is often on the military weakness of the Israelites. In 1 Kings 20:27, the Israelites were encamped "like two little flocks of goats, while the Arameans filled the country." Nevertheless, the Israelites won a great victory, because YHWH said to them, "I will give all this great multitude into your hand, and you shall know that I am the Lᴏʀᴅ" (20:28). Once again in 2 Kings 6 and 7, the Arameans sent a huge army to surround the Israelites and lay siege to their city. Famine grew so great that the people were reduced to cannibalism. The siege was broken when YHWH caused the Arameans to hear the sound of a great army, horses and chariots, so that the Arameans thought the Israelites had enlisted the help of the Hittites and the Egyptians to defeat them. The Arameans retreated in haste. The Israelites' vulnerability is not remedied by for-

---

11. John Howard Yoder, *The Politics of Jesus* (Grand Rapids: Eerdmans, 1972), pp. 80-82.

eign allies and their armies, but by YHWH's trickery. YHWH is the only ally the Israelites need.

In the Old Testament accounts, military misfortune is invariably explained by Israelite self-reliance and refusal to obey the command of God. In 2 Chronicles, for example, the alliance of King Asa of Judah with King Ben-hadad of Aram against the Northern Kingdom is condemned by the seer Hanani in the following terms: "Because you relied on the king of Aram, and did not rely on the LORD your God, the army of the king of Aram has escaped you. Were not the Ethiopians and the Libyans a huge army with exceedingly many chariots and cavalry? Yet because you relied on the LORD, he gave them into your hand. For the eyes of the LORD range throughout the entire earth, to strengthen those whose heart is true to him. You have done foolishly in this; for from now on you will have wars" (16:7-9). This motif is common in the prophetic literature. As Isaiah has it,

> Alas for those who go down to Egypt for help
>   and who rely on horses,
> who trust in chariots because they are many
>   and in horsemen because they are very strong,
> but do not look to the Holy One of Israel
>   or consult the LORD!
>
> (Isa. 31:1)

The commandment against killing is based in a respect for life as a gift of God. Human life itself, however, has no absolute value, but is always to be measured in relation to the will of God. The examples of the martyrs suffice to show that there are circumstances under which the preservation of physical life is not the highest value. The recognition that life is a gift of God may require under certain conditions that a free gift of one's life be made.[12] The authors of the Old Testament believed also that obedience to the will of God might require one not merely to surrender one's life but to kill. This can be squared with the Decalogue's "You shall not kill" only if we assume that killing may be done only when God commands it. If it is ever justified for a

12. See Barth, pp. 334-35.

human to kill a fellow human, it can only be out of obedience to the
word of God.

III. Rival Loyalties

At this point one can imagine that the good, sensible, rational people at the *New York Times* are shaking their heads in disgust. They
might not wish to quibble with my reading of the Old Testament
narratives, but they might recoil nonetheless from the fanaticism
and violence that such a view will, in their view, inevitably produce.
Rather than see the Old Testament view that life belongs to God
alone as a way of limiting violence, many today contend that such a
view makes violence more intractable because it gives it divine
sanction. The sense that one is operating on God's orders to kill produces an absence of constraint and an easy confidence in the justice
of even the most frightening slaughter. One need look no further
than terrorist attacks by Islamic militants to see the awful consequences of such a view.

Over the last several years I have been reading, for another project, every book and article I can find arguing that religion causes violence. There are a great many, both academic and popular. Their arguments tend to be of three types: (1) religion is absolutist, (2) religion is
divisive, and (3) religion is irrational. The implication of these arguments is that the use of force should be secularized. Though I cannot in
so brief a space give a full accounting of each type of argument, I will
give one example of each.

1. Religion Is Absolutist

In an essay entitled "The Non-Absoluteness of Christianity," John
Hick indicts claims of the uniqueness and ultimacy of revelation in
Jesus Christ for inciting Christians to violence against Jews in Europe and non-Christians throughout the Third World. Hick makes
clear that this is not a dynamic unique to Christianity, but is en-
demic to religion as such. "It should be added at this point that the
claims of other religions to absolute validity and to a consequent su-

periority have likewise, given the same human nature, sanctified violent aggression, exploitation, and intolerance. A worldwide and history-long study of the harmful effects of religious absolutism would draw material from almost every tradition."[13] According to Hick, it is a constant temptation to mistake the way for the goal, to absolutize what is merely relative to the Ultimate. This temptation is by its nature a temptation to violence. Hick advocates what he calls a "Copernican Revolution" in which we begin to see that one's own religion does not occupy the central place, but rather the various religions of the world in fact orbit around the Ultimate.[14] The Word of God, both Christ and Bible, are thus relativized in the face of the unknowable Ultimate.

2. Religion Is Divisive

Here the indictment of religion is based on religion's tendency to form strong identities exclusive of others, and thus divide people into us and them. The famed historian of religion Martin E. Marty wants to allow a public political presence for religion, but only after it is chastened by evidence of its divisiveness. Under the heading "Religion Divides," Marty puts the argument this way: "Those called to be religious naturally form separate groups, movements, tribes, or nations. Responding in good faith to a divine call, believers feel themselves endowed with sacred privilege, a sense of chosenness that elevates them above all others. This self-perception then leads groups to draw lines around themselves and to speak negatively of 'the others.' . . . The elect denounce 'others' for worshipping false gods and often act violently against such unbelievers."[15]

13. John Hick, "The Non-Absoluteness of Christianity," in *The Myth of Christian Uniqueness: Toward a Pluralistic Theology of Religions,* ed. John Hick and Paul F. Knitter (Maryknoll, N.Y.: Orbis, 1987), p. 17.
14. Hick, p. 34.
15. Martin E. Marty with Jonathan Moore, *Politics, Religion, and the Common Good* (San Francisco: Jossey-Bass, 2000), pp. 25-26.

3. Religion Is Irrational

The claim here is that religion is especially prone to violence because it produces a particular intensity of nonrational or irrational passion that is not subject to the firm control of reason. "Fervor," "rage," "passion," "fanaticism," "zeal," and similar words are used to describe the mental state of religious actors who are driven to violence. The following passage from political theorist Bhikhu Parekh sums up much of this line of thinking: "Although religion can make a valuable contribution to political life, it can also be a pernicious influence, as liberals rightly highlight. It is often absolutist, self-righteous, arrogant, dogmatic, and impatient of compromise. It arouses powerful and sometimes irrational impulses and can easily destabilize society, cause political havoc, and create a veritable hell on earth. . . . It often breeds intolerance of other religions as well as of internal dissent, and has a propensity towards violence."[16]

Now, there is no doubt that absolutism, divisiveness, and irrationality can lend themselves to violence. The problem the above theorists and others like them have is in trying to separate out a religious violence that is absolutist, divisive, and irrational from a secular violence that is not. The problem arises in the dubious distinction between the religious and the secular. Hick, for example, is forced to admit that it is impossible to give a definition of religion or identify any essence of religion. If religion is meant to indicate belief in a God or god, Hick recognizes that some things called religions, such as Confucianism and Theravada Buddhism, have no such belief. As a result, some so-called "secular" phenomena such as Marxism are given the status in Hick's scheme of "distant cousin" within the extended family of religions. Hick tries to maintain the distinction between religious and secular, but the border is constantly shifting depending on little else than what Hick wants to include or exclude. Hick claims Confucianism as a central "world religion" and Marxism as peripheral, even though, by his own admission, there is no essence of religion and therefore no criteria for separating center from periphery.

16. Bhikhu Parekh, "The Voice of Religion in Political Discourse," in *Religion, Politics, and Peace,* ed. Leroy Rouner (Notre Dame: University of Notre Dame Press, 1999), p. 72.

139

Martin Marty has similar problems. Although he wants to pursue an argument about the violent tendencies of religion in general, he admits that "[s]cholars will never agree on the definition of religion," and so he decides to forgo a precise definition and list five "phenomena that help describe what we are talking about": (1) religion focuses our ultimate concern, (2) religion builds community, (3) religion appeals to myth and symbol, (4) religion is reinforced through rites and ceremonies, and (5) religion demands certain behaviors from its adherents. Then, however, Marty proceeds to show how "politics" also meets all five of these criteria. For example, "ultimate concern," a term explicitly borrowed from Paul Tillich, applies not merely to belief in deities but more generally to answers to questions such as "What do we most care about? For what would you be willing to die?" Marty proceeds similarly through the rest of the five features. Religion builds community, and so does politics. Religion appeals to myth and symbol, and politics "mimics" this appeal in devotion to the flag, war memorials, and so on. Religion uses rites and ceremonies such as circumcision and baptism, and "[p]olitics also depends on rites and ceremonies," even in avowedly secular nations. Religions require followers to behave in certain ways, and "[p]olitics and governments also demand certain behaviors."[17] Marty is trying to show how closely intertwined are politics and religion. What he fails to do is provide any criteria for separating the two. If politics fulfills all the defining features of religion, why is politics not a religion?

Parekh does not define religion, but assumes the validity of the religious/secular distinction. Nevertheless, he admits that "several secular ideologies, such as some varieties of Marxism, conservatism, and even liberalism have a quasi-religious orientation and form, and conversely formally religious languages sometimes have a secular content, so that the dividing line between a secular and a religious language is sometimes difficult to draw."[18] If this is true, where does that leave his searing indictment of the dangers peculiarly inherent to religion? Powerful irrational impulses are suddenly popping up all over, including in liberalism itself, forcing the creation of the category

17. Marty, pp. 10-14.
18. Parekh, p. 74.

"quasi-religious" to try somehow to corral them all back into the category of "religion."

There is a growing number of scholars who would like to scrap the term "religion" altogether because it produces more confusion than clarity.[19] It is not my purpose to enter into that debate here. What I want to argue is that there is no reason to suppose that so-called secular ideologies such as nationalism, patriotism, and liberalism are any less prone to be absolutist, divisive, and irrational than belief in the biblical God. As Marty himself implies, belief in the righteousness of the United States and its solemn duty to impose liberal democracy on the rest of the world has all the ultimate concern, community, myth, ritual, and required behavior of any so-called religion. Recently revived debate over a ban on flag burning is replete with references to the "desecration" of the flag, as if it were a sacred object.[20] Secular nationalism of the kind we are currently witnessing can be just as absolutist, divisive, and irrationally fanatical as anyone who believes he or she is responding to the will of the biblical God.

Let us consider the question of absolutism. The problem with this term is that it is vague and quantitative. It tries to gauge a depth of commitment or intensity that does not admit of easy measurement. Of course, Christians would want to make the theological claim that God is absolute in a way that nothing else is, just as the distinction of Creator and creatures makes all that is created merely relative to God. The problem, as the first table of the Decalogue makes plain, is that humans are constantly tempted to idolatry, to putting what is merely relative in the place of God. It is not enough, therefore, to claim that worship of God is absolutist. The real question is, what god is being worshiped? Today, Caesar and Mammon, even in their supposedly secularized forms of the liberal nation-state and capital, are just as

19. For an excellent example of this type of argument, and a survey of the state of the conversation, see Timothy Fitzgerald, *The Ideology of Religious Studies* (Oxford: Oxford University Press, 2000).

20. Sheryl Gay Stolberg, "Given New Legs, Old Proposal Is Back," *New York Times*, June 4, 2003, p. A28. See also Carolyn Marvin and David W. Ingle, *Blood Sacrifice and the Nation: Totem Rituals and the American Flag* (Cambridge: Cambridge University Press, 1999). Marvin and Ingle study American society just as anthropologists study "primitive" societies, and argue that American patriotism is a religion of blood sacrifice that has the flag as its totem symbol.

prone to being absolutized as ever. In fact, if we try to measure absolutism with a neutral criterion, such as "What one considers absolute is that for which one would kill," then it is clear that, in our society at least, the nation-state is by far subject to the most absolutist fervor. We live in a society in which missionary work or spreading the Word of God in public is considered in poor taste, and yet most people would not hesitate to kill whomever the president asked them to make war against. For the most part, people are willing to kill, but only in the name of a false god.

The title of Andrew Sullivan's article has it exactly right: this *is* a religious war, one that pits the religion of liberal democratic capitalism against the religion of Islam. If this is so, what we are witnessing is widespread idolatry, for the ideal of the liberal nation-state is to separate violence from the will of the biblical God and to put violence in the hands of the secular state. The argument that taking God's will seriously causes violence is used as a way of reinforcing the transfer of the Christian's ultimate loyalty to other gods. The nation-state is not only a false god, it is a jealous god: you shall kill only in the name of your country, and not in the name of the God who brought you out of Egypt. The vision of the Decalogue has been turned upside down. Rather than restricting the authority to kill to God's command, we now evacuate God's command of its authority and place our lethal loyalty only in human hands. The nation-state has become, as Thomas Hobbes said, that "mortal god" whose monopoly on violence is absolute.

IV. What Our God Commands

All kinds of people do violence for all kinds of beliefs — both "religious" and "secular" — that they hold as absolute. People kill in the name of all kinds of false gods. This does not necessarily mean, however, that those who kill in the name of the true God are acting rightly. Having argued that if any killing is justified it must be killing in conformity with the command of God, it remains to address the question, what does God actually command of Christians? Is there any killing that can actually be justified as in conformity with God's will?

The Christian must base the answer to this question in Christ. We must look at the overall trajectory of salvation history from Sinai to Calvary and beyond. What we see is a progressive broadening and deepening of the prohibition against killing. The commandment is seen by many Old Testament scholars in the context of the move beyond clan-based blood vengeance. The right to avenge the death of one's kin was removed from the clan and placed in the hands of tribal judges who were representatives of YHWH. The commandment against killing is set in the context of a widening of blood safety from the clan to the whole people.[21] Over the course of Israelite history, we see a progressive mitigation of capital punishment, beginning with the requirement that there be two witnesses for a capital sentence (Num. 35:30). In postexilic Judaism, lesser punishments following the *lex talionis* were progressively converted into fines. By Jesus' time capital punishment for cases other than murder had fallen into disuse.[22] When Jesus commands his followers to turn the other cheek (Matt. 5:39) and love their enemies (5:44), he is moving with, not against, the grain of the revelation of God to Israel, not abolishing but fulfilling the Law (5:17). The coming of the Messiah has broken open history and radically expanded the idea of the sacredness of life. As Yoder says, "As the Decalogue had expanded blood safety from the family to the tribe, now love of enemy and the universalizing of the faith community make the concept of the outsider, out-law an empty set."[23]

With the coming of the Messiah in the incarnation of God in Jesus Christ, God signals that human life has been definitively accepted into the divine life, and that human life therefore is to be respected and protected as belonging to God.[24] The cross is even more central to understanding God's command, for it is as an executed criminal that the retributive justice of God found final expression, and expiation accomplished. The forgiveness of all has already been achieved through the nonresistance of Jesus Christ to the homicidal intent of human beings. In Christ's death at the hands of others, death is abolished. Karl Barth asks, "From this standpoint, can we speak of the justifiable killing of one man by another? Can there be any necessary or

21. John Howard Yoder, "Exodus 20:13 — 'Thou Shalt Not Kill,'" *Interpretation* 34, no. 4 (October 1980): 396.
22. Yoder, "Exodus 20:13," pp. 397-98.
23. Yoder, "Exodus 20:13," p. 397.
24. Barth, pp. 397-400.

commanded extinction of human life? What would be its purpose now that by the extinction of this one human life that which is necessary and right for all has already taken place?"[25]

If the killing of Christ does not put an end to killing, then it is difficult to see how the cross could be construed as a victory. It seems very difficult indeed to reconcile the kind of victory that the cross is with the kind of victory that we encounter in the books of Kings, where thousands fall in battle before the Israelites. They are reconcilable only if one bears in mind that it is God who fights in the Old Testament. The point of the narratives is that Israel is preserved not through military preparedness and strength, but through the miraculous hand of God. It is not unreasonable, then, for the New Testament church to have seen in the Old Testament stories a paradigm for how the kingdom of God would be inaugurated not by military means, but solely by the worthiness of the slaughtered Lamb (Rev. 5:12). The early Christians seem not to have regarded the apocalyptic vision as something to be consummated outside of history. They did not regard the love of enemies as an "interim ethic" available to a few for a short time. They rejected all killing and refused, by and large, to serve in Caesar's army well into the third century, and often paid for their refusal with their lives.[26] They understood that the cross had changed history, and that the killing and resurrection of the Father's only Son had opened the commandment "You shall not kill" to its broadest and deepest extent.

Where does that leave us as Christians today? Christian reflection on war must go beyond merely ticking off the just-war criteria as a preliminary step to supporting the military adventures of the nation-state. Radical obedience to God's command must be the beginning and end of Christian reflection on war. Specifically, we must take seriously the teaching of Jesus that love of enemies is the fulfillment of the Law, that the prohibition against killing has been extended to the prohibition of anger and hatred, that the *lex talionis* has been fulfilled in the commandment to turn the other cheek (Matt. 5:17-48). All the ways we have of excusing Jesus' commands — they are meant for individuals, or only for the perfect, or apply only within the Christian community, or are meant as hyperbole, or are meant to set the bar unrealistically high in order to convict us of our

25. Barth, p. 400.
26. Yoder, *The Politics of Jesus*, pp. 86-89.

unworthiness — must be regarded as attempts to evade the command of
God, and therefore to violate not just the commandment against killing
but the prohibition against worshiping other gods.

In this light Karl Barth says that killing in war calls into question
"the whole of morality, or better, obedience to the command of God in
all its dimensions. Does not war demand that almost everything that
God has forbidden be done on a broad front? To kill effectively, and in
connexion therewith, must not those who wage war steal, rob, commit
arson, lie, deceive, slander, and unfortunately to a large extent forni-
cate, not to speak of the almost inevitable repression of all the finer and
weightier forms of obedience?"[27] Barth comments that even a qualified
Christian defense of participation in a particular war must be even
more difficult to make than exceptions to the ban on suicide and abortion. Barth admits that we must begin from the assumption that paci-
fism has "almost infinite arguments in its favour and is almost over-
poweringly strong."[28] Barth does allow the possibility of exceptions to
the ban on war. He believes we cannot allow the letter of the law to re-
strict the freedom of the Spirit of God to make exceptions to the ban on
killing.[29] Nevertheless, Barth says we must always claim that war is an
exception, never normal, always admitted only in extremis. Furthermore, the state exercises power only as an *opus alienum,* and never as a
right to be claimed on its own. It is always the task of Christians to
question the necessity for war, and go to war only if it is in obedience to
the will of God, not to the state. The Christian must also be prepared to
be a selective conscientious objector, and refuse to fight in any war that
results from mere human command and not the command of God.[30]

In admitting the possibility that the Christian might kill for the
state, Barth seems to step back from the radical and logical conclusion
of his own reflections on the command of God in the New Testament.
In my judgment, Barth underestimates the idolatrous temptation at
the heart of the modern nation-state, which is founded on war.[31] How-

27. Barth, p. 454.
28. Barth, p. 455.
29. Barth, p. 433.
30. Barth, pp. 456-63.
31. Michael Howard sums up the historical evidence of the origins of the
state this way: "the entire apparatus of the state primarily came into being to enable princes to make war" (*The Invention of Peace: Reflections on War and International*

ever, Barth is helpful for focusing our attention away from the state's fulfillment of just-war criteria and back onto the command of God. Pope John Paul II is helpful here as well, for in his reflections on war and the commandment against killing, the pope makes it clear that killing is not a right to be exercised once certain minimum criteria have been met. As the pope explains in *Veritatis Splendor,* the commandments do not simply establish minimal standards but are "a path involving a moral and spiritual journey towards perfection, at the heart of which is love." The commandments are an invitation to follow Jesus, who has become the living Law. As the pope says, the commandment against killing thus "becomes a call to an attentive love which protects and promotes the life of one's neighbor."[32] The Vatican's extreme skepticism about the use of military force — even going so far as to question the very possibility of a "just war"[33] — must be read in this light.

Order [New Haven: Yale University Press, 2000], p. 15); Charles Tilly says, "War made the state, and the state made war" ("Reflections on the History of European State-Making," in *The Formation of National States in Western Europe,* ed. Charles Tilly [Princeton: Princeton University Press, 1975], p. 26). The connection between the liberal nation-state and war is not accidental, for liberal polity is based on tragedy, that is, the ultimate inability of people to agree on the good. In the absence of a shared conception of the good, there is no way to adjudicate disagreements among rival wills nonviolently, so violence can only be displaced, directed against a common external enemy in war.

32. Pope John Paul II, *The Splendor of Truth (Veritatis Splendor),* para. 15.

33. For an analysis of the Vatican's progressive tightening of conditions for justifiable use of force, see William L. Portier, "Are We Really Serious When We Ask God to Deliver Us from War? The Catechism and the Challenge of Pope John Paul II," *Communio* 23 (spring 1996): 47-63. Cardinal Ratzinger called into question the very possibility of a just war in a recent interview with the Zenit News Agency. When asked if the March 2003 war against Iraq fit the just-war criteria, Ratzinger responded, "The Pope expressed his thought with great clarity, not only as his individual thought but as the thought of a man who is knowledgeable in the highest functions of the Catholic Church. Of course, he did not impose this position as doctrine of the Church but as the appeal of a conscience enlightened by faith. The Holy Father's judgment is also convincing from the rational point of view: There were not sufficient reasons to unleash a war against Iraq. To say nothing of the fact that, given the new weapons that make possible destructions that go beyond the combatant groups, today we should be asking ourselves if it is still licit to admit the very existence of a 'just war'" ("Cardinal Ratzinger on the Abridged Version of Catechism," May 2, 2003, at http://zenit.org/english/visualizza.phmtl?sid=34882).

According to a recent survey by the Pew Forum on Religion and Public Life, only 10 percent of Americans said their religious beliefs were the most important influence on their thinking about the war against Iraq. For those who attended religious services regularly, the number rose to only 17 percent. The overwhelming opposition of church leaders to the war against Iraq largely fell on deaf ears among the faithful; Christians supported the war by a large majority, and were apparently content to place the judgment of the state over that of the church regarding the justifiability of the war. If the argument of this paper is correct, then we have little choice but to warn against wholesale idolatry. If killing can be justified only if it comes from the direct command of God, then Christians have transferred the interpretation of God's will from the church to the secular state, and thereby have created an idolatrous "mortal god" in the nation-state. For many, the nation-state has become the god of life and death, the arbiter of who is allowed to live and who is required to die. It is for precisely this reason that arguments such as Andrew Sullivan's are so dangerous; in condemning killing in the name of the biblical God, they give free rein to killing in the name of a false god.

What, then, are we to conclude about the commandment against killing in the context of contemporary war? At the very minimum we should conclude that the church, and not the state, should judge — with a great deal of skepticism — whether or not any particular act of mass slaughter is in conformity with the will of God.[34] If we move beyond the minimum and see the commandment against killing, with Pope John Paul II, as an invitation to follow Jesus Christ, then we may conclude that it is simply not possible to reconcile the will of God with killing for a state whose *very ideal* is the separation of violence from the will of God.

---

34. I make this argument in detail in my article "At Odds with the Pope: Legitimate Authority and Just Wars," *Commonweal* 130, no. 10 (May 23, 2003): 11-13.

You Shall Not Kill — What Does It Take?
Why We Need the Other Commandments
If We Are to Abstain from Killing

Bernd Wannenwetsch

The richness of the Decalogue comes into view only when it is not understood as just a list of individual commandments nor merely an order in which we encounter the divine imperatives — as the two-table account suggests. Rather, the "Ten Words" must be seen as setting up an interrelated environment, only within which the individual commandments are comprehensible in their fully rounded completeness. This "environmental" account of the relationship of the Decalogue's commandments suggests itself with particular force if we look at the fifth commandment.

In what follows I first try to analyze important steps in the traditional discourse on this commandment by looking at and comparing Luther's and Aquinas's interpretations. Luther's understanding of the abstention from killing as a matter of the *heart* will prepare us for the recognition of what I have labeled the "perichoretic" nature of the Decalogue in which each individual commandment does not appear as a self-contained entity but as "nesting" in the others. The perichoretic quality of individual commandments is based on the foundational role that the first commandment assumes for the whole Decalogue. It is by virtue of an "enhypostatic" relation to the first that each and every other commandment assumes a similar interrelation with all the others. For the fifth commandment this perichoretic quality may be demonstrated in relation to a number of other commandments, naturally more easily for some than for others. To clarify how this works, I will focus attention on a not-so-obvious relation: the way in which the fifth depends on the fourth. What does it take to abstain from killing? In the light of my analysis, the answer will be: as a prerequisite, it will need the honoring of parents, parenthood, and the family.

While this particular relation can be illuminated in a topical way by analyzing the degree in which recent problems in biotechnology and medical ethics betray a significant though largely unacknowledged dependence on questions and practices that fall under the rubric of sexual and family ethics, the following argument can also be read as a preliminary contribution to the question of the unity of the Christian moral life. If the Decalogue is amongst the prime Christian moral concepts describing the whole orbit of this unity, the question to raise will be: What sort of unity does it present us with?

1. The Most Important and Easiest Commandment?

It is obvious that the whole human race, not only Jews and Christians, regard this commandment as of the highest importance. A transgression of the fifth is the most severe in kind, and is deserving of the most severe punishment. It appears then to be pivotal for the Decalogue, at least as regards the second tablet, which deals with our relation to fellow human creatures. If this command is not kept, there seems to be little point in keeping the rest. "You shall not kill" seems then to be the most basic of precepts, as it protects in general what the other commandments protect in a variety of more particular aspects: life itself. Presented in the Decalogue's typical apodictic mode, this precept belongs, claimed Thomas Aquinas, to the class of absolute necessities of which we know "that without it the order of virtue would be destroyed."[1] Hence, it seems fitting to find the fifth commandment listed first amongst those commandments which order human relations outside the home, since in the Decalogue we "find the order to be according to the gravity of sin."[2]

---

1. *Summa theologiae* I/II, q. 99, art. 5, resp. (hereafter *STh*); quotations follow the translation by the Fathers of the English Dominican Province, rev. Daniel J. Sullivan.
2. *STh* I/II, q. 100, art. 6, resp. Luther speaks in a similar vein about the "apt order" of the second tablet that the prohibitions, outside the household, start with

It is fortunate, we might say, that in being the most important and severe, the fifth commandment is at the same time the easiest to keep. This is partly due to its very severity that sends out, as is evident to all, a particular strong caveat. The other reason why it seems the easiest to keep results from its negative formulation. Abstention is generally easier to conceive than are positive commands, which is why we usually find it easier to keep to the (negatively worded) precepts than the commandments that call for acts or behavior of a specific shape. Lining up nicely with the assumptions that it is the most severe and easiest to keep is the fact that it springs first to Jesus' lips when he reminds the rich man of what God requires of him (Matt. 19:18). To this the man easily responds: "These I have all kept" (v. 20).

"Never have I killed a human being, nor have I slept with another man's wife" we can hear resonating in his mind. Since these prohibitions are clear-cut, it seems quite possible to keep them; in fact, abstaining from killing appears to be the easiest of moral tasks. It only asks from us exactly the behavior we are used to. Yet, we might ask, is what Jesus is asking for really that easy? While Jesus chose not to argue with the rich man's claim to have kept the commandments, we nevertheless find our notion of an "easy" command challenged when listening to the preacher of the Sermon on the Mount.

"You have heard that it was said to the people long ago: 'Do not murder, and anyone who murders will be subject to judgment.' But I tell you that anyone who is angry with his brother will be subject to judgement. Again anyone who says to his brother 'raka' is answerable to the Sanhedrin. But anyone who says 'you fool' will be in danger of the fire of hell" (Matt. 5:21f).

Interestingly, a look into the history of Christian teaching on this commandment reveals that the great theologians such as Aquinas or Luther typically focus more on Jesus' rendition of it than on its original context in the Old Testament. Luther, for example, holds that one must understand this commandment "through Christ" and "according to

---

the biggest concern (killing) and proceed to the smaller ones. "Sermon on the Ten Commandments" (1516), quoted after the edition *Luthers Sämtliche Schriften,* ed. J. Georg Walch, reprint of the 2nd rev. ed. (St. Louis: Concordia, 1880-1910), 3:1246. References to volumes of this edition are given under the siglum "Walch"; translations are mine.

the Spirit" as opposed to the letter.[3] If we listen to the antithesis of the Sermon on the Mount, it presses the question: What is Jesus doing with the fifth commandment when he is drawing a direct line from murder to anger?

It seems obvious that he did not intend to do away with all those necessary features of a sound judicial practice which exactly depend on the distinction between acts and motivation and that of various degrees of severity. Instead of a *moralization* of the *juridical* usage of the law (which would be of disastrous consequence), we may say that Jesus *radicalized* the *moral* understanding of the law by invoking judgment on types of actions that we would not normally count as falling under the remit of the fifth commandment. And he did so by distinguishing between the external and the internal aspect of an act. As regards the latter, the internal movement of volition and intention, Aquinas remarks: "Divine law alone, and not human law, is able to judge. For human law does not punish the man who wishes to slay but slays not, whereas Divine law does, according to Matthew 5:22: Whosoever is angry with his brother, shall be in danger of the judgment."[4]

Having spoken of radicalization, we must now try to understand its nature. Does the radicalization of the fifth merely mean that Jesus counts more types of actions amongst transgressions of this commandment? There is more to it than this, as we shall see with the aid of Martin Luther's exegesis.[5]

2. A Matter of the Heart

The true radicalization that Jesus wrought in the commandment is shifting the focus of moral analysis from the typology to the psychology of action. His interest is not only in the type of action performed but in the kind of person who performs it. In short: abstention from killing becomes a matter of the heart.

3. Walch, 3:1247f.

4. *STh* I/II, q. 100, art. 9, resp.

5. For the wider context, see my *Luther's Moral Theology*, Cambridge Companion to Martin Luther, ed. Donald K. McKim (Cambridge, New York, and Melbourne: Cambridge University Press, 2003), pp. 120-35.

Luther took this point from the saying that parallels our passage, in which Jesus radicalizes the sixth commandment: "It is said: You shall not commit adultery. But I tell you anyone who looks at a woman lustfully, has already committed adultery *in his heart*" (Matt. 5:27-28). As with all evil, adultery and killing have their beginning in the heart. Though they are recognized by others only when performed through bodily action, what is said in 1 Samuel 16:7 remains essential: "Men look at the outward appearance, but God looks on the heart." Taking up a traditional interpretation descending through Augustine, Aquinas, and Bonaventure, Luther discerns in Jesus' odd saying about killing an order of graduation[6] which leads from the anger of the heart by way of degrading mimics and gestures ("raka") to assaulting words that come out of the mouth and finally to the actual raising of the hand against the neighbor. What are the consequences that Luther draws from this? We can identify five main points.

The commandment to abstain from killing addresses

  (i)   *the whole person,* with a special
 (ii) *focus on the affections;* as such, it carries
(iii) *positive inclusions,* reveals
 (iv) radical *dependence on grace,* and subsists
  (v) in a *perichoretic relationship* with the other commandments.

Let us look at these points in turn.

a. The Whole Person

"Do you think he speaks of the fist if he says, 'you shall not kill'? What does it mean 'you'? Not merely your hand, nor foot, tongue or any other member, but all that you are of body and soul."[7] The soul, the in-

---

6. For example: *manu — ore — adiutorio — consensu — corde;* Thomas Aquinas, *Duo praecepta* §1262; cf. also Augustine, *Contra Faustum* M.I. XIX, c. 23; *De sermone Domini in monte;* see further: Albrecht Peters, *Kommentar zu Luther's Katechismen,* vol. 1, *Die Zehn Gebote* (Göttingen: Vandenhoeck und Ruprecht, 1990), p. 220.

7. Weimarer Ausgabe (ed.) of Luther's Works (hereafter WA), 32.363.2, exegesis of Matt. 5–7, 1530/32, my translation.

ward man, is no less capable of murder than the bodily man.[8] Luther concludes with a critical move against the tradition that held that the commandment can be fulfilled by merely abstaining from homicide. "Therefore, it is not enough not to be a murderer outwardly."[9] The requirement is more radical, he says in a summary statement: "This commandment is simple enough. . . . We must not kill, either by hand, heart, or word, by signs or gestures, or by aiding and abetting. It forbids anger except . . . to persons who occupy the place of God, that is parents and rulers. Anger, reproof and punishment are the prerogatives of God and his representatives."[10]

The real substance of the commandment, as Luther sees it, is in fact not the act of homicide but the affection that begets it, with the exception of those in the position of authority — from parents to governors — who are, by virtue of their stewardship of those entrusted to them, entitled to "just anger" on behalf of their protégés.[11]

b. Anger and Revenge as the Heart of the Matter

As far as I can see, this formulation marks a major shift away from the high medieval interpretative tradition of the commandment that had focused on act and intention, the latter understood as a movement of the rational will toward a perceived good, the telos of the act. Those within this tradition felt no need to make the affections a central part of the analysis of acts, as they perceived them to be subject to the control of the rational will. In late scholastic theology with its dominance of Scotism, the natural ability of the indeterminate will was seen as capable of eliciting not only good works but even the required love of

8. In this context Luther quotes 1 John 3:15: All who hate a brother are murderers; Walch, 3:1251.

9. "Sermon on the Ten Commandments" (1526); Walch, 3:1114.

10. *Large Catechism,* quoted after *The Book of Concord, the Confessions of the Evangelical Lutheran Church,* trans. and ed. Theodore G. Tappert (Philadelphia: Fortress, 1959), p. 389.

11. This *zelus iustus* Luther understands also as "necessary" or even "divine," "a Christian and brotherly, even fatherly anger" that is eventually conceived as "love's anger." WA, 32.362.18, 25 (exegesis of Matt. 5–7); see Peters, pp. 219f.

God.[12] Luther deliberately breaks with this tradition when stating that, while the first four commandments "have their works in the understanding . . . so that he [man] rule not himself . . . but allow himself to be led that pride be prevented . . . the following commandments deal with the passions and lusts of men, that these also be killed."[13] Accordingly, for Luther the subject matter of these divine precepts is "the passions of anger and revenge, of which the Fifth Commandment says 'Thou shalt not kill.'"[14]

It must be understood from this focus on the affective dimension of the commandment "that this commandment includes also all the sins of anger and hatred,"[15] that Luther's translation of the Hebrew term *raṣaḥ* employs the more sweeping notion of "killing" instead of the seemingly more precise notion "murder." The Hebrew term as used in both versions of the Decalogue, Exodus 20:13 and Deuteronomy 5:17, is relatively rare compared to the more usual verbs *(harag* or *hemit)* for killing. In a significant contrast to these verbs, *raṣaḥ* does not address killing in warfare or within a legal penalty system but focuses on private killing of personal enemies.[16] It encompasses both intentional killing and unintentional manslaughter, yet in both cases with an emphasis on the tendency of these actions to induce a chain reaction of revenge (Num. 35:19, 27). It is within this background that we have to understand the thrust of the commandment. Together with institutions such as the asylum cities, the fifth commandment means to cut through this chain of revenge in that the issuing of judgment and punishment is wrestled from the hands of private agents or groups and confined to public authorities and legal practices.

Yet if the paradigmatic situation to which the commandment re-

12. Gabriel Biel, for example, stressed that to love God over all things can be elicited of the faculty of the human will "without the infusion of grace." "Posset actum dilectionis Dei super omnia elicere ex suis naturalibus, etiam si gratia non infunderetur." *In sent. Lib.* II dist. 28 qu. un. art. 3.

13. *Treatise on Good Works, Second Tablet,* p. xxi, quoted after the Philadelphia edition *(Works of Martin Luther* [Philadelphia: Muhlenberg, 1943ff.], 1:271).

14. *Works* (Philadelphia ed.), 1:272.

15. "A Brief Explanation of the Ten Commandments," in *Works* (Philadelphia ed.), 2:361.

16. Werner H. Schmidt, *Die Zehn Gebote im Rahmen Alttestamentlicher Ethik* (Darmstadt: Wissenschaftliche Buchgesellschaft, 1993), pp. 107f.

fers is revenge and the chain reaction of mutual bloodshed, then we can legitimately say that the predicament the commandment addresses is not only injustice but also anger and hatred. When we suffer a wrong, we desire not only to repay the wrong, but the pleasure of inflicting pain, as the anger and hatred in us call for a return and even a surplus of the pain inflicted. Revenge is not just driven by the desire to restore justice but reflects the disordered state of desire in the human heart. It is along these lines that Luther understands the paradigmatic situation of the commandment as the lust for revenge — and not merely the inordinate desire for some specific "good" which would be covetousness.

Therefore, as we can infer from this, it is not enough to keep the other commandments as a healthy environment for the keeping of the fifth — as important as this remains. What needs to be addressed in addition is our basic instinct for self-defense which breeds anger and hatred. Luther, rather annoyingly, makes his example of this point as radical as possible: if we are innocent but are attacked by an enemy who means us evil, it is exactly our natural instinct to defend ourselves, our life, our reputation, possessions, etc., that the commandment is forbidding.

Correspondingly, Luther makes his positive formulation equally radical, understanding the love of the enemy as the touchstone and core content of this commandment. If we believe the Sermon on the Mount to be the authentic interpretation of the commandment according to the Spirit, Luther says, we are compelled to see that "You shall not kill" means nothing less than "Love your enemy"![17] In fact, the Reformer describes the transgressor of the fifth commandment with the following summary statement: "He who forgives not his enemies, nor

17. While Luther will later, in the wake of the peasant revolt and spiritualist revolution of the 1520s, tend to more strongly emphasize that political authority has the right and duty to protect society and citizens against assault, it marks a lasting difference of Reformation theology that for Luther the right to warfare is not, as it is for Thomas Aquinas, associated with a natural-law-derived right to self-defense (which Luther does not assume to exist for Christians), but is understood solely from the duty to protect those entrusted. At the very heart of the discussion about the fifth commandment and its scope, Luther is outspoken that the insistence on a right to self-defense is no less than revenge and hatred. *Large Catechism*, pp. 389f.

prays for them, is not kindly disposed toward them and does them no good."[18]

c. Overcoming the Affirmative-Negative Distinction

As with all the commandments of the Decalogue, Luther assumes that any prohibition includes a positive claim, just as any positively worded precept excludes certain affections and actions. He therefore rejects the traditional distinction between negative and positive commandments (*negativa* and *affirmativa*) which is false in keeping only to the outward shell of the syllabi. "For through this commandment 'thou shalt not kill,' he expresses the strongest command (*affirmativam*), which is: You shall be meek and generous of heart, patient, still and peaceful."[19] The traditional distinction between negative and positive commandments reflects in Luther's opinion a nonspiritual reading that is enslaved to the surface of the language. Yet this commandment is a prohibition only according to the letter, but according to spirit the "most noble and greatest works of God" are positively required if it is to be fulfilled.[20]

Luther is particularly critical of the distinction between positive and negative commandments on the grounds that it leads at the end of the day to a denial of grace. There are those "most excellent" amongst theologians who "dream" that the commandment is exhaustedly kept by the sheer abstention from killing even if this abstention is combined with anger,[21] and hence "grace is not necessary for the commandment nor intended."[22] In contrast, for Luther the commandment "requires a pure heart, not merely a pure hand,"[23] according to Psalm 24:4 that envisions one "who has innocent hands and a pure heart," and therefore the theological result is inevitable: we all are guilty since "this spirit of revenge clings to everyone of us,"[24] and in regard to Matthew 5:21f.:

18. "A Brief Explanation of the Ten Commandments," in *Works* (Philadelphia ed.), 2:361.
19. Walch, 3:1262.
20. Walch, 3:1264.
21. Walch, 3:1260f.
22. Walch, 3:1261.
23. Walch, 3:1283.
24. *Large Catechism*, p. 390.

"Here, is no-one excluded, we are all guilty. For even if the fist, mouth and other limbs hold still, the heart is still full with anger, envy and hatred."[25]

d. Spirit and Grace

As radical as the enslavement to sinful desire is, so radical is the dependence on God's grace: "This spirit of revenge clings to everyone of us," yet "God wishes to remove the root and source of this bitterness toward our neighbour."[26] Though it may be (to some degree) within man's capacity to have the rational will directing intentions and actions, there is no way of controlling the basic affective responses in a healthy way. *Affectus affectu vincitur* — the affect can be overcome only by another, stronger affect, as Luther's friend Philipp Melanchthon famously stated.[27]

Nothing less is required than the taking on of Christ's own affect of holy charity if anger, hatred, and the desire for revenge are to be discarded. What the commandment calls forth is a renewed heart that endows its bearer with novel affections.[28] This, of course, is the subject of the first commandment, which requires nothing other than faith which can be only a gift coterminous with a new heart. Or in Luther's words: "He always wants to remind us to think back to the First Commandment, that he is our God; that is, he wishes to help and protect us, so

---

25. "Sermon on Ex 20:13," Walch, 3:1114.

26. *Large Catechism*, p. 390.

27. Philipp Melanchthon, *Loci Communes, I. De hominis viribus*, 44: "Contra interni affectus non sunt in potestate nostra. Experientia enim usque comperimus non posse voluntatem sua sponte ponere amorem, odium aut similes affectus, sed affectus affectu vincitur." See my "Affekt und Gebot. Zur ethischen Bedeutung der Leidenschaften im Licht der Theologie Luthers und Melanchthons," in *Passion, Affekt und Leidenschaft in der frühen Neuzeit. Kongreßband des Wolfenbütteler Arbeitskreises für Barockforschung*, ed. Anselm Steiger (forthcoming).

28. Augsburg Confession XX: "It is only by faith that forgiveness of sins and grace are apprehended, and because through faith the Holy Spirit is received, hearts are so renewed and endowed with new affections as to be able to bring forth good works." Quoted after the more precise Latin version; *Book of Concord*, p. 45. See also my "Caritas fide formata. 'Herz und Affekt' als Schlüssel zum Verhältnis von 'Glaube' und 'Liebe,'" *Kerygma und Dogma* 46 (2000): 205-24.

that he may subdue our desire for revenge."[29] It is ultimately from this connection with the first[30] that the fifth commandment comes into view as anything but easy. "Hence," Luther summarizes, "this commandment is a very profound one, and there is nobody who is capable of fulfilling it without grace. . . . Since without love it is impossible that this commandment is not transgressed."[31]

3. Luther and Aquinas on the Interrelatedness of the Commandments

It is instructive to compare Luther's emphasis on grace and love with Thomas Aquinas's discussion of the precepts of divine law in his *Summa theologiae*. At first we note a basic consensus. Aquinas, in discussing "Whether the Mode of Charity Falls under the Precept of the Divine Law," states: "Man cannot fulfil all the precepts of the law unless he fulfil the precept of charity, which is impossible without charity. Consequently it is not possible, as Pelagius maintained, for man to fulfil the law without grace."[32] He discusses "contrary opinions" on the matter and takes issue with those who hold that it is "possible for one not having charity to fulfil this precept." Aquinas concedes a moment of truth in the latter opinion insofar as a narrower focus on the "act of charity" itself may suggest understanding it as falling only under the actual precept to love God and neighbor. Yet he favors the theologically more sensitive reading of charity "as being the mode of the acts of the other virtues, that is, according as the acts of the other virtues are ordered to charity, which is *the end of the commandment.*"[33]

---

29. *Large Catechism*, p. 391.

30. "All works remain in the First Commandment and in faith, and that faith, for the sake of which all other commandments and works are ordained, exercises and strengthens itself in them." *Treatise on Good Works*, in *Works* (Philadelphia ed.), 1:248.

31. Walch, 3:1251. Cf. another summarizing formulation with a clearer christological emphasis: "Ergo sententia est: praeceptum dei nemo implet, nisi habeat charitatem dei et spiritum sanctum, quae veniunt ex charitate Christi." WA, 15.649.8 (sermon on Matt. 5:20 of July 3, 1524).

32. *STh* I/II, q. 100, art. 10, ad 3.

33. *STh* I/II, q. 100, art. 10, resp.

A closer look, however, suggests that Aquinas is not as radical as Luther, as he maintains this dependency on charity and grace only in a *general sense* for the whole of the Decalogue as a result of the overarching importance of the double-love command which the Christian constantly has to bear in mind, while Luther sees it as *inherent in every individual commandment itself.* For Thomas there is a sense in which the fourth commandment, for example, is capable of being fulfilled in its own right without charity. "Honour thy father, does not mean that a man must honour his father from charity, but merely that he must honour him. Therefore, he that honours his father, yet has no charity, does not break this precept."[34] Though Thomas adds: "although he breaks the precept concerning the act of charity for which reason he deserves to be punished," there prevails a sense in which both precepts may assume a relative independence — an independence Thomas describes in temporal terms. "Since these are two affirmative precepts not binding for all times, they can be binding each one at a different time, so that it may happen that a man fulfils the precept of honouring his father and mother without at the same time breaking the precept concerning the omission of the mode of charity."[35]

This difference between the two grand theologians also pertains to the related question of the interrelatedness of the commandments, as to whether and how the fifth is dependent on others. Due to his focus on the heart, Luther assumes that the ban on killing exists in a perichoretic relation with other commandments: "This commandment includes also all the sins of anger and hatred, such as murder, war, robbery, arson, quarrelling, contention, envy of a neighbour's good fortune and joy over his misfortune."[36] While this statement explicitly mentions coveting, the ninth and tenth commandments, elsewhere Luther includes the eighth commandment when he says a slanderer is in fact a threefold manslaughterer: he murders himself, the one to whom he addresses his slandering, and finally the one about whom he slanders.[37]

34. *STh* I/II, q. 100, art. 10, resp.
35. *STh* I/II, q. 100, art. 10, ad 2.
36. "A Brief Explanation of the Ten Commandments, the Creed and the Lord's Prayer" (1520), in *Works* (Philadelphia ed.), 2:361.
37. WA, 1.474.1ff. In yet another perspective he sees the ninth and tenth included in the sixth and seventh; see Walch, 3:1341.

Aquinas, on the other hand, holds that the fifth commandment need address only the deed, not the desire. For the kind of action to which it refers, it "was necessary to proscribe, not sins of thought, but only sins of deed," since it belongs to another class than, say, adultery. While adultery must be forbidden not only as a deed but also as a desire, because the accompanying pleasure is itself an "object of appetite," with murder it is different. "Since it is natural for man to love his neighbour," Aquinas states, this act is "desired only for the sake of something else."[38]

We must understand this distinction as arising from the particulars of Aquinas's philosophy of action which, in turn, dictate his account of sin. In a compressed rendering of his account, the logic unfolds like this: the fifth commandment is concerned with (the avoidance of) action; action is intelligible only on the basis of the will forming a specific intention; intention is always shaped by and directed to a specific telos; as an object of desire, every telos of an act is per definition (perceived as) a good. "No one acts intending evil," as he approvingly cites Dionysius.[39] This is why, for Aquinas, sin "is not a pure privation but an act deprived of its due order,"[40] i.e., deprived of the true order of reason dictating the will to form the intentions adequate to human nature. Hence, it is established for Aquinas that in principle "every sin consists in the desire for some changeable good for which man has an inordinate desire."[41]

This formally positive construal of sin explains why Thomas emphasizes that the ban on killing is a precept that contents itself with the prohibition of the act as such and has no need to include thought or affection, as the commandments against adultery and stealing necessitate, since the sixth and seventh deal with "objects of appetite" while the fifth addresses only "objects of repulsion." "Consequently," Aquinas summarizes, "with regard to sins of murder . . . it was necessary to proscribe, not sins of thought, but only sins of deed."[42] We kill not be-

---

38. *STh* I/II, q. 100, art. 5, ad 5.

39. *Div. nom.* 4, quoted in *STh* I/II, q. 72, art. 1, resp. Cf. also the following statement: "The intention of the sinner is not directed to the point of straying from the path of reason; rather is it directed to tend to some desirable good from which it derives its species." *STh* I/II, q. 73, art. 1, resp.

40. *STh* I/II, q. 72, art. 1, ad 2.

41. *STh* I/II, q. 72, art. 2, resp.

42. *STh* I/II, q. 100, art. 5, ad 5.

cause we like it or because we like to inflict evil, but only in pursuit of a perceived good the possession of which deems us good.

The difference to Luther is subtle but striking. In tracing back the transgression of the fifth commandment to an unordered state of desire, Aquinas seems to suggest something very similar to Luther's account of killing as a matter of the corrupted heart. Yet his philosophical framework does not appear to allow a diagnosis as radical as Luther's, which detects as the core of the moral predicament the *immediate captivity* of the heart *in* hatred. What is often superficially invoked in terms of the more "optimistic" anthropology of the Aquinate, is perhaps more adequately seen to be rooted in a philosophical framework whose parameters are ill equipped to account for the phenomenon of hatred in a *theological* way.[43] What "good" has hatred other than the evil delight in the pain inflicted on the other? In the light of Luther's biblical account, the distinction that Thomas's framework offers collapses. Hatred is not sinful because it desires an improper object or aims at a wrong end, but is sinful in itself.

It is on the grounds he established in his consideration entitled "Whether All Sins Are Connected with One Another?"[44] that Aquinas, contrary to Luther, retains the customary distinction between affirmative and negative precepts, "when one is not comprised in the other." Reflecting under the heading "Whether the Precepts of the Decalogue Are Suitably Distinguished from One Another?" he is ready to concede that *some* precepts *can* in fact be comprised in another. Yet, he nevertheless acknowledges the general validity of the distinction. As a proof, he picks the fourth and fifth: "That man should honour his parents does not include that he should not kill another man, nor does the latter include the former."[45]

Though Aquinas falls short of the more radical perichoretic ac-

43. Aquinas's explicit discussion entitled "Of Hatred" in the *Summa* remains fairly pale as it hardly transcends the parameters set by the anthropological framework of the two antagonistic inclinations of the "natural appetite." The formal ordering suggests that "every hatred arises from some love as its cause," but Aquinas's cautious "Whether a Man Can Hate the Truth" does not even remotely resemble Luther's bold claim that self-love actually engenders hatred of God (*STh* I/II, q. 29, art. 1, 3, and 5).

44. *STh* I/II, q. 73, art. 1.

45. *STh* I/II, q. 100, art. 4, ad 2.

count that Luther gives on the interrelatedness of the commandments, we must not fail to validate the points Thomas makes and the reason he gives for them: as we have seen, he does acknowledge that there are certain commandments which explicitly address a state of mind including the affective dimension, as do those which warn of adultery or coveting. The ban on killing, however, belongs to another type, since nobody really desires the killing itself but only as a means to get hold of something else, which is the true object of his desire. In this vein, we may say that *we kill because we covet.* Aquinas allows us to maintain that the commandments on adultery and coveting are actually "comprised within" the fifth. If we are to abstain from killing, we must learn to abstain from coveting and lusting. This is an insight worth pausing on. The Bible has no shortage of narrative accounts indicative of this interrelationship. Just think of the story of King David and Bathsheba in the second book of Samuel.

4. A Matter of the First: The Dynamics of Sin

In this narrative we see the dynamic of sin unfolding when the transgressing of one commandment provokes the transgression of another. Some say it all started with the king's idleness that made him into a voyeur from the top of his palace. Watching bathing Bathsheba creates desire, desire becomes coveting, coveting begets adultery, perhaps rape, which is followed by lying, deceit, murder, and making others complicit in the king's sin.[46] Though we are certainly right to recognize in this plot a dynamic of sin that culminates in murder, we should not assume an automatism in terms of the simple unfolding of a chain reaction. Though every individual transgressing seems to gravitate to another, the acting subject is still accountable for every individual act in its own right. This is particularly apparent when the narrative pictures Uriah twice displaying reluctance to play David's game. And it is only the king's failure to recognize this as a warning that leads to the

---

46. Luther: "No sin comes alone, but it always prompts another one after it. . . . Who does not soon get up again and recognizes it, will soon fall into another temptation. The sin of lust and adultery is followed by lie, and after that comes manslaughter and bloodshed and finally despair." WA, 44.369.5-9.

most serious step being taken and Bathsheba's husband becoming the victim of a murderous plot. Though David may have been tempted to employ the well-worn rationale of "having seen no other way out," there is still a strategic mind at work that elaborates the plot. This is what we usually define as the difference between murder and manslaughter, as the latter does not feed on strategy but typically emerges and concludes in a single situation.

As important as it is to acknowledge and understand this dynamic of sin as narrated in 2 Samuel, we must resist the temptation to construe the unity of the Decalogue by way of a psychological account of the unity of sin as in a chain reaction model. The unity that binds the Ten Words together lies not on psychological but on theological grounds. It is a unity that subsists in the universality of dependence which binds all commandments back to the first. The 2 Samuel narrative prepares this point in its own way. This comes out in the divine judgment pronounced by the prophet Nathan on David's serial sin.

Though the prophet does not hesitate to name what David has done in its full thrust, "You have struck down Uriah the Hittite with the sword" (2 Sam. 12:9), oddly enough both the prophet's parable that leads to the king's conviction and the divine address after David's surrender do not focus on murder, not even on adultery or deceit, but on coveting: "I gave you your master's house, and your master's wives into your bosom, and gave you the house of Israel and of Judah; and if that had been too little, I would have added as much more. Why have you despised the word of the LORD, to do what is evil in his sight?" (2 Sam. 12:8f.).

Here we have, on the one hand, a narrative confirmation of the account we have developed with Luther's help: that the commandment pertains not only to the act of transgression but to the causes that lead to the transgression, the root of which is located in the coveting of the human heart. Yet the divine judgment delivered by Nathan implies another connection in that it identifies coveting as a *fundamental distrust in God's generosity and grace.* Coveting does not expect everything and more, the full comfort and fulfillment of God, but assumes the necessity of projecting one's own pursuit of happiness. In other words, coveting as a fundamental distrust in God's sufficient love and grace exactly withholds from God what the first commandment requires.[47] We kill since we do not know how to abstain from coveting. And we covet since we do not trust in God's grace. Given the backdrop of this connection, we can also see that ultimately coveting is an equivalent to the desire for revenge. In both cases, we have an affective impulse formed from a lack of trust in God. We cannot keep the fifth commandment, or the ninth and tenth, or any other, as long as we do not keep the first.

If we consider this connection with the first commandment to be as pivotal as it was for Luther, we understand why Luther had to be more radical than Aquinas in his account of the perichoretic relation the fifth commandment enjoys with the others. By constituting all the commands as a matter of the heart and the first commandment, all commandments must be said to be "comprised in one another" even though this may in some cases be less obvious than in those which Aquinas also acknowledged. From their common dependence on the first, all commandments of the Decalogue assume theological depth and width that allows and challenges us to inquire into the variety of their bilateral interrelation. In other words, a perichoretic account of the Ten Words maps out acres of new and fertile ground that Christian moral inquiry needs to dig and exploit. It triggers the imagination of the moral theologian in a way that allows her to identify and name secret spheres and patterns of interconnection that must otherwise remain in the dark with which sin clothes our perception of reality.

Let us take as a test case the one commandment Aquinas explicitly exempted from such a perichoretic relation with the fifth: the command to honor one's parents. If our overall assumption is right, we should, contrary to Aquinas's expectation, be able to demonstrate how the fifth nests, amongst others,[48] in the fourth. As we shall see, this is not only possible; it even seems that the connection between those two commandments is given a particular sharp relief through recent devel-

---

47. For a more detailed account of covetousness as the explicit idol of our time, see my "The Desire of Desire: Idolatry in Late Capitalism," in *Idolatry,* ed. Stephen Barton (London and New York: T. & T. Clark, forthcoming).

48. Another example that may trigger our imagination would be the second commandment. The ban on making idols constitutes an essential prerequisite for the ban on killing, since the most spectacular and brutal cases of transgressing the fifth have tended to happen in the name of "higher values" or other idols such as "civilization," "class-free society," or — worst of all — in the name of God.

opments within our liberal societies, especially in the field of medical ethics. Perhaps we will hardly be capable of understanding what is going on in contemporary culture unless we inquire into the dynamic relationship between these two commandments.

5. How the Fifth Commandment Nests in the Fourth

A first indicator of this relationship is given in the wider context of the Decalogue itself, when in Exodus 21 a list of casuistic laws that follows the promulgation of the Ten Words in the preceding chapter and which addresses issues of violence, murder, and manslaughter, features two definitions that prescribe capital punishment for the one "who strikes father or mother" or "who curses father and mother" (Exod. 21:15, 17). This is not only a possible specification of the fourth commandment that indicates that the "honoring" of parents must include their bodily and spiritual integrity. Given the often highly tense relations between the generations, these prescriptions also suggest that only those who have exercised themselves in honoring their parents as the fourth commandment requires will be able to refrain from cursing or striking them (to death), should the temptation become overwhelmingly great in a particular situation.

It would seem obvious that one could explore the topical significance of the interrelation of both commandments along the lines suggested by these Old Testament precepts. Just think of recent discussions in some Western countries about the "adequacy" of access to expensive health care for the elderly or the "soft imperatives" to the terminally ill perceived to be inherent in the "euthanasia" legislation to "think constructively" about the burden their prolonged existence places on family members and so forth.

a. A View from Nowhere

Richard Neuhaus reports a telling example that clarifies how these trends toward a loosening of limits of the "license to kill" are, amongst other things, rooted in a theoretical disregarding of the family. The disregard of the family as a divinely assigned place of particular responsibility for particular people who are entrusted to us, makes way for a highly abstract construal of both human nature and responsibility. Neuhaus highlights a passage in an interview that Peter Singer gave to the *New Yorker:*

> There was a spot of unpleasantness in the debate. Singer's Benthamite principle that each counts as one and none as more than one has led him to insist again and again that, from an ethical viewpoint, our duties to friends and family are not different from our duties to strangers. That is part of what it means when he says his ethical theory is universal. One has no more ethical duty, for instance, to one's own daughter than to a girl of the same age ten thousand miles away in Bangladesh whom one has never seen and whose name one does not know. My family, my friends, my country — each must give way to the universal. Each person counts as one and no more than one. But then, in a long and generally sympathetic interview in the *New Yorker,* the question came up about Singer's devoting many thousands of dollars and elaborate nursing care for his own mother who had Alzheimer's. In the interview, Singer is reported to have explained, "Perhaps it's more difficult than I thought before, because it is different when it is your mother."[49]

Of course, from a theological point of view, Singer's admission strikes us as thoroughly positive — another indication of the well-attested fact that moral instinct is often more sensitive to the real world than moral theory. Yet the fact that this moment of sudden recognition of the particular moral significance of his own son-mother relation came as a surprise to the moral philosopher is indicative of a general point that is more disconcerting as it brings the theoretical disregard of the family within the horizon of euthanasia and abortion. If the family is not honored by acknowledging the moral commitment this given (for Christians: divinely ordained) relationship claims by its sheer existence, we are left, as Neuhaus puts it, with a strange "view from nowhere" — a view that lends itself to abstract utilitarian principles that will eventually breed indifference and violence. While the ab-

49. Richard John Neuhaus, "A Curious Encounter with a Philosopher from Nowhere," *First Things* 120 (February 2002): 77-96.

stract principle of universal responsibility, in theory, commits us to care for anyone, we face the fact in practice that we cannot care for everyone. Thus it is understandable that given the natural limitedness of our resources to care, this view from nowhere must produce other reasons and means that will allow us to be selective about where to grant and where to withhold care. Singer's own answer is well known. By distinguishing between members of the human species and (developed) persons, of which only the latter group is entitled to be bearers of human rights, Singer offers theoretical legitimating for dramatically extending practices of abortion and euthanasia. Though Singer's position is not necessarily widely shared, what many, in particular Kantian, critics of his account tend to overlook is the degree to which it is rooted in an original disregard of the type of *given* social relationships of which the family is representative.

Less obvious though no less dramatic than these trends at the end of life must the interrelation between killing and dishonoring the family appear if we look at recent trends surrounding the beginning of life. How could a designer baby, whose bodily features including her sex have been destined to live up to other people's desires, truly honor her parents for what they are if she must face the fact that the circumstances of her coming into being were marked by the unwillingness of her progenitors to honor her for what she might become? And as the birth of the first human clone seems only a matter of time: How could a clone ever honor her father and mother if there aren't any, as she would be not begotten, just made? We need not entertain a strong Freudian view with fantasies of patricide to see the difficulty. If, on the other hand, the fourth commandment is to protect the family by calling forth an active honoring of father and mother, it must certainly include the provision of the most fundamental circumstances that enable any child to fulfill it — which simply means: to have and to know his or her parents as those who are to be honored.

b. Reproductive Technologies and the Imperative to Kill

Several things result from the dishonoring of the family as the divinely assigned way for a new human being to come into life as the fruit of the loving embrace of a man and a woman who form a unit of care.

One result is that we become accustomed to using such abstract ideas as the "right to a child," just as we have become accustomed to the idea of "the right to have sex" as a result of disregarding what the sixth commandment protects. If having sex and procreating are defined as human rights in the abstract, they can be claimed by anyone in whatever circumstance, whether married or unmarried, single mothers who want a baby without a man, or homosexual couples. In the light of this, we should not be surprised to see cases like the recent one in which a couple of blind lesbians claimed a right to have a baby via in vitro fertilization (IVF) that would be destined to share their fate as a result of selecting a blind semen donor.

Liberal societies have actively (though not necessarily intentionally) promoted the disintegration of the family[50] as the natural context of gestation from begetting to birth, not least through the promotion of technologies that make this process increasingly independent of the family. It is here that we can identify a prime point of connection between the disregard of the fourth commandment and the implicit imperative to transgress the fifth. Having employed reproductive technologies such as IVF for an extended period of time, we have found ourselves producing a surplus of zygotes and embryos who are never meant to live; these human beings are not meant to exist as ends in themselves but are brought into being as mere means to serve the lives of others. More recent developments make us note a certain vicious circularity here: while the production of superfluous embryos required in the name of the "right to a child" as the material base for IVF inherently already suggests killing,[51] with the more recent call to and

50. Stanley Hauerwas, "The Radical Hope in the Annunciation: Why Both Single and Married Christians Welcome Children," in *The Hauerwas Reader,* ed. John Berkman and Michael Cartwright (Durham, N.C., and London: Duke University Press, 2001), pp. 506ff.

51. The Catholic Information Network (CIN) newsletter, edited by Fr. Richard W. Gant, reported on November 27, 2002, that Centers for Disease Control statistics indicate that in 1999 some 21,501 children were born in the United States using assisted reproductive techniques. They failed to report another fact. Extrapolation from those figures shows that about 170,000 human embryos actually died in the attempts by doctors to bring about the birth of a child through in vitro fertilization. This calculation was made in an article by Dr. James P. Toner on progress on IVF in the journal *Fertility and Sterility,* and reported by Life-Site. Voicing the church's condemnation of IVF, John Paul II said at the Jubilee for Families in 2000: "The tendency

established practice of a consumptive use of these superfluous embryos for the sake of genetic research, another intensified imperative to kill is created. Furthermore, the resulting insights into genetically codified diseases will stimulate a massively increasing demand for prenatal genetic screening that will, in turn, ultimately result in another leap in abortion figures.

So we are caught up in a circularity in which death is born of desire and desire is born of death. It is abortion that originally provided the material that now makes possible the creation of genetically risk-free offspring or even "designer babies" via preimplantation diagnostics with its concurrent imperative to selection. And it is the very possibility of producing babies according to one's own individual or society's image that will eventually result in another imperative to kill, if something is threatening to turn out a little below our standards. If killing begets killing, though not as in the ancient circle of blood revenge but in a civilized manner through the amplification of technological knowledge put forward in the name of "health," "quality of life," etc., it seems not inappropriate to speak of a "culture of death" as John Paul II has done.[52] A culture of death does not "fall into" the sin of killing, but organizes it in grand style: as a high-tech affair under protection of the juridical system. Of course, in order to promote killing in civilized societies it must be legalized under deceitful names. Yet liberal societies seem happy to be deceived exactly to the degree to which they have developed into societies of covetousness.[53] In capital-

---

to use practices which are morally unacceptable in the generation [of children] betrays the absurdity of the 'right to a child,' which takes the place of the correct recognition of the right of a child to be born and then to grow in a fully human way." The pope encouraged couples unable to conceive a child to turn to adoption, a "true exercise of charity that places children's well-being before parental needs." Web source: http://www.cin.org/archives/cinjub/200211/0109.html.

52. Encyclical letter *Evangelium Vitae,* English: *The Gospel of Life* (1995).

53. A more charitable account of liberal society's tendency to self-deception is offered in Hans S. Reinders's *"The Future of the Disabled in Liberal Society": An Ethical Analysis* (Notre Dame: University of Notre Dame Press, 2000). In this compelling analysis, Reinders points to the irredeemable antagonism between the two forces that have driven liberalism: the desire for justice, which calls for equal rights for the retarded, and the desire for freedom, which when spelled out as procreative freedom (including selection and abortion), cannot but eventually undermine the actual status of the disabled in society and hence the state of justice.

ist societies we are busily organizing disordered desire, on the perpetuation of which the survival of society as a functional politico-economic unit is believed to depend.

c. The Power of Definition and the Imperative of Self-Deceit

Therefore the culture of death is essentially marked by the business of redefinition. In defining our own humanity we claim the property rights that entitle us to distribute life and death according to the self-images we draw[54] — just as the "giving names to all the animals" in the beginning was seen as a license to kill. Part and parcel of this business of redefining humanity is to usurp the definition power over the goods which the individual commandments aim to protect: for example, if the sixth commandment meant to protect marriage and the good of proper use of our sexuality, we now insist on our own definition of what this good must be like:

"Sex," they now say, is a fun thing that must be always available and exciting. Likewise, the goods protected by the fourth and fifth commandments are willfully redefined.

"Family," they now say, is no longer where parents can be honored by their children, but simply "wherever children are cared for."

"Life," they now say, is actually what is "worth living," i.e., in full possession and actualization of our potential.

From these redefinitions of goods flows a redefinition of what we are (and are entitled) to do with them. For example, as embryos and fetuses do not have or show off the qualities we look for in a person, to perform an abortion is not killing a fully human being but merely changing a state of affairs: "termination of pregnancy." Similarly, we do not kill thousands of human fetuses but we undertake "consumptive research" on "embryonic material" or engage in "therapeutic cloning." This defining "aright" of reality is itself a violent act, directed against reality as God has created and protects it. And insofar as we refuse to enjoy it as it is destined to be, insisting instead on our redefinition, we cannot avoid killing. In particular, we must kill those whose

---

54. See my "What Is Man? That You Are Mindful of Him! Medical Aspirations in the Light of Psalm 8" (Farmington Papers, 2004, forthcoming).

very existence is threatening to give the lie to the virtual reality we have created through our defining imagination: the unwanted unborn, the disabled, and the terminally ill.

In liberal societies we are faced with a real dilemma: on the one hand, as agents and slaves of a technologically sustained culture of death, it has become virtually impossible for us to abstain from killing. And as a result, the fifth commandment must appear as anachronistic, since it cannot be kept under the circumstances of modern life. On the other hand, as heirs of the Enlightenment project, we still cling to the idea that killing is alien to our humanity, unnatural or even irrational — which ironically results again in the fifth commandment perception as an anachronism, since it formulates only what is self-evident to the modern mind anyway. As civilized people we hate to kill as much as we hate death. Yet we cannot abstain from killing, because we cannot abstain from coveting and revengeful hatred. Being caught up in this web, even our hatred of death becomes a motive to kill — when, for example, we cannot stand the slow advent of death in the suffering of a terminally ill person and therefore must bring it prematurely to an end.

As a result of this dilemma created by two irreconcilable tendencies, we must take great pains at concealing what we do. In order to deceive ourselves about the reality we create, we *cannot but* buffer our killing with a language which suggests that we are doing something else: hence we invest our language with academic unintelligibility ("consumptive research on embryonic material," "collateral damage"), with euphemistic attributes ("emergency contraception," "therapeutic cloning"),[55] or with a perverted grammar, as when our soldiers "die" on the battlefield or our terminally ill "die" with the help of a merciful drug.

If this analysis of our current culture has any merit, we must conclude that Aquinas was wrong in assuming a nonintegral relation between the fourth and fifth commandments. We may, of course, exempt him from blame, granting that he could hardly have foreseen a culture

55. Robert Spaemann has pointed out ("Gezeugt, nicht gemacht," *Die Zeit,* January 4, 2001) that the language of "therapeutic cloning" is deceiving, since the act of cloning is not therapy but killing — the killing of the embryos whose genetic material is exploited for the sake of (a future possibility of) therapy of *other* persons.

like ours in which the interrelation would take on such a dramatic dynamic. Even though we can hardly claim more than a preliminary attempt at inquiring into the critical relationship between these individual commandments, we have found enough ground to suggest that it should be perceived an ongoing task of those engaged in Christian moral reasoning to discern which particular aspect of the Decalogue's *perichoresis* is at stake at a given time and situation. It may well be that the prerogative of our generation is to become alert to the explosive interrelation of those two commandments in particular, while other generations will have to focus on the same imaginative alertness elsewhere in the Decalogue.

As we have seen, one important feature of this ministry of moral inquiry will be a theological criticism of the language employed by a culture of death. The discernment of which commandment is at stake in a given course of action[56] will enable us to truthfully describe what is going on and to name the particular sin at stake. Nathan's famous cry, "You are the man," identified what the king had done: You are the man who killed his neighbor. *You* killed him — and not the swords of the enemies. You *killed* him — and not just advised someone else to expose him to higher risk. And the same clarity about the nature of the object of an action is required in regard to liberal societies' state of confusion when it comes to legalized abortion, euthanasia, and conduct in warfare. Do we really just "preserve the eventual future baby's right to be a child that is really wanted," do we really simply "end a patient's suffering," are we really just "putting up with collateral damage" when in fact we are killing innocent life?[57] Of course, clarifying is not yet curing, but without recognizing and naming killing where it occurs, abstention will be practically and theoretically impossible.

---

56. In 2003 the Pontifical Council for the Family of the Vatican published a critical glossary that offers the interpretation of seventy-eight "ambiguous terms" involved in "discussion of the family, life and ethical questions." The 876 pages of the Italian edition are currently near translation into English and other languages. *Lexicon. Termini ambigui e discussi su famiglia, vita e questioni etiche,* ed. Dehoniane (Bologna, 2003).

57. See my "Intrinsically Evil Acts; or: Why Euthanasia and Abortion Cannot Be Justified," in *Ecumenical Ventures in Ethics: Protestants Engage Pope John Paul II's Moral Encyclicals,* ed. R. Hütter and T. Dieter (Grand Rapids: Eerdmans, 1998), pp. 185-215.

6. Dwelling in the Torah

We have analyzed the fifth commandment from its location right in the middle of the Decalogue, as buffered, so to speak, on all sides by the surrounding precepts; and we have particularly inquired into the relation this commandment has with the fourth. I hope this analysis has in all its tentativeness become somewhat illustrative of what it means to "walk" or "dwell" in the Torah, as a preeminent biblical image suggests. In this sense the moral meaning of Torah is not confined to "showing the way" by providing a map or functioning as a signpost; rather Torah is itself perceived as a "way." Hence exploring the interrelatedness of individual commandments by virtue of the assumed perichoretic nature of the Decalogue can be seen as a genuine theological way of exploring the world as it appears in the light of God's Torah.

A related methodological gain of this analysis, I hope, will be that the theological validity of Luther's famous claim that all the commandments find their center in the first could be demonstrated not, as it is usually done, from the immediate perspective of faith, which as love of God necessarily implies the love of his decrees, but mediated through the perspective of an individual commandment and its dependence on another. That ultimately everything, the keeping of every individual commandment and the Decalogue as a whole, depends on faith and love is as true a statement as it tends to be a rushed one that is often more prone to eclipse than illumine the fine topography of the moral life. The unity of the Decalogue cannot be construed in psychological terms (according to a dynamic of sin or something of this kind),[58] but it should also not be understood as being derived from a single unifying first principle. The first commandment and the faith it calls forth is not such a principle that provides unity to the rest by applying to all in the same fashion. Rather, as we discovered in our exploring of the concrete perichoretic relation of two particular commandments, the *dependence on the first is spelled out in the concrete*

---

58. Aquinas seems to point in a similar direction when drawing out the categorical difference between virtues and vices in terms of their respective unitive quality: while the "love of God is unitive, in so far as it draws man's affections from the many to the one . . . self-love disperses man's affections among different things. . . . Hence vices and sins, which arise from self-love, are not connected together." *STh* I/II, q. 73, art. 1, ad 3.

interdependence of the other commandments. We never "keep the Decalogue" but always only an individual commandment as it addresses
us in a particular life situation. Yet we are to keep any individual commandment as one of the Ten Words, and we do so by accounting for
the critical relation it shares with any other. This is "our" immediate,
human way of accounting for the unity of the Decalogue which is possible even on this side of a final settling of the speculation about the
unity of virtues.

By doing so we acknowledge that we "through faith" are not capable of abstaining from killing, as faith is not available to us as a
means, but that we can hope to abstain from killing only by abstaining
from coveting, dishonoring our parents, and so forth — all of which, in
turn, are impossible without faith. Our *mediated* acknowledgment (mediated through exploration) of this *immediate* fact becomes ever deeper
as we discover the *different* ways in which faith is required and in
which grace is operating in the concrete dealings with the world as the
commandments address them. To account for the interdependence of
individual commandments within the Decalogue is, on the other
hand, precisely what prepares us to understand and acknowledge
their fundamental dependence on the first.

So, in conclusion, what does it take to keep the fifth commandment? The answer is: All the others — every other commandment,
plus the first. The first is not included in "all the others"; rather these
are included in the first. We need to keep them all, but in a way that
keeps them as the fulfillment of the first, of which we are made capable by virtue of the renewal of the heart that Jesus gives.

Male and Female He Created Them

Robert W. Jenson

I will start with the commandment itself. The assigned title allows me room to do otherwise; but in the case of the particular matter assigned me there is reason not to take advantage of that freedom, for the dominant heresy of the contemporary Western church is of course antinomianism, and it is in the commandment not to commit adultery that our antinominianism finds its chief occasion. We are still, for the most part, willing to say that killing someone without legal mandate is a bad idea, indeed a crime, which is to say, that it is a matter for law, for a commandment — or rather, we are willing to say that with one multimillion-victim exception. The same goes, still at this moment anyway, for stealing and false witness. But when we get to law about sex, the underground current of antinomianism breaks out into an aboveground torrent, whose billows and eddies you do not need me to describe to you.

So directly to the commandment. "You shall not commit adultery." Like most of the commandments, the commandment in its stated form is negative. Adultery is copulating with someone else's spouse, or if married with anyone but the spouse. No one is to do that, according to God according to Moses, on pain of God's extreme displeasure. Indeed, throughout Scripture and tradition adultery is prominent on the list of those sins the doers of which will "not inherit the Kingdom of heaven."

In its negative form the commandment is blunt, but the commandment is also in one way indeterminate, since it does not stipulate what counts as a spouse. In different societies spousehood comes in different forms, several of which appeared even within the chosen people to whom the commandment was given, and without explicit rebuke. Solomon, celebrated in Scripture precisely for wisdom, had a harem the sultans never matched, at least according to an obviously envious report.

The various peoples have socialized and ritualized the procreative, passionate, and companionate power of our matched plumbing variously. What the commandment says in its immediate negative form is that whether monogamy or polyandry or polygamy obtains, violation of spousal units thus established is a crime against God and humanity.

In considering this immediate negative force of the commandment, I have used the word "crime," a legal term. Theology has often regarded the Ten Commandments, or at least the second table, as a statement of universal natural law, or of whatever term you prefer for universally heard deontic mandates. No society that dishonors the continuity of the generations, or relies on vendetta instead of police and judges, or does not protect property, however defined, or honors greed, can long perdure — except perhaps as what Luther called a rout of swine. The crimes prohibited from Sinai, at least those of the second table,[1] are those that undermine human society itself, and are thus crimes in every perduring society, just because it has perdured.

Prominent among such crimes is adultery. Whatever spousal and familial form a society ordains, it must, as a matter of the community's life and death, enforce it. And in fact, "You shall not commit adultery" is basic law in every viable civilized community, just because it is viable; that venerable cliché, that "the family is the foundation of society," is a cliché because it is so obviously true to all experience and investigation.

It is, I think, worth a paragraph of emphasis at this point. A society that gives up the legal shaping of sexual behavior — which perhaps, in terms of our society, regards divorce as a matter with "no fault," or grants legal advantages equivalent to those granted marriage to whatever human amalgamations present themselves — can-

---

1. I think an argument can be made to establish this point also about the first table, but do not need to make it here.

not be a just society or indeed a viable civilization. When asked why the world of Islam hates us, our pundits hardly know what to do with one obvious part of the answer: Islamic societies regard us as sexually corrupt and try desperately to protect themselves from our influence. Their cause is probably hopeless and their measures are usually, but it is hard to dispute the judgment itself — which may very well turn out to be the judgment of God.

II

But now we must observe that the commandments, and again most especially this one, do not, despite their immediate formulation, function only as universally necessary prohibitions. They were given to specific communities, to Israel and the church; and in Israel and the church, and to some extent in other cultures exposed to Torah, they acquire complex positive meanings specific within the lives of these communities. Thus "You shall not kill" comes to mean not only that vendetta is prohibited, but that, as Luther's catechism has it, "We should so fear and love God, that we do our neighbor no bodily injury or harm, but *help* and *assist* him in every bodily need." Our present commandment, the command against spousal unfaithfulness, "You shall not commit adultery," has acquired in Israel and the church positive force of especially great scope and complexity.

Israel experienced the favor of her God as his passionate love for her: as Deuteronomy insists, it was not because Israel was the greatest of the nations that the Lord made her his own, but because he loved her. The Lord's election of this people was neither a rational decision nor an arbitrary one, it was of another sort altogether: he fell in love with her — and if anyone is about to cite recently standard, though surely odd, exegetical opinion and say that "love" in Deuteronomy is not a passion, I will refer him to the work currently being done by Jacqueline Lapsley of Princeton Seminary. Thus the analogy between the Lord's relation to Israel and conjugal love appears early and often in Israel's Scripture.

But now, if the sexual relation of spouses can provide an analogy for the Lord's relation to Israel, the analogy must have some impact also the other way around. And in that direction it will open as a moral opportunity: the sexual relation of spouses can be modeled on the relation of the Lord and Israel. In this modeling of spousal attraction and union on the attraction and union between the Lord and Israel, as it happened in Israel and derivatively in the church, two aspects of the relation between the Lord and his people have been decisive: first, there is but *one* God and *one* people of God; and second, the virtue which the specifically biblical God practices with his people and demands from them is *faithfulness*. Thus one woman and one man becomes over time the normative pattern of marriage in Israel and the church, and in societies decisively shaped by them, as it rarely is elsewhere; and faithfulness becomes the great sexual virtue, as yet more rarely elsewhere — demands for virginity in brides and purdah or its equivalent in marriage are another matter altogether. In Israel and the church, "You shall not commit adultery" comes to mean, again in Luther's words: "We should fear and love God, so that we live chaste and disciplined lives in word and deed, so that each one *loves and honors* the spouse."

And that is about as far as we get by concentrating strictly on the commandment. Of course if we could get that far in churchly practice it would be a major reformation; and if we could get that far in society it might be the foundation of another Renaissance of the West.

Nevertheless, many arguments in the church about human sexuality end in stalemate between inveterate antinomianism and what does indeed sometimes sound like a rather nitpicky use of the Bible, because they do not proceed from staring at the commandment itself to the context within which the commandment in its affirmative forces makes sense: the Bible's construal of what it means to be human as male or female. It is that to which I must now turn.

III

The first thing to be said about the Bible's understanding of human life is that it is thoroughly theocentric: we are what we are because God relates to us as he does. We are, in the famous biblical passage, made "in the image" of God.[2] What the philological exegesis of the passage

2. Gen. 1:26-27.

should be is disputed, but so much is plain from the whole context of Scripture: what we are and are to do is determined by what God is and does and by a relation of correspondence to his being and action. In any case, it is Scripture's whole following story of the relation of the Lord to his creatures that then in fact determines what "in the image" means. Thus there is indeed a very specific and clear biblical anthropology — though it will be discovered neither by passage hunting nor by hermeneutics of suspicion, nor yet of course by standard liberal carelessness. It is one aspect of that anthropology that interests us here.

"In the image of God he created him (singular); male and female he created them (plural)." The arresting syntax and diction of this passage are, I think, deliberate and precise; we must remember that the passage does not come from some "primitive" stage of Israel's history or from freely storytelling tradents, it is from "the Priestly Document," which, however shadowy its existence as an actual entity may currently look, does stand as a convenient label for the most careful and theologically reflected of the Pentateuch's strands or layers of material and editing. The passage in Genesis is nothing less, it seems to me, than a piece of strictly dogmatic theology, a summing up of everything on the subject in earlier formulated Scripture, from cultic purity laws to the narratives of patriarchal and royal marriage to old men's rueful wisdom to the prophet's acted parables.

Humans come in two sorts, female and male, differentiated in the plainest possible way: if we now took off our clothes, there is one way of sorting us into two groups that would not take much thought. Precisely in the plumbing that so crudely differentiates us, there are located *both* the most intense physical pleasure of which we are capable and our power to continue the human race. And these differing apparatus *fit* each other in again the plainest possible way; in a set of verses on the six days, I once referred to "the cabinet-catch mechanism of our joy." Now according to the priestly wisdom of Genesis 1, only when we are created in these two forms is "the man," *ha-adam*, created at all. We are human only as male or female, and just so we are human only as both together; the Bible knows no gender-neutral humanity.

Now why ever did God do it this way? It is surely one of his more peculiar ideas — the old crack about the pleasure — for all its wonder — being fleeting, the position ridiculous, and the cost ruinous goes right to several points. Something can, I think, be said on the matter; Karl Barth said most of it, and in other writing I have tried to polish a point or two. So for some readers there will be a bit of repetition in the following.

Our creation as two different kinds of bodies, paired to each other by the paired shape and function of blatant bodily phenomena, is the way God keeps our reality as *communal* beings from being a mere mandate or ideal, and makes it be a fact about the actual things we are. Over against a physically undifferentiated and just so spiritualized humanity, our self-love would inevitably make directedness to one another at best a desirable virtue. But the material apparatus of sexual differentiation does not permit us thus to postpone our directedness to each other — I mean, there are the appendage and the orifice, part of the things we are and manifestly made for pairing. And that God not allow us to evade our mutuality is necessary to our salvation. For that we are communal, that we are our human selves precisely as *we*, that we are directed to each other for good and ill, is a necessary condition of God's relation to us.

This is so because the actual God is triune. Which is to say, the actual God is in himself a community: the Father is the Father only as the Father of the Son, and only in that he is Father is he God; the Son is the Son only as the Son of the Father, and only in that he is Son is he God; the Spirit is the Spirit only as the mutual spirit of this Father and this Son, and only as he is Spirit is he God; and only as each of these three is in his way God is there God at all.

God then relates *ad extra*, to what is other than God, to creatures, only and precisely as *this* God, not as if he were a monad. The way this God relates to creatures is that he lets the relations that make the triune community intersect with the relations that make the created community: thus, e.g., the Spirit, who is the love between the Father and the Son, gives himself to be the bond of love between creatures and between their community and the Father and the Son — or at least so Augustine and Luther taught.

Were we not communal in fact but only in aspiration, we would not as we are placed and found in the world be entities appropriate to the Spirit's work. So also the Son, on whom the Spirit rests and who is the Father's own Expression, is one of us: his body is among us, and all our religious life, centered of course in prayer and oblation, depends on joining our physical voice with his and our offering of his body and our bodies with his offering of them. Were we not communal in fact but only in aspiration, the Son could at most belong only to an elite human community — as some otherwise wonderful thinkers of the church have been seduced into thinking — and poor sinners would have neither access to the Father nor the availability of the Spirit. These dialectics, once observed, can be spun out endlessly.

Thus whether or not we accept Karl Barth's contention that our reality as male and female is itself a reflection of the inner-triune life and constitutive of the image of God, a smaller claim can be made with confidence: it is as bodies inescapably ordered to each other by vagina and penis that our adaptation to correspondence with the himself communal God is made part of what we simply and without choice *are*. If God then chooses to address us, we are available to be the special creatures he indeed addresses at the end of the sixth day.

There are of course other bonds of mutuality, most of them also in one way or another bodily. But marriage is the only one that creates an actual new bodily unit — the old myth of the creature with two backs who was forcibly divided to make woman and man rested on simple observation. The two bodies envelop and enter each other in a fashion provided for not only by shape but by their function beyond pleasure, the function of this orifice and this member of maintaining God's human creation — for which in evolutionary view the pleasure is just a kind of bait. And before and around and after the unifying gesture of copulation, a faithful union of one woman and one man develops an entire repertoire of unifying gestures unique to this one singular relation. It is the drive to sexual union — and the anticipation of sexual union and perhaps especially the faithful memory of sexual union — that makes our mutuality a fact of our created existence.

Or we can cast the matter in semiotic fashion. Our life is not a life with the whole of humanity as a unit, it is a life in families, enterprises, cults, etc. After the family, the most determinative of these are those groups, whether tribes, firms, or whatever, that have cultures. A culture, by a usual definition, is a spiderweb of mutually enabling signs.

Here it helps to borrow some key observations from Augustine. There are various sorts of signs in the web of a culture. Some compose its language; in Augustine's terminology, they are "words." Some are objects or gestures not linked in a general syntax; in Augustine's terminology, they are "visible" signs. We have many such signs, gestures of mutual commitment, movements of the body toward the other, that in a culture are so understood. Not just coitus, but the whole pattern of spousal movements that develops in a marriage — perhaps sleeping spoon-fashion, or a certain kind of kiss, etc., etc. — produces a movement toward one another which, at least in Israel's and the church's culture, becomes the visible sign of the sexual virtue enabled in God's people, of faithfulness, of the virtue by which marriage in Israel and the church patterns itself on the faithfulness of God's own life. The specifically spousal pattern of movement to one another is that movement of two to each other which is the end of such movement, the movement of two to each other after which there is no way for creatures to go further.

We can, to be sure, make sex mean less than faithfulness; we can even make it mean the opposite. We can make it mean "I really like you for tonight" or "There's one more for my list." But then we have no gesture left to mean faithfulness, and a culture — or a person — bereft of a sign for faithfulness is incapable of it, since faithfulness is the sort of thing which does not exist without a sign. *Sex in the City* is indeed remarkably written and fetchingly acted — and our film-professional daughter and son-in-law commend its technical virtues to us — but it makes me shudder for the city in question.

IV

All of which brings us to the jewel of the Bible's construal of human sexuality, the Song of Songs, which is Solomon's. When folk, especially combatants in the sex wars that tear our churches, set out to assemble canonical resources, both sides usually assemble a rather puny set, because they leave out the most important document.

The Song is obviously love poetry, and of a fairly unabashed sort. Let me cite a verse or two from the first pages, just to remind you: "Oh, give me of the kisses of your mouth. . . . My beloved is a packet of myrrh, lodged between my breasts."

The question has always been: Who are the lovers? Israel's rabbis said they were the Lord and Israel, and this reading appears to have been the justification of the book's appearance in the canon; according to one of the ancient sages, anyone who says the book is just love poetry forfeits his share in the world to come — which is going to damn just about the whole membership of the Society of Biblical Literature. The traditional exegesis of the church followed the rabbis, with the usual claim of the church to be Israel: the lovers are Christ and the church, or, therein comprised, Christ and the believing soul.

Modern exegesis has supposed this had to be wrong. The poems, according to modernity's exegetes, must have been secular love poetry, later misread by the rabbis and the church's exegetes as religious; or for a while some thought they were indeed originally religious but must have been liturgy for some other religion than that of Israel, a fertility religion, again later appropriated by the rabbis.

The warrants of these "must's" are, however, on examination rather feeble. Chief among supposed warrants for the first opinion is the existence in other cultures of love poetry that does not celebrate love between God and his creation. The refutation of that warrant is a simple "So what?" That there exists love poetry between creatures scarcely means there can be no love poetry between Creator and creatures; indeed, the contrary is plainly the more plausible. Next comes the — very Protestant — feeling that Israel just *could* not have produced love poetry between the Lord and herself. But if the rabbis could appropriate love poetry for the love between the Lord and Israel, why could an Israelite poet not have written such poetry in the first place?

There are in any case three fatal problems with the modern exegesis. First, it has been pointed out, by André LaCoque and Ellen Davis,[3] who otherwise interpret the Song oppositely, that the author of the Song, more than the authors and tradents of any other part of the OT, lived in the language and imagery of the *rest* of the OT; it is, in Davis's phrase, the "most biblical" of the biblical books, a tissue of biblical reference and pastiche, in both language and imagery. Whatever the Song's author or authors may originally have intended to write, he, she, or they were thorough, Bible-reading Israelites, who cast their love poetry in the language of texts saturated with the Lord's love for Israel. Second, Davis makes a trenchant following point: Why *shouldn't*

3. André LaCoque, *Romance She Wrote* (Harrisburg, Pa.: Trinity International Press, 1998); Ellen Davis, *Proverbs, Ecclesiastes, and the Song of Songs* (Louisville: Westminster John Knox, 2000).

ROBERT W. JENSON

such an Israelite poet have written love songs between the Lord and Israel?

And of course third, and independently of Davis's observations, if indeed the rabbis did appropriate poetry originally about human lovers only, or even a chunk of someone's fertility ritual, and include it in the canon to celebrate the love between the Lord and Israel, then it is the love between the Lord and Israel that the *canonical* text is in fact about; here as elsewhere a reconstructed precanonical status of the text could at most serve to detect subtleties of the canonical presentation.

So the young woman is Israel or the church, and the young man is the Lord; and this is not an "allegorical" reading of the text, it is the plain sense of the canonical text, which itself of course makes that sense indeed by a fabric of images. Yet neither do we want to turn the poem into a record of disembodied religious experience, as churchly exegesis sometimes has done. The poem remains, whosoever affair it narrates, sensual love poetry. It is about body parts and aroma seduction and lovers looking for a place to be alone and frustration and satisfaction.

Whether the author or authors intended it so, or the rabbis did it, the canonical text of the Song posits an analogy between the relation of human lovers to each other and the relation between God and his people, precisely as both relations are — analogously — erotic. We should moreover note that by the classic doctrine of analogy this does not mean that we are the originals of eroticism and God's relation to his people is an attenuated version thereof; it means rather that human lovers' relations to each other are recognizable as erotic only by distant resemblance to a true eroticism which is God's alone.

It is the shaping of human eroticism thereby accomplished, and not so much or initially God's own eroticism, that belongs within the scope of my assignment. So first, and longest, that side of the matter.

If erotic love is an analogue of God and his people, then the way we shape it must in some part shape our relation to God. Just as our faulty righteousness can nonetheless be an anticipation of our eschatological sharing in the righteousness of God, so our frail erotic faithfulness can, despite its frailty, be an anticipation of our eschatological sharing in God's absolutely faithful love for his people in the Son. The deepest reason why God is concerned with monogamy and faithfulness is that our arrangements here must shape the form and intensity of our relation to him — whether overly ideological children of the Reformation like it or not, it is after all said that some will take fewer of their works through the fire into the kingdom than will others. Given the Lord's saying, I will not speculate about how our marriages will reemerge on the other side of judgment, but I am quite sure our divorces and infidelities, however passionate and committed, etc., will make it only as very much scorched by fire.

How then should we shape our marriages? We should *seek* each other, as the Lord and Israel seek each other in the Song; and we should faithfully persist in seeking each other, again like the lovers in the Song. We should cherish each other's bodies and the presence they constitute, as the Lord washes and nourishes our bodies and as we cherish his body on the altar. The language of the genuine *Book of Common Prayer,* even allowing for older uses of "worship," is drastic and precisely to the point: "With my body I thee worship." We should sing praises to each other, like the lovers in the Song and like the Lord's love poetry to Israel in the prophets and like Israel's psalm poetry to the Lord. Write your lover some doggerel, however unskilled — I am not sure Blanche Jenson would be best pleased were I too slavishly to imitate the Song and salute her with *some* of its similes, but so long as nobody reads my twice-yearly effusions but she, I can find my own. We should seek and find places to be alone.

One specific matter is decisive here: if erotic love is an analogue of God and the church, then no shame can be intrinsic to the activity. In his exegesis of Genesis, Martin Luther said that had Adam and Eve not disobeyed, sexual congress would have been sheer openly enjoyed duty and delight, with neither any need to hide itself nor yet — we may add — the defiance with which shame now is often — as they say — transgressed. Davis asks us to note that the scene for much of the poetry is a garden; she calls it the third garden, after Eden and the temple, which latter, you will remember, was decorated as a simulated garden. Where were the lovers making love? Davis suggests: in remembered Eden and in the poetically evoked temple. The Song's poesy of sheer bodily delight, invoked in order to speak of the Lord and his people joined passionately in the temple, simultaneously evokes human love as it would be, were we lovers in Eden or in the garden the temple depicted: it would be the joyous image of God's love for Israel.

Given that Eden and the temple are not now extant, the garden is eschatological, and so then must be the Song's depiction of love. Human eroticism as now practiced and experienced is an indeed unreliable image of divine love; in the West and Islam oppositely and equally we are well along to making it an image of satanic hate. The image will be clear only in the kingdom; and that it is in the present age simultaneously a uniquely potent and uniquely unreliable image of our relation to God, is what curtains it with a unique fabric of shame.

We have of course no notion of what the eroticism of the kingdom will be like, and indeed are dominically instructed not to form any notion. But also the dominical saying about likeness to the angels does not presuppose that eroticism is simply absent from the kingdom.

V

Here, undoubtedly, is the place to say something about celibacy, as it has long been practiced and praised in the church. Through antiquity and the Middle Ages, exegesis of the Song was especially a work of monastic theology; it was above all the heirs of Anthony and Benedict who pondered the love between God and the soul, under the imagery of love between man and woman. It is of course easy to make jokes about men self-deprived of women contemplating breasts and thighs under the cover of biblical scholarship. But even if that was sometimes a factor, again, so what?

Far more important is what the celibate tradition's love for the Song tells us about celibacy: for those called to it, celibacy is not a renunciation of sexuality but a pressurized form of it, a reduction of eroticism to that eros between God and his people that is the enabling archetype of all eroticism. And then also the other way around: the celibate tradition's love for the Song tells us something about spousal love, that for those called to it spousal eroticism is a discipline at least as rigorous as that of the monastery. That at least is how Luther, who invented the Protestant pastor's-family, thought about the matter; turning the Augustinian priory into a family home and boardinghouse, he did not think he was leaving a heavy priestly discipline for a lighter one. Just the opposite. Thus marriage and celibacy should be understood as alternative callings within one understanding of sexuality — an understanding displayed to us above all in the Song.

VI

This section is an excursus from the main line of my discussion: in present circumstances it is probably necessary to say something about homoerotic practice. For a first point, it is indeed practice — and not orientation — that is the proper subject of ethical inquiry. If indeed there are various sexual orientations, and whatever their cause, they are not what is to be ethically or morally judged — unless, to be sure, they are *acquired,* as "habits" in the medieval sense, in which case they must be either virtues or vices.

Homoerotic practice, described simply as what is overtly done, is an attempt to treat a member of the same sex as if he or she were of the other sex, or to provide the partner with the simulacrum of the other sex without presenting the partner with the actually other. That is, homoerotic practice is *substitution for the created other,* of access to whom one has in some way been deprived, whether by one's own choice, or by circumstance or societal influence, or indeed by genetic inheritance if that is sometimes or always involved.

Homoerotic practice thus attempts to contravene God's imposition of embodied directedness to the other. A homoerotic act is a rebellion against the Creator, however otherwise benign. That said, it should be noted that I here make no suggestion about how church or society should socialize persons given to such practice. Nor do I wish to suggest that homoerotic practice is more to be condemned than the heteroerotic rebellions more immediately prohibited by our commandment. Thus someone who — like a recent candidate for the episcopacy — has left spouse and children for a lover should not be in the clergy; the gender of the lover hardly matters.

VII

And now at the end I must say something about what the Song teaches us about *God* and eros: that Nygren was wrong. "Agape" and eros are supposed to be opposite phenomena, for which the common English translation of both with the same word, "love," is at best greatly misleading. Agape is disinterested self-giving to the other; eros is needy desire for the other. The biblical God, according to

Nygren, is all agape and no eros; and his disciples should strive for a similar condition.

But surely God's love for us is *not* agape sheerly without eros, is not sheerly disinterested self-giving. When you think about it, who indeed would want to be disinterestedly loved? By God or anyone? If I didn't think Blanche Jenson had *something* to get from our marriage, that I was all and only need and she all and only beneficence, living with her would be a crushing obligation, it would be "all law and no gospel." And indeed, it seems to be an essential aspect of the good news: the God of the gospel narrative freely determines himself to need us.

The Father would not be the Father without the Son, and so would not be God. The Father *needs* the Son to be God. The Son would not be the Son without the Father, and so would not be God. He needs the Father to be God. The Spirit would not be the Spirit without the Father and the Son, and so would not be God. He needs the Father and the Son to be God. And if these three were not God, there would be no God. Thus need for the other, longing for the other, eros, belongs to the very being of God.

The Son is not the Spirit and the Spirit is not the Father; these needs are not interchangeable. Therefore the differentiation of male and female does have some analogy to the differentiations of the triune identities, and so erotic faithfulness also belongs to the being of God.

And then — the death and resurrection of the incarnate Son take us into this life: thus, given the incarnation, God loves us also with a needy love. Jonathan Edwards said it was the great saving effect of the incarnation that God can as incarnate be "passionate" to his own, can love us with a love we can recognize as love.

So why, finally, should "each one love and honor the spouse," as Luther said? To be *godlike*, "perfect, as [our] heavenly Father is perfect."

The Tongue — Fallen and Restored:
Some Reflections on the Three Voices
of the Eighth Commandment

Reinhard Hütter

We have come a long way so far and have covered most of the commandments, either explicitly or by *perichoresis,* to use Bernd Wannenwetsch's felicitous expression.[1] Now, in a seemingly indistinct position comes the eighth commandment: "You shall not bear false witness against your neighbor." As do the other commandments of the Decalogue's second table, this one pertains to a particular bodily member of the human being. Even if it is only a matter of pushing a button or using a computer keyboard, it takes hands to kill and to steal, eyes to covet, and sexual organs to commit adultery — except for adultery in the heart, for which the eyes suffice.

The eighth commandment focuses our attention on another part of our body: the tongue. The tongue is the organ par excellence of human intersubjectivity. With the tongue we praise, we curse, we speak truth, and we lie. In his *Large Catechism,* Martin Luther ends the exposition of the eighth commandment with a pertinent remark in which James 3:5 strongly resonates: "There is nothing about a man or in a man that can do greater good or greater harm, in spiritual and in temporal matters, than this smallest and weakest of his members, the tongue."[2] This all too well known intersubjective liability of the tongue

---

1. Cf. Bernd Wannenwetsch's essay on the fifth commandment in this volume.
2. Martin Luther, *The Large Catechism,* trans. Robert H. Fischer (Philadelphia: Fortress, 1959), p. 48.

would be a simply trivial matter and an exclusive concern for social and political engineering if the human being were indeed just an accident of the evolutionary process. However, if the world — in and through the process of its distinct becoming — is understood as God's creation, everything in general and everything about the human in particular must be understood in light of God's providential intention and care. And if indeed the tongue also must be thought as subject to divine intention and providence, this smallest and weakest member gathers significant theological and metaphysical weight. For the tongue is the organ of speech, and the point of speech is nothing less than truthful communication, from the simple "Watch your step" to the significant "I love you."[3] Because the intersubjective world depends so profoundly on truthful communication, it is such truthful communication that sustains and edifies any human community.

It is for this reason that Thomas Aquinas discusses the vice of lying in his *Summa theologiae* in the context of those virtues that sustain and edify the life of the human community. For Aquinas the intersubjective vice of lying is opposed to the intersubjective virtue of truthfulness or veracity.[4] And it is Calvin who in his *Sermons on the Ten Commandments* most explicitly and forthrightly articulates the intersubjective character of truth telling:

> Now if we want to observe what this text contains, we need to consider a higher principle, that is to consider why God created our tongues and why he gave us speech, the reason being that we might be able to communicate with each other. Now what is the purpose of communication if it isn't our mutual support and charity? Consequently, then, it is essential for us to learn to bridle our tongues to the extent that the union which God commands us may constantly be nurtured as much as possible. And that is why Saint

3. There is probably no theologian who has probed the theological nature of human speech and its trinitarian root in the relationship between the Father and the Logos more profoundly and more rigorously than Saint Augustine in his two treatises on lying. For what amounts to simply the best treatment of Saint Augustine on lying and simultaneously the philosophically and theologically most rigorously argued book on lying, cf. Paul Griffiths, *Lying: An Essay after Augustine* (Grand Rapids: Brazos, 2004).

4. Cf. Thomas Aquinas, *Summa theologiae* II-II, q. 110, art. 1.

190

James employs such vehemence when he speaks of evil reports. He says that the tongue, which is such a little member, or such a small piece of flesh, can start such a fire as to ravage the largest forest of the world. Therefore let us come back to our principle knowledge that God provided us with a unique gift when he gave us a means of being able to communicate with each other. So, on the one hand, men's affections may be hidden, but on the other the tongue exists to reveal our hearts. Therefore let us be encouraged to use such a gift and not to soil it with our vices and deplorableness. And seeing that God has given it to us for the purpose of nurturing tender love and fraternity with each other, may we not abuse it in order to gossip and bustle about here and there, so perverting our speech as to poison ourselves against each other.[5]

It seems like everything worth saying on this topic Calvin has said rather straightforwardly in his sermon on the eighth commandment. But it only seems so. To be sure, in the sermon passage just quoted, Calvin touches upon all the topics that we rightly should expect from a catechetical sermon on the eighth commandment. However, in the following remarks I do not simply want to expound upon extant interpretations of the eighth commandment, even if such influential ones as Luther's or Calvin's. Nor do I want to belabor again the classical and by now outworn philosophical debate about lying that has preoccupied deontologists and utilitarians for such a long time.[6] Rather, I want to focus on the way in which the eighth commandment encounters *us*. That is, I want to pay attention to the distinctly *theological* dynamic of this commandment as we find ourselves addressed by it. For we all too easily forget that we do not meet the Decalogue as abstract modern subjects on some allegedly neutral ground. To the contrary, the Ten Commandments encounter us in a highly charged theological context.

This theological context has a surprising and deeply disquieting contour, although it appears in a narrative clothing that is seductively familiar to many. According to the biblical witness, and more precisely

5. *John Calvin's Sermons on the Ten Commandments,* trans. Benjamin Farley (Grand Rapids: Baker, 1980), p. 216.

6. For the best recent treatment of this discussion in the middle of a clear and concise discussion of the whole spectrum of lying, cf. Sissela Bok, *Lying: Moral Choice in Public and Private Life* (New York: Vintage Books, 1989), pp. 32-56.

Genesis 3, mendacity already emerges in the Garden of Eden, that is, in the state of original human righteousness before God. And what is even more significant, mendacity does not emerge just somehow, but in precise relationship to God's commandment "You may freely eat of every tree of the garden; but of the tree of the knowledge of good and evil you shall not eat, for in the day that you eat of it you shall die" (Gen. 2:16-17 NRSV). As we know all too well, Eve's interlocutor, the serpent, deconstructs this unequivocal commandment as a concealed way of protecting divine self-interest: "God knows that when you eat of it your eyes will be opened, and you will be like God, knowing good and evil" (3:5 NRSV).

Subsequently disobeying God's original commandment, Adam's and Eve's eyes are instantaneously opened to their profound estrangement from God. It is not that they are naked, but that they *feel* naked — exposed, because estranged. Eve, being asked by God to account for her act of disobedience, responds with "The serpent tricked me, and I ate" (3:13 NRSV). We must grant that Eve's insight into the serpent's activity is perceptive and accurate. Having been tricked means having been lied to — this Eve now understands. And her understanding matches exactly what Thomas Aquinas understands to be the perfection of a lie, namely, a successful deception.

Three things need to come together, according to Aquinas, to constitute a lie in all respects: first, falsehood of what is said; second, the will to tell a falsehood; and third, the intention to deceive.[7] While the narrative account of Genesis remains silent about the serpent's explicit intentions, the lack of any attempt at a defense on the serpent's part and, moreover, God's punishment are more than telling of the serpent's intention. To quote Aquinas, "the will to impart a falsehood" and "the intention to cause another to have a false opinion" must have been constitutive of the serpent's communication with Eve. According to Aquinas, deception is a perfection of the species of lying, and it is precisely the perfection of this vice that we encounter in Genesis 3 for the first time. From here on things decline dramatically and rapidly to Cain's murder of his brother Abel in Genesis 4. The first blatantly explicit lie from a human in relationship to God interestingly occurs immediately after the first homicide. I do not need to remind you that ac-

---

7. Thomas Aquinas, *Summa theologiae* II-II, q. 110, art. 1 corp.

cording to the narrative account of Genesis 4, God asks: "Where is your brother Abel?" and Cain answers, "I do not know; am I my brother's keeper?" (4:9 NRSV). In this lie that is as short as it is insolent, we encounter the intimate commerce between mendacity and murder. Coveting, lying, and murdering emerge as fundamental and ultimately lethal contours of a life profoundly estranged from God, a life under the condition of sin. It is telling that right after the first homicide has been committed and the first blatant human lie has made its appearance in the world, the NRSV introduces the following heading, suggesting a transition in chapter 4 of Genesis: "Beginnings of Civilization." While the committee of translators of the NRSV might not have intended it, this heading suggests that the distinct brew of mendacity and murder narrated in Genesis 4 forms the secret underground, the repressed past, the concealed core of every civilization, past, present, and future. It took a René Girard to remind us of this fact.

This, in short, is the theologically charged context in which the eighth commandment encounters and addresses us — as human beings under the condition of sin. We are estranged from God and afraid of each other, and lying becomes a mode of survival. Being truthful can be dangerous, indeed suicidal, and lying, in contrast, a useful, even beneficial practice, or so it seems in a world full of potential competitors and enemies. And indeed, if God did not exist and if every human just acted according to the laws of self-preservation and self-enhancement, or according to the logic of contemporary sociobiology, in order to expand his or her own genetic pool, truthfulness and lying would be nothing other than functions of such self-interest.

No one has seen the profound implications of radical sociobiological reductionism more clearly than Friedrich Nietzsche in his early essay "On Truth and Lies in a Nonmoral Sense." Just one short sampling will suffice: "What then is truth? A movable host of metaphors, metonymies, and anthropomorphisms: in short, a sum of human relations which have been poetically and rhetorically intensified, transferred, and embellished, and which, after long usage, seem to a people to be fixed, canonical, and binding. Truths are illusions which we have forgotten are illusions; they are metaphors that have become worn out and have been drained of sensuous force, coins which have lost their embossing and are now considered as metal and no longer as coins."[8] Nietzsche draws out the ultimate consequence of a knowledge of good and evil that is severed from its root, the obedience to God's original commandment. Truth and lying become functions of personal or collective utility and thus contingent aspects of the endless play of the will to power, celebrated by the human, that claims to stand beyond good and evil. And Nietzsche says it straightforwardly in a note published posthumously in the volume *The Will to Power:* "If the morality of 'thou shalt not lie' is rejected, the 'sense for truth' will have to legitimize itself before another tribunal: — as a means of the preservation of man, as *will to power.*"[9] And yet while Nietzsche seems right, especially in light of the terrors that the twentieth century brought upon humanity, not the least by Nietzsche's own fatherland, he nevertheless is wrong. The reason is a simple one to be found right there in the narrative of Genesis 4. While God punished Cain, God did not abandon him so that he might perish by also being murdered. Rather, God protected Cain in and under the condition of his punishment. Similarly, God does not abandon humanity under the condition of sin. Rather, God gracefully sustains humanity even under the condition of profound estrangement from and outrageous rebellion against God. Nietzsche seems right in so much of what he wrote because he was so acutely aware of part of the theological context we inhabit — the history of human sin finds its expression in both the form of ressentiment and the *will to power.*

Yet because Nietzsche got only part of the theological context right, he had to reinterpret the history of human misery and rebellion for it to read as a genealogy of morals, thereby giving voice only to his own deep longing for empowerment as well as to his own deep-seated ressentiment against the Christian faith. For Nietzsche was fully aware that the Christian gospel claims unequivocally to disclose the theological context in which the Decalogue addresses us. In light of the narrative account of Genesis 3 and 4 and resonating James 3, I shall characterize this context with the appropriate abbreviature, namely, "fallen tongue." Having served as catalyst of the first, aboriginal sin, mendac-

8. "On Truth and Lies in a Nonmoral Sense," in *Philosophy and Truth: Selections from Nietzsche's Notebooks of the Early 1870's,* trans. and ed. Daniel Breazeale (Atlantic Highlands, N.J.: Humanities Press, 1979), p. 84.

9. Friedrich Nietzsche, *The Will to Power,* trans. Walter Kaufmann and R. J. Hollingdale (New York: Vintage Books, 1968), aphorism 495.

ity has become a characteristic expression of life under the condition of sin. Although mendacity was not caused by the tongue but by the intention to deceive, we still most appropriately name the lie after the organ that initially carried out, and in most instances still carries out, this intersubjective vice. Hence, in the following remarks, the "fallen tongue" shall designate the theological context in which the eighth commandment encounters and addresses us.

The commandment's address occurs, I will argue, in a threefold way. First, the commandment serves as a heuristic device, pointing out to us what is "natural" according to God's good creation and what therefore needs to be morally demanded and even legally enforced to sustain human life under the condition of sin. In my own, that is, the Lutheran, tradition, this is called the *political use of the law*. Here the commandment speaks in the voice of "You shall not lie."

The commandment encounters us, secondly, by holding the mirror before our own face and thereby unmasking and convicting *us* as its violators. In the Lutheran tradition, this is called the *theological use of the law*. Here our commandment speaks in the voice of "You must not lie." The Letter to the Hebrews gives us an idea of how deep God's Word encountering us in this unmasking and convicting use of the law cuts: "Indeed, the word of God is living and active, sharper than any two-edged sword, piercing until it divides soul from spirit, joints from marrow; it is able to judge the thoughts and intentions of the heart. And before him no creature is hidden, but all are naked and laid bare to the eyes of the one to whom we must render an account" (4:12-13 NRSV).

Thirdly, and now in a fundamentally different and completely new voice, one never heard before, the commandment encounters us by teaching us the genuine gestalt of the life with God in faith. In this form the commandment announces the future of the life with God that already becomes present in the life of faith. Hence, the commandment takes on the voice of a parenetic prophecy: "You will not lie." In contradistinction to the disciplining and enforcing political use and the unmasking and convicting theological use of the law, some Lutherans have called this voice of the commandment the "second or parenetic use of the gospel"[10] while Calvinists have tended to call it the third or genuinely spiritual use of the law.

---

10. As did William H. Lazareth and Wilfried Joest.

Passing in silence over this interminable debate between Lutherans and Calvinists about the legitimacy or illegitimacy of a third use of
the law, I will turn now to our commandment's first voice, encountering us in the form of the law's political use. In this voice the eighth
commandment works heuristically. That is, it functions as an explicit
reminder of something humanity should and indeed does know in
light of creation's inner law, in light of what is "natural" to creation.
And, sure enough, it is not difficult to find thinkers in antiquity who
were concerned about the destructive impact of lying and the con-
structive and edifying character of truthfulness, such as Aristotle and
Sallust.[11] Precisely in light of the largely correct but also largely inef-
fective moral insight of ancient sages, however, Christian theologians
from Ambrose and Augustine on held that due to the continuously
bad habits of mendacity, humanity's collective memory about truthfulness as "natural" to what creation is about had become more and
more unreliable. In short, despite the individual knowledge of some
sages, humanity in general was increasingly in need of an explicit divine reminder of what is "natural" to human creatures in relation to
God and neighbor. Hence, the classical Christian tradition, which included Aquinas and Luther, understood the Decalogue as God's condensed salutary reminder to humanity, given first of all, yet not exclusively, to the particular people God had chosen as his witness of
holiness to all the nations. As God's revealed reminder to humanity,
the Decalogue amounts to the most authoritative and clearest summary of the natural law readily grasped and easily memorized by the
common person. In a most straightforward and condensed form, the
Decalogue points out what is "natural" to God's good creation and
also under which masks of moral demand and legal enforcement the
commandment must appear in order to sustain human life under the
condition of sin.

Regarding the eighth commandment, we find this heuristic function well reflected in the old German proverb *"Lügen haben kurze
Beine"* — "Lies have short legs." That means lies will always eventually be outrun by the truth. Lies are parasitical on truth; they depend

---

11. Aristotle, *Nicomachean Ethics* 4, cap. 3 (referred to by Aquinas, *Summa
theologiae* II-II, 110.3 corp.); and Sallust, *Bellum Catilinae* 10.6-7 (referred to by Augustine, *Enchiridion* 18).

on the ontological as well as communal primacy of veracity. The proverb itself thus echoes what humanity should and can know about veracity and mendacity in light of creation's inner law. Life in community can only be sustained on the basis of a sustained practice of truth telling that is habitualized in the virtue of veracity or truthfulness. Every basic communication, every basic economic interaction, every basic political act is built upon trust, a trust that in turn presupposes truthfulness. Every act of economic, political, medical, or other form of public mendacity, be it perjury or fraud or tax evasion, has an immediate destructive impact on the community at large. Whenever deception in the form of balance manipulation occurs on large economic scales, it has a devastating effect destroying the economic existence of thousands upon thousands of people, not to mention the long-range economic effects of these forms of criminal mendacity. Whenever lying occurs on a large political scale in national or even international dimensions and if corruption becomes a way of life among a political elite, as it continuously happens around the globe, it poisons the political culture, encourages a pervasive hermeneutics of suspicion by the electorate, and thereby undermines the basic trust necessary to uphold and sustain a body politic. The heuristics of the eighth commandment thus helps us see the ways in which this particular commandment has encountered us long before, under the mask of laws that prohibit and legally prosecute all forms of giving false witness that undercut or damage the common good as do perjury, fraud, tax evasion, public defamation, slander, and libel. In the body politic, in the economy, in the church as an institution of law and public accountability, and wherever else justice and the common good are at stake, lying must be denounced and appropriately punished in order to deter and undercut all habits and structures of mendacity and in order to sustain the veracity necessary to the flourishing of human life together. For the "fallen tongue" and its concomitant vices are a deadly danger for any human community. If mendacity takes over and gains broad public acceptance, it will eventually destroy any particular human community, a lesson easily learned from history.

But, you might ask, if lies indeed have short legs and are always eventually outrun by the truth, why worry about the "fallen tongue" and its destructive consequences? Doesn't God's sustaining rule of creation always eventually let truth win over? Doesn't God assure that the ontological primacy of truth always asserts itself sooner or later? So why is there the heuristics of the eighth commandment, pointing out the masks of the legal forms of enforcement under which it always already encounters us? Here we need to understand that what is "natural" to creation is not a quasi-physical, self-sustaining mechanism. Rather, we come to reappreciate the ontological and communal primacy of veracity only after we have suffered under the destructive consequences of mendacity. That is, God's providential political use of the law works not like a law of physics but rather draws upon the experiences and reasoning capacity of human beings. A society in which political and economic mendacity take over the public life will eventually collapse, disintegrate, or be taken over by others — or it will recover on the grounds of a collective repentance initiated by a sustained witness to truthfulness. Teaching the Decalogue to all the faithful and moreover witnessing the Decalogue as God's revealed reminder to all humanity are therefore crucial services the church must offer to every society in which it dwells. For the eighth commandment does not just belong to Judaism and to the church. It rather commands unequivocally what is natural for the human being as God's creature. Therefore, each and every society is in need of being reminded most sharply and forthrightly of what it should and indeed can know on its own. In the long run veracity, that is, habitual truthfulness, not only is politically and economically beneficial, but also is the very lifeblood of human life together. To put it differently, because truthfulness is constitutive of the ontology of any community of persons, systemic and sustained mendacity willfully denies and betrays that ontology and subsequently poisons the lifeblood of any community of persons to the point of killing the community itself. I think I do not need to belabor the more than obvious point that systemic mendacity is indeed a pressing and urgent challenge for the CEO elite in contemporary American business life.

In short, public lies are intolerable because of the political and economic damage they cause. They are rightly labeled "criminal" and prosecuted appropriately. In the voice of the political use of the law, the eighth commandment therefore encounters us salutarily under the mask of those laws that allow for the prosecution of perjury, fraud, tax evasion, public defamation, calumny, and slander.

Yet God's commandment not only reminds us of what is "natural" to humanity as God's good creation. Under the general condition of human sinfulness, God's commandment cuts much deeper. It also addresses us individually and directly as those who are affected by the rule of the fallen tongue. Here neither the common good nor justice is at stake. Rather, what is at stake now is the source from which all lies well up: the human heart as that unfathomable depth of the human being from which our thinking and willing are troubled and directed in ways we are hard pressed to account for. The fallen tongue is fed by a fearful and restless heart that is not at rest in its true source, its maker and redeemer, but is uneasily afloat and tirelessly at search for false securities.

How easy it is to point to fraudulent CEOs and corrupt politicians and at the same time to forget how extremely widespread among all citizens the willingness is to commit tax evasion or insurance fraud whenever possible without impunity! Who does not know the temptation to commit the small fraud that no one will ever find out about? Whence do these temptations arise but from our restless hearts that are disclosed to none besides our own troubled consciences — and God.

The eighth commandment encounters us here in the form of the *theological use of the law.* It unmasks and convicts us by holding the mirror in front of our face in order that we come to the awareness that we of all people are its violators. In light of this mercilessly clear mirror, reflecting back to our conscience not only our actions but also the unfathomable depths of our heart, we come to understand that even not having spoken a single lie in all of our lives does not suffice in front of this mirror insofar and as long as mendacious thoughts continue to well up from the depths of our hearts. By unconditionally commanding in the voice of "You must not lie," the commandment convicts my own heart. I indeed live under the power of the lie insofar and as long as I am cut off from the truth to which I owe my existence, and which alone can liberate me to live a life free from mendacity and free for truthfulness. This way, the eighth commandment turns us back to the first commandment. Only if my heart comes to rest in God can I afford the truth about myself. Cut off from its ground, the truth is too hard to bear: my utter contingency and vulnerability coming to a terminal peak in my mortality, my dependency upon, and subsequent indebtedness to, others — all of this becomes unbearable.

It is this very inability to face the truth of our own lives from which arises the mendacity of moral euphemisms that are so pervasive in our contemporary culture. What do I have in mind with "moral euphemisms"? I mean the subtle form of euphemistically redescribing the moral character of what we are doing or neglecting to do. And precisely because moral description is the first act of moral judgment are these euphemisms so effectively mendacious. Let us call them the phenomenon of moral new-speech, ingeniously anticipated in Aldous Huxley's *Brave New World* and in George Orwell's *1984*. Instead of dying we pass away, instead of committing adultery we have an affair, instead of fornicating we engage in pre- or extramarital sex, instead of killing in war we "gain ground," instead of having an abortion we terminate a pregnancy, instead of killing embryos for scientific purposes we are simply doing consumptive research, instead of committing tax fraud we "keep what is our own." Instead of spouses we have partners, best of all, "life-segment-partners" (an all too literal translation of the trendy German *Lebensabschnittbegleiter*). Instead of children we have offspring. Only in the case of divorce has the moral notion itself turned into the moral euphemism! That is, getting a divorce still is getting a divorce, only it has become as morally significant as having a tooth pulled — uncomfortable, possibly hurtful, but completely insignificant morally. These and endless other moral euphemisms allow us conveniently to practice a form of moral mendaciousness without explicitly lying about anything. As soon as we come to appreciate the depth of the collective complicity in the practice of moral euphemization, we come to understand how our society collectively violates the deep sense of the eighth commandment — as much as each of us is unmasked at least as a potential violator. Our fearful hearts and our fallen tongues betray us, and our conscience, faced with the mirror of God's law, convicts us.

However, while unmasking and convicting us, the law cannot transform our hearts but only locks us deeper and deeper into our violation of the law. Only God, touching us directly through his Spirit, can transform our hearts. Only when God's Spirit is poured out over all human beings do we receive new, living hearts instead of our rebellious hearts of stone. The Spirit's eschatological earnest is faith, the faith that is the fulfillment of the first commandment. And while God's Spirit rested upon many patriarchs, prophets, and saints of Israel, his full and unequivocal coming is intrinsically connected to the mission of Christ. The Father's Spirit who rests upon and is sent by the Father and the Son re-creates those ossified hearts so that they become temples of the Spirit rejoicing in God through Christ. Having been reconciled with the Father through Christ and thus having become a new creation through the power of the Spirit, we have become, Luther would say, new persons, who now can delight in God's law because we now hear it in a completely new way, fundamentally different from its first demanding and disciplining voice and its second unmasking and convicting voice. There are those who insist that there can be no third voice to God's commandment because where the Spirit is, there is freedom. And the genuine freedom of the Spirit is in no need of any commandment or guidance. It acts completely spontaneously, motivated exclusively by love. However, this is an antinomian and ultimately gnostic misunderstanding of genuine creaturely freedom, mistaking the human being for an angel. Whoever is yearning for a freedom without its gestalt is yearning for a disembodied existence, is yearning for the sovereign self that instead of being embodied uses the body as its first and foremost tool of self-realization. The gestalt of freedom is the link between the liberating truth and the path on which genuine freedom is exercised as a reconciled life with God.

Hence, we need first of all to appreciate that the very core of any positive freedom — not the freedom from, but the freedom for — is the truth. If it is the case that Christ is the truth, as the whole Gospel of John ceaselessly confesses, then it is the case that those who have received Christ in faith and therefore continue in his word are free in the most profound sense: "You will know the truth, and the truth will make you free" (John 8:32 NRSV). The positive character of freedom becomes concrete only if it receives a gestalt that enacts as well as protects it. Without its embodied gestalt, this freedom would actualize itself only punctually and hence come under the sovereignty of the self that interprets itself by spontaneous acts of freedom. The freedom of the truth that sets us free, however, is the freedom that is actualized in the life with God. And as a continuous reality, this freedom must be received together with its peculiar gestalt appropriate to the creature's finite and embodied nature. It is this peculiar, received gestalt that enacts as well as protects the truth that set us free in the first place. How does the commandment do this?

In its third voice the commandment announces the future of the life with God that already has become present in the life of faith. Hence, the commandment takes on the voice of parenetic prophecy: "You will not lie." The disciplining, enforcing, unmasking, and convicting voices have vanished. And if we understand "law" to be just that, disciplining, enforcing, unmasking, and convicting, it indeed is the case that wherever the Spirit of Christ has set us free, the law has passed away. Yet what cannot and will not pass away is the prophetic announcement and parenetic teaching of the very gestalt that the reconciled life with God takes. We find this voice most beautifully expressed in Psalm 15:

> O LORD, who may abide in your tent?
>> Who may dwell on your holy hill?
> Those who walk blamelessly, and do what is right,
>> and speak the truth from their heart;
> who do not slander with their tongue,
>> and do no evil to their friends,
>> nor take up a reproach against their neighbors;
> in whose eyes the wicked are despised,
>> but who honor those who fear the LORD;
> who stand by their oath even to their hurt;
> who do not lend money at interest,
>> and do not take a bribe against the innocent.
> Those who do these things shall never be moved.
>
> (NRSV)

Psalm 15 offers a prophetic parenesis of what the eighth commandment looks like when it completely shapes the way of a reconciled life with God, when it, in short, is fulfilled. Moreover, in Psalm 15 we encounter a reconciled intersubjectivity because the tongue has been restored to its original purpose, or as the psalmist puts it: "Those who . . . speak the truth from their heart; who do not slander with their tongue."

What is "natural" to God's good creation encounters us here in the mode of fulfillment: no perjury, no fraud, no corruption, no defamation, and no slander are committed. This is why those who are freed by the truth do not need a law. They know what is natural to God's good creation because they walk in the freedom of the children of God. Yet this freedom is precisely free for the joyful embodiment of the creaturely gestalt that God has granted this freedom. This is the true sense of torah, the telos and fulfillment of which is Christ and his messianic announcement of God's reign as embodied in the Sermon on the Mount.

Luther and Calvin perfectly understood this aspect in their respective interpretations of the Decalogue by turning the commandment around, by turning it from an unequivocal prohibition into a limitless invitation to good works. For our eighth commandment it sounds the following way in Luther's *Large Catechism:* "A person should use his tongue to speak only good of everyone, to cover his neighbor's sins and infirmities, to overlook them, and to cloak and veil them with his own honor."[12] And Luther concludes his exposition of the eighth commandment thus: "This commandment, then, embraces a great multitude of good works which please God most highly and bring abundant blessings, if only the blind world and the false saints would recognize them."[13]

It seems as if we have exhausted the third voice of our commandment. Almost, but not quite yet. For in a final step we need to ask whether there is a specific characteristic to the tongue as restored to its original purpose and glory, whether there exists a practice that circumscribes its restored splendor. And indeed there is. The practice that embodies the tongue's restored splendor is praise or adoration. Drawing upon an extraordinary insight from Saint Augustine, Paul Griffiths puts it the following way: "The only possible response is praise. As Augustine says, 'non solum non peccemus adorando, sed peccemus non adorando.' Not only do we fail to sin by adoring, but we sin by failing to adore. . . . If you are not adoring God, you are sinning; lying is incompatible with the adoration of God."[14] Turned around positively into the voice of parenetic prophecy, Saint Augustine's insight means that the tongues of those who have become a new creation in Christ will not lie anymore because they have been restored to their primary and original vocation, that is, ceaseless adoration.

---

12. Luther, *The Large Catechism,* p. 47.
13. Luther, *The Large Catechism,* p. 48.
14. Paul Griffiths, "The Gift and the Lie: Augustine on Lying," *Communio: International Catholic Review* 26 (1999): 3-30; here 30.

In Psalm 119 we find a stunning example of this ceaseless adoration, praising the glory of God's word.

> I rejoice at your word
>   like one who finds great spoil.
> I hate and abhor falsehood,
>   but I love your law.
> Seven times a day I praise you
>   for your righteous ordinances.

(119:162-164 NRSV)

And

> My lips will pour forth praise,
>   because you teach me your statutes.
> My tongue will sing of your promise,
>   for all your commandments are right.

(119:171-172)

Luther insisted that every student of theology should meditate on Psalm 119 once a day, and of course, this psalm is sung daily in the monastic liturgy of the hours. Adoration directs our tongue primarily and ultimately toward God as the giver of all intersubjectivity. All creaturely intersubjectivity is received gratuitously. Living truthfully and hence freely means that all our relationships must be transparent to their gratuitous reception. This is why worship — "Seven times a day I praise you for your righteous ordinances" — is the most important and primary context in which our tongue is healed and trained in the truthfulness that grows out of adoration.

We need to end our meditation on the three voices in which the eighth commandment addresses us with a cautionary note — a note that prevents the subtle self-deception of a realized eschatology in matters of speaking truth and lying. If we think the three voices of the commandment amount to an irreversible narrative of progression from external compliance to crisis to spiritual fulfillment, if we therefore think the third voice amounts to a precise description of our present state of being, we deceive ourselves and the truth is not in us. Forces of sin still oppose the power of the Spirit from without and within. External and internal *Anfechtungen,* temptations of fame and wealth, unrestrained passions such as anger and fear, or the seductive lullabies of a false security, might turn us at any time into violators against the eighth commandment. We only need to ask ourselves honestly: Do we Christians always speak truthfully? Do we give a truthful witness to the gospel? Do we cut through the cloud of moral euphemisms? Are we free of gossip, flattery, backbiting, bickering, not to mention flat-out lies? Because the report will be a very mixed one at best, collectively as well as individually, and because we know that we are in ongoing need of forgiveness, Christians still need to hear the eighth commandment in its first and second voices, disciplining and unmasking the sinner in light of what is natural to God's good creation.

We live by the trust in God's assurance that because of the power of God's Spirit working in our lives, the third voice will increasingly become a solo while the two other voices will recede more and more into the background and eventually fade away. Yet as long as the power of sin is still active, as long as we feel the pull and lure of the power of the lie, it is crucial that the church proclaims and teaches the eighth commandment in all three voices — lest our proclamation and catechesis violate the eighth commandment. As Stanley Hauerwas and Will Willimon so perceptively put it: "But to go to church on a summer Sunday, to settle down for a pleasant hour with people like us, planning to be soothed by the music of the organ, lulled by the mellifluous words of the preacher — then to be told the truth, and to be told it straight, thereby to discover we are called to truthful witness, is grand."[15] This is why we cannot do with less than all three voices of the eighth commandment.

15. Stanley M. Hauerwas and William H. Willimon, *The Truth about God: The Ten Commandments in Christian Life* (Nashville: Abingdon, 1999), p. 128.

Sins of the Tongue

Carl E. Braaten

You shall not bear false witness against your neighbor.

Exodus 20:16

Introduction

The title of my address is taken from Martin Luther's explanation of the eighth commandment: "This commandment forbids all sins of the tongue by which we may injure or offend our neighbor. False witness is clearly a work of the tongue. Whatever is done with the tongue against a neighbor is forbidden by God. This applies to false preachers with their corrupt teaching and blasphemy, to false judges and witnesses with their corrupt behavior in court and their lying and malicious talk outside of court. It applies particularly to the detestable, shameful vice of back-biting or slander by which the devil rides us."[1]

The apostle James says this of the power of the tongue:

> So also the tongue is a small member, yet it boasts of great exploits. How great a forest is set ablaze by a small fire! And the tongue is a fire. The tongue is placed among our members as a world of iniq-

1. Martin Luther, "The Large Catechism," in *The Book of Concord*, Tappert edition (Philadelphia: Fortress, 1959), p. 400.

uity; it stains the whole body, sets on fire the cycle of nature, and is itself set on fire by hell. For every species of beast and bird, of reptile and sea creature, can be tamed and has been tamed by the human species, but no one can tame the tongue — a restless evil, full of deadly poison. With it we bless the Lord and Father, and with it we curse those who are made in the likeness of God. From the same mouth come blessing and cursing. My brothers and sisters, this ought not to be so. (James 3:5-10 NRSV)

Each of the commandments, at least of the second table of the Law, highlights something fundamental to all human community — the relation between children and parents, every individual's right to life, the sanctity of marriage, the right to make a living and own personal property. The eighth commandment highlights the importance of trust and truthfulness in public life. Some contemporary ethicists debate whether these commandments are meant exclusively for the Christian community or are universally relevant for the whole of human society. In their book *The Truth about God: The Ten Commandments in Christian Life,* Stanley Hauerwas and William Willimon tell about a commencement address delivered some years ago by Ted Koppel at Duke University. They write: "After enumerating various signs of moral decay in America, Koppel asked, 'What is the solution for all these problems?' He then proceeded to list each of the Ten Commandments, briefly explaining how, if Americans would only follow these ethical guidelines, we would have no moral problems."[2] Koppel was assuming that the Ten Commandments are morally instructive for all Americans, not only for Christians. Hauerwas and Willimon disagree. They write: "We disagree with Koppel's implied characterization that the Ten Commandments are timeless ethical principles that are applicable to all Americans. . . . We cannot understand the commandments, the Decalogue, apart from the worship of the true God. . . . The Ten Commandments are meant for those who are known by the God of Abraham, Isaac, Jacob, and the God of Jesus Christ."[3] I disagree. The Ten Commandments were given by God to his people Israel as a republication of the law of creation *(lex creationis)* embedded in struc-

2. Stanley Hauerwas and William Willimon, *The Truth about God: The Ten Commandments in Christian Life* (Nashville: Abingdon, 1999), p. 14.
3. Hauerwas and Willimon, p. 14.

tures of life common to all human beings, whether they live in Jerusalem, Athens, Tokyo, or Baghdad. The Ten Commandments specify the moral foundations, the bedrock, of every human society. The law of God the Creator functions in, with, and under the common structures of human existence, and is the indispensable condition of the possibility of social life. Everyone who exists participates in some way or other in the legal, economic, political, and family situations to which the commandments speak. And God's law mediated through the structures of common human existence impinges on the conscience of every human being. On the eighth commandment, one scarcely needs to be a Jew or a Christian to know that lying is wrong and perjury is a threat to the social order.

I agree, however, with Hauerwas and Willimon when they say: "We believe that recovery of the Commandments is crucial for our survival as a people called Christian in the face of today's challenges."[4] But I also agree with Ted Koppel that the people who call themselves American need to reclaim the commandments of God for public instruction and observance. And therefore, unlike these good fellows from Duke, I have no problem with seeing the Ten Commandments on the walls of public schools and courtrooms. I do not see them as privy to a religious sect or belonging only inside the walls of a church.

I. The Eighth Commandment in the Bible

The original setting of the eighth commandment applies to the giving of testimony in a court of law. Next to their horror of idolatry and blasphemy, the Hebrews had a profound abhorrence of false witness.

> A faithful witness does not lie,
> but a false witness breathes out lies.
>
> (Prov. 14:5)

According to Proverbs, there are six things that God hates, and one of them is "a lying witness who testifies falsely" (6:19).

In the New Testament the meaning of this commandment is not

4. Hauerwas and Willimon, p. 13.

restricted to legal testimony in a court, but Jesus extended it to include every aspect of human speech. "Let your word be 'Yes, Yes' or 'No, No'; anything more than this comes from the evil one" (Matt. 5:37). The early Christians retained the Hebrew abhorrence of false witness. They had a special reason to do so because their Lord, Jesus himself, was condemned to death on false testimony solicited by the Sanhedrin (Matt. 26:59). Jesus knew what it felt like to be the victim of false witness. He had been falsely accused of gluttony, drunkenness, blasphemy, demon possession, and sedition. He fulfilled the prophecy of the suffering servant of the Lord, who was brought

> like a lamb that is led to the slaughter,
>   and like a sheep that before its shearers is silent,
>   so he did not open his mouth.
> By a perversion of justice he was taken away.
>   Who could have imagined his future?
> For he was cut off from the land of the living,
>   stricken for the transgression of my people.
> They made his grave with the wicked
>   and his tomb with the rich,
> although he had done no violence,
>   and there was no deceit in his mouth.
>
> (Isa. 53:7b-9)

So Christians will always think of bearing false witness not only as a sin against the eighth commandment, but as a sin against Jesus himself. In becoming a human being Jesus became our neighbor, becoming himself forever the object of the witness of others, whether true or false. Thus the meaning of this commandment expands into life in all its relationships *sub specie Christi*. It is not enough to refrain from telling outright lies about your neighbor; instead, we should speak the truth and speak it in the spirit of love (Eph. 4:15). The latter is an important qualification because sometimes to blurt out the whole truth about others is intended not only to hurt them but also to make oneself look good.

The New Testament tells the story about Jesus, as well as the entire sweep of human history, in terms of a dramatic conflict between God and Satan, between good and evil, between light and darkness, between truth and falseness. Jesus stood before Pilate, who cynically asked, "What is truth?" (John 18:38). Pilate did not realize he was confronting in person the truth of God incarnate, and that Satan, who is a liar and the father of lies (John 8:44), was the directing agent behind his back. Jesus was "the light [that] shines in the darkness, and the darkness did not overcome it" (John 1:5). Jesus came into a world that did not care for the truth; no wonder he was rejected by all around him. The chief priests, the whole council of elders, the crowd, the soldiers, the false witnesses, and even his disciples — all of them were on the wrong side in the struggle of truth against falsehood. Jesus — only he was the light of the world — was full of grace and truth on that dark day when the world unknowingly witnessed the eclipse of truth.

II. Sins of the Tongue in a Culture of Lying

That was then; we are now into the now generation. We are engulfed in a postmodern culture all around, in which truth lies by the side of the road in need of a good Samaritan. Under the spell of postmodernism the view is popular in many philosophy and English departments that truth is something we construct out of our imagination, not what we discover in the way things really are. The idea catches on: the truth of the Bible is what we say it is. It is like a wax nose that we can mold in our own image.

Since the eighth commandment originated in another time and place, three thousand years ago and ten thousand miles away, in the context of an ancient religion and antiquated culture, one might be inclined to regard its truth as obsolete, no longer relevant. Nothing could be more wrong. Even the most nihilistic of postmodernists whine when their books receive a bad review. Christians who take a long view of history, who believe that the criterion of truth has already arrived at the midpoint of history, know that the alpha and omega of all reality are united in Christ. Truth has arrived in the One who declared, "I am the Truth." Truth is a person and an event. Truth is an event that happened in history, in the coming of a special person. In Christian faith the opposite of truth is the lie. The decision for or against the truth is a life-and-death decision to accept Christ or to reject him. He is not one teacher of truth among many; he is the one and only Teacher of

Truth because along with the Fourth Gospel, we confess he is the perfect embodiment of truth.

So what has changed in the intervening twenty centuries? It seems we are not far removed from the original apostolic situation when it comes to basics. We find ourselves living in a world of mendacity in all spheres of life, in both its secular and religious dimensions. False witness is the norm, not the exception. We read the daily newspaper, watch TV, log on to the Internet, and find ourselves inundated by the diabolical spam that lies about everything: low interest rates, pharmaceutical deals, breast enhancement, penis enlargement, Russian beauties, and whatnot. We are living in what Paul Weaver, writing from his own personal experience about how journalism really works in our time, calls a culture of lying.[5]

Many of us are all too prone to gorge ourselves on the so-called news. We click on one news station after the other — CNN, Fox News, Headline News, MSNBC, CNBC, C-SPAN — especially when the airwaves are flooded by riveting reports of crisis or scandal. We have the impression, though we cannot prove it, that only C-SPAN comes close to conveying the unvarnished truth. Weaver argues, rightly I think, that the news is not what we are supposed to think it is; it's not simply an objective report of what happened. He writes: "It's a *story*, with characters, action, plot, point of view, dramatic closure."[6] The stories that pass for news are mostly fabrications by officials and journalists, who are in bed with the powers that control the media. "The news stops representing the real world and begins to falsify it. The barter transaction between newsmaker and journalist degenerates into an exercise in deceit, manipulation, and exploitation. . . . The word *lying* is harsh, but it's the correct term for the behaviors we are talking about here."[7]

What Weaver means by a culture of lying is that the purveyors of the news are not personally corrupt with the intention to "break the rules and falsify facts."

> I am talking about what happens when people follow the rules . . . about the behaviors that prevail and the consequences that flow

5. Paul H. Weaver, *News and the Culture of Lying* (New York: Free Press, 1994).
6. Weaver, p. 1.
7. Weaver, pp. 2, 4.

when officials and journalists work within the framework of accepted practice, when everything is on the up-and-up, when the facts are right and the relevant people have been contacted and the story has been told straight. I am arguing that in such circumstances, officials and journalists are usually lying. . . . Fabricated politics and journalism . . . constitute what I believe can fairly be described as a culture of lying. The culture of lying is the discourse and behavior of officials seeking to enlist the powers of journalism in support of their goals. . . . We encounter the culture of lying in the contrived statements of government and corporate officials in trying to look good on the nightly news.[8]

Public opinion surveys indicate that people have a massive distrust of the major institutions and elite professions in America. The *Arizona Republic* recently reported on the extent of plagiarism going on at the state universities, under the headline "Institutions of Higher Cheating." Not so long ago the medical profession was rated up there with the clergy in public trust and integrity. Now both have plummeted to near the bottom of the scale. And what about the legal profession and the justice system? Nobody believes that because a person swears to tell the truth, the whole truth, and nothing but the truth that the person won't lie. If a person is lying, the defense attorney will make it appear to be the truth. If a person is telling the truth, the prosecuting attorney will do everything to make him look like a liar. And let the jury decide. The Johnnie Cochrane and O. J. Simpson fiasco exploded the myth that juries can be trusted to reach a just verdict. And if hundreds of inmates on death row have only recently been proved innocent by DNA testing, how many innocent people heretofore lost their lives in a system that pays big money for false testimonies, sins against the eighth commandment? Mistrust of the major players in the American system of justice has reached crisis proportions.

Perhaps nothing has etched public mistrust so deeply in the American consciousness as the lies told by the presidents to the American people, starting with Franklin D. Roosevelt. While moving the country closer to participation in World War II, Roosevelt assured the American people when he ran for reelection, "I have said this before,

8. Weaver, pp. 4, 13.

but I shall say it again and again: Your boys are not going to be sent into any foreign wars."[9] And recall how Americans were shocked when they learned that Dwight D. Eisenhower — beloved Ike — lied about the U-2 incident, when an American spy plane was forced down in the Soviet Union. Running for president, John F. Kennedy asserted that the Eisenhower-Nixon administration had allowed a "missile gap" to occur to the advantage of the Soviet Union, claiming the support of a secret Pentagon study. After he won the election he announced that he was mistaken and there was no missile gap. During his campaign for president Lyndon Johnson assured the American people that Barry Goldwater was a war hawk and would escalate the war in Vietnam. He, on the contrary, promised that he would not widen the war and would never "send American boys to die in Asian jungles." The election turned on that issue, but within weeks after Johnson won, the administration proceeded to execute the plan that sent over half a million soldiers to fight the immoral war in Vietnam. Richard Nixon's presidency became unraveled in the lies and deceit of Watergate. And there was Ronald Reagan, who pledged, "I cannot recall," when interrogated about the Iran-contra affair. We had an interlude of sorts with Jimmy Carter, who ironically was ridiculed by the media precisely for telling the truth in his *Playboy* confession, that he had indeed lusted in his heart. Then there was George Bush's campaign theme: "Read my lips, no new taxes." A year later he flip-flopped. The little liberties Bill Clinton took with the truth still ring fresh in our memories; "I did not have sexual relations with that woman." And now Americans have fought a war predicated on the absolute certainty of finding the weapons of mass destruction in Iraq that allegedly constituted an imminent threat to our national security. Still we cannot locate them, after having ridiculed Dr. Blix and the U.N. inspectors who had been given a much shorter period of time to find them. Little wonder that polls indicate that the American people do not believe that their political leaders are trustworthy. Al Franken reflects a large part of American public opinion in his highly partisan best-seller entitled *Lies and the Lying Liars Who Tell Them*. Whether Republican, Democratic, or Independent, voters are finding it increas-

9. *The Public Papers and Addresses of Franklin D. Roosevelt*, 1940, 8:517 (October 30, 1940).

ingly more difficult to find candidates running for high office whom they can trust.

III. The God of Truth and the Church's Witness

Why should we care whether we live in a society riven by scams, cover-ups, cheating, and corruption involving politicians, presidents, professors, prelates, and other professionals in high places? What does all that have to do with theology and the church? The answer is, truth is at stake. The church and its theology are servants of truth. Wherever truth is at stake, whenever truth is being distorted, the church is called to exercise its prophetic ministry.

The holy people of God are called to bear witness to the God of truth who wills that truth shall flourish in all human relationships. All moral responsibilities and human rights are grounded in the law of God, not in the laws of the state. Lying is wrong not only because of what it does to society, but because it is contrary to truth, and truth is an essential attribute of God. All things stand under the judgment of God's truth (Ps. 96:13). A lie is an offense against truth, and therefore an offense against God. Only God is absolutely trustworthy because truth is his very being. When God acts true to his nature, his word is trustworthy; he means what he says.

When God created the world, he established both the laws of nature and laws of morality. If we disregard the law of gravity, we will not survive. If the world of commerce and industry does not observe the rule of law, people lose confidence in the economy and that, we are told, is the chief cause of the troubled stock market. Why swear by almighty God to tell the truth, the whole truth, and nothing but the truth if we do not believe in the God of truth and in the God who will punish liars? Revelation 21:8 says liars go to hell, right along with murderers, fornicators, and idolaters.

We the church — God's people — have received the Spirit of truth who comes from the Father, sent by the Son, to guide us into all truth (John 15:26; 16:13). God's Spirit is the spirit of truth at the heart of the universe. The admonition to Timothy applies to all Christians: "Do your best to present yourself to God as one approved by him, a worker who has no need to be ashamed, rightly explaining the word of truth"

(2 Tim. 2:15). We should prove ourselves better than the world in our love for the truth, in our ability to distinguish between truth and false-hood, accompanied with courage to call a spade a spade. So how are we doing? Are we as a church compromising the truth? Are we faith-ful witnesses to the truth? Are we also guilty of scams and cover-ups? Are ecclesiastical officials more believable in the public mind than government officials? Is the church a safe place for people to live by the truth, or do we have to watch what we say for the sake of political correctness? Or is it not often the case that in our mad pursuit of rele-vance and of trying to be in touch with reality, we trim the truth to suit the tastes of those around us?

I read this parable somewhere, which has a point I wish to make. A stranger arrives in town. He brings with him a watch that keeps per-fect time. Upon his arrival he looks at the clocks in the church steeples and finds that they are half an hour fast. The townsfolk have set their watches by these clocks. Consequently, the whole town is living in a system of false time. So the stranger tries to tell them. "Hey, people, my watch is accurate. This is the truth. I came with the true time." But the people ridicule him and make him feel out of touch. In the end he begins to wonder. "Maybe my watch is not accurate after all. Maybe they are right." And so he resets his watch to conform to the watches of the townspeople.[10] I would submit that this is strikingly apropos to how many churches today discount the truth entailed in each of the commandments, in order to appear more attractive to the people to whom they have a truth to tell. It's like resetting the watches to the clock in the town square. We skip the hard-nosed truth of the law that offends and go to the sugary sweet words of grace and acceptance.

Even more worrisome than shaving the truth of God's law to conform to the passions of the crowd is the falsification of the gospel in a lot of the church practices that take place for the sake of evangelical outreach, church growth, and contemporary worship. The power of the lie is at work not only in the realm of the law but in the realm of the gospel. When I was a beginning student of theology at Luther Semi-nary in the early fifties, Professor Herman Preus had us outline the en-tirety of C. F. W. Walther's *The Proper Distinction between Law and Gos-*

10. I found this parable in a book on the Ten Commandments by Jozsef Farkas, *Bench Marks* (Richmond: John Knox, 1969), p. 100.

pel, chapter by chapter, for which I got the worst grade I ever got in my life. But later I came to see the point of the exercise and to believe that preaching today could use a good dose of Walther's ideas on law and gospel.[11]

All Christians are commissioned by the risen Jesus to be bearers of truthful witness everywhere and always. He promised, "You will receive power when the Holy Spirit has come upon you; and you will be my witnesses in Jerusalem, in all Judea and Samaria, and to the ends of the earth" (Acts 1:8). He chose ordinary folks whom he trusted with the truth to tell what they had seen and heard, led by the light of the gospel and the power of the Spirit. We have the same call today as the first-century witnesses to give faithful testimony to Jesus Christ, to his gospel and to his church, by our words, actions, and attitudes. This pope, John Paul II, has canonized 469 persons to sainthood during his twenty-five-year papacy, many of them martyrs. We need to give more time in our worship services to commemorating the acts of the martyrs. Martyrdom is the supreme witness given to the truth of the faith, even unto death. People do not lay down their life for a lie unless they are crazy or possessed by the devil, the father of lies.

As Christians we lie when we are ashamed of the gospel of Christ, when we detract from its uniqueness in order to appear open to the pluralist view that all religions are equally valid ways of salvation. The gospel handed down to us by the apostles is a scandalous message to profess, because we are born into a mendacious world in which the devil is prowling around, tempting us to play fast and loose with the truth. When the church bears true witness to the gospel, she will attend not only to the words she speaks, but to many other forms of expression. Truth, goodness, and beauty, like the triune God, are three in one. Truth is good and truth is beautiful.

When I was a student at St. Olaf College, there occurred a lively debate emanating from the art department about architecture. What kind of architecture is appropriate for this college? Looking around, we saw many beautiful buildings. What can be wrong in sticking with what we've got? I didn't know a thing about it, but I was told in no un-

---

11. To be honest, I should add that my agreement with Walther does not extend to his views on Scripture and the church. He embraced the theory of biblical inspiration and taught the delegation theory of the ordained ministry.

certain terms, "What's wrong is that it's pseudo-Gothic." "Pseudo" means "false, spurious, sham." A church college should not engage in pseudo-like forms of expression. The implications are far-reaching for the church in general. There are ways of bearing false witness by the way our churches are designed for worship, by the songs we sing, and by the art works we display. These things should serve to reflect the transcendent mystery and awesome glory of God and his holy name. We should take care that everything tawdry and ugly be removed from our worship and that the beauty of our music and architecture corresponds to the truth God has revealed in Christ, who "is the reflection of God's glory and the exact imprint of God's very being" (Heb. 1:3a).

I will end with a word from Martin Luther's preface to the *Small Catechism*: "This much is certain: anyone who knows the Ten Commandments perfectly knows the entire Scriptures. In all affairs and circumstances he can counsel, help, comfort, judge and make decisions in both spiritual and temporal matters. He is qualified to sit in judgment upon all doctrines, estates, persons, laws, and everything else in the world."

If we pastors, teachers, and parents take Luther's words to heart, we in our time will become more diligent in our study of the Ten Commandments, and indeed the whole catechism, to equip ourselves better to teach them to our children and to all our people and to train them to live obediently to the glory of God and his coming kingdom. 1 John 5:3 sums it up beautifully: "For the love of God is this, that we obey his commandments. And his commandments are not burdensome."

God or Mammon

R. R. Reno

The Ten Commandments structure our lives in different places. I want to focus on the commandments concerning possessions, the tenth commandment primarily, along with the eighth, but as we shall see, the whole of the second table implicitly, and the first table as well, especially the second commandment. This final word of the ten words delivered on Mount Sinai gives direct expression to the perfection of heart that is entailed within the two tablets taken as a whole, made explicit in Jesus' strenuous words in the Sermon on the Mount. "Do not lay up for yourselves treasures on earth, where moth and rust consume and where thieves break in and steal," Jesus advises us, "but lay up for yourselves treasures in heaven, where neither moth nor rust consumes and where thieves do not break in and steal" (Matt. 6:19-20). Echoing the moral ambiance of the Ten Commandments, Jesus links covetousness to adultery and idolatry as he completes the thought, "For where your treasure is, there will your heart be also" (v. 21). A covetous heart is an adulterous heart that wishes to enjoy the pleasure of one while feigning a loyalty to another. The wandering eye of lust is closely linked to the greedy eye of avarice, as well as the transfixed and captive eye of idolatry, and as Jesus warns, "If your eye is unhealthy, your whole body will be full of darkness" (v. 23). Just as a man cannot vow himself to a woman and chase skirts, just as he cannot fast to purify his soul and parade his sanctity before others, so also he cannot seek the treasure of heaven while turning his heart and mind to acquiring the treasures of this world. "No one can serve two masters," Jesus teaches, "for either he will hate the one and love the other, or he will be devoted to the one and despise the other. You cannot serve God and mammon" (v. 24). Thus, as is always the case, the commandments of God and our obedience to them turn on the first commandment. Will we love the Lord our God with all our heart and all our soul and all our mind? This is the crucial question, for the second great commandment is like unto it, and on them hang all the law and the prophets (Matt. 22:40).

It is telling that Jesus does not say that we cannot serve God and Baal, or God and Caesar, or God and Dionysus, for it is quite obvious that we can. This is fitting. In our time, priests and theologians are most often servants of Baal. Few lust for power and surrender themselves to Caesar. Most of us suffer from the wandering eye of sexual desire, but it is notoriously fickle. In contrast, the eye of greed is widespread, and it can become fixed, constant, and dominant. The keen moral psychologist John Chrysostom saw how avarice can trump. "So tyrannical is the passion" for wealth, he notes, "that it sometimes prevails over lust." For this reason the strict taskmaster Mammon can create the illusion of virtue. As Chrysostom observes, some, "to spare their money, may indeed have bridled their unchastity."[1] The expense of the swinging life may be its greatest deterrent. Surely, if it can restrain lust, the greedy reign of Mammon is powerful indeed.

It is cruel as well. Chrysostom observes in the same homily that the desires of the body admit of temporary satisfaction, but the avaricious soul always wants more. Quoting from Sirach and exploiting the tradition that places greed among the sins of the eye, Chrysostom evokes a powerful scriptural image of avarice: "He sees with his eyes and groans as a eunuch groans when embracing a girl" (Sir. 30:20). The image of unconsummated — unconsummatible — desire reflects the literal meaning of avarice. It comes from the Latin verb *aveo*, "to crave." The term translates the Greek term *pleonexia*, the desire to have more. Both words suggest a state of desire that, unlike lust and glut-

---

1. *Homilies on Matthew* 83.2. My use of patristic sources throughout this essay is deeply indebted to Richard Newhauser's invaluable monograph, *The Early History of Greed: The Sin of Avarice in Early Medieval Thought and Literature* (Cambridge: Cambridge University Press, 2000).

tony, seeks no specific object of pleasure and admits of no satiated satisfaction. Instead, avarice aches ever for more.

The church fathers understood the internal dynamics of avarice. They also saw the scope and depth of debilitations and depravities wrought by love of Mammon. Their insights, like the Sermon on the Mount, are shaped by the Ten Commandments. Basil links avarice to theft and false testimony: "Who is the father of lying? Who is the maker of forgeries? Who brings forth perjury? Is it not wealth? Not a zeal for wealth?"[2] Others list violence and murder as fruits of greed. Still other early Christian writers follow Colossians 3:5: "Put to death, therefore, whatever in you is earthly, fornication, impurity, passion, evil desire, and greed (which is idolatry)." For example, Chrysostom observes, many possess wealth and dare not use it, "but consecrate it, handling it untouched, not daring to touch it, as though it were some dedicated thing."[3] Indeed, many pagans will sell their idols for the value of the gold rather than disobey the commands of Mammon. Not only are the second, sixth, and eighth commandments violated by greed, but the fifth as well. Chrysostom observes that often men do not honor their fathers and mothers. Because they covet their inheritance, many resent any financial liabilities that arise from aging parents.

The specific fruits of avarice involve a wholesale violation of the Ten Commandments, and this wickedness is summed up in the most common images of greed in Christian literature, ancient and medieval. Not only is avarice pictured as a transfixed eye that is bewitched by the luster of gold, it is also seen as a gaping mouth that consumes the poor. The former symbolizes a wholesale transgression of the first table of the Decalogue, and the latter a systematic transgression of the second table. Truly, the rule of Mammon runs against the grain of divine legislation.

Those of us trained in the Augustinian-Gregorian tradition will tend to think that pride is the basic sin from which all others flow. Surely pride is a moral acid, but we should not let ourselves complacently imagine that Prometheus is more dangerous than Mammon. Following 1 Timothy 6:10 ("love of money is the root of all evil"), we

---

2. *Patrologia Graeca*, 31:297. I draw this quote from Newhauser, p. 65.
3. *Homilies on John*, Homily 65, para. 3.

might do well to follow the guidance of some of the old writers, to consult the vast store of Christian moral wisdom laid up in countless treatises and sermons, letters and poems that treats avarice as more decisive than pride. We should listen to this wisdom because our middle-class society is defined far less by honor — the dry tinder which the sparks of pride can turn into a raging fire — than by wealth. The dangers we face are many, but the danger most pressing may be Mammon's command over our lives.

I

For some of the old writers, greed is directly equated to a love of earthly things. Just as gold is mined from the bowels of the earth, so does the love of money draw us down into the caves of worldliness. This assessment is especially true of the monastic writers. Chrysostom, for example, is constantly juxtaposing the monks of the deserts who have renounced all possessions with the grasping townspeople who listen to his sermons. The same holds for John Cassian, who traveled to live with the desert monks for many years and then returned to Italy to teach their wisdom. For Cassian, avarice is directly linked to money and the workaday world of commerce. Cassian's assumptions about the link between commerce and greed influence his account of the proper strategy for overcoming avarice. Lust and gluttony stem from enduring bodily desires, and those who seek perfection must plan for a lifetime of struggle against temptations. However, Cassian reports the confidence of the monastic teachers of the East, that a disciplined monk can put the temptations of wealth behind him by abandoning his property and fleeing into the desert, far from the world of commerce (*Conferences* 5.8). The implication is clear. Mammon has a limited kingdom. If we cast aside our gold coins, we will not be transfixed by their luster.

I recount Cassian's analysis because it has an important modern analogue. For Marxists and leftist fellow travelers, the luster of coins is a purely social construct that has no intrinsic beauty. We need only smash the idols of capitalism and the charm will be broken. This promise is the key to the enduring appeal of leftist thought. Even though historical materialism is an utterly failed theory of history, and actually existing socialist countries were and continue to be moral and economic failures, the dream lives. Put an end to capitalism and greed will die. This social iconoclasm always gives the left-wing activist a sense of moral superiority. He is not renouncing commerce and fleeing to the desert, as Cassian would advise. The activist is strategizing to find a way for society as a whole to renounce commerce and usher in a new age of human social relations free from the base metals of gold and silver. Instead of rushing to the desert, the goal is to bring the desert and its absence of tempting conventions of private property to the workaday world.

I have little doubt that the radical renunciation of the world entailed in Cassian's vision of monastic life fundamentally alters the shape of temptation. Perhaps Mammon was unable to insinuate himself into the lives of the Desert Fathers. However, in our age, I have never found the Marxist moral analysis of wealth and its grip on the human soul persuasive. I have not been edified by the many sermons I have heard, few self-consciously Marxist but all shaped by a general leftist sentiment, that have attempted to shift the dangers of our desire for wealth onto the supposed injustices of our economic system. I have found Boethius, the fifth-century Christian philosopher, more persuasive. To him I now turn.

Boethius wrote his influential treatise, *The Consolation of Philosophy*, in the dungeon of Alvanzano, where he had been sent by the emperor Theodoric and from which he would not emerge until the time of his execution. The substance of his reflections concerns misfortune and the saving power of true wisdom. The treatise begins with Boethius bewailing his circumstances, the injustice of his imprisonment, and the ill fortune he has suffered. It is in the mournful state that a woman appears before him, the beautiful and commanding countenance of Lady Philosophy.

In the course of his discussion with Lady Philosophy, Boethius laments that the world is against us, for Fortune spreads her benefits in a fickle and unjust fashion. The wicked prosper and the righteous often suffer defeat. Wealth and honors go to those who do not deserve them, while the meritorious receive no reward. Boethius's complaint is parallel to the soft moralism of the left. Structures of society are unjust. Honest labor is exploited and human need is neglected, while the accidents of birth and accumulative desire are rewarded. But for these unjust structures, virtue would flourish and human relations would be properly ordered toward the common good.

Lady Philosophy defends the vagaries of Fortune against Boethius's complaint, and by extension against the complaints of so many social critics in our day. True, she says, wealth and honors are spread unevenly and without consistency. But, she continues, our complaints are based upon spiritual fantasies. We imagine that Fortune should solve our problems by being more evenhanded. Against this dream, Dame Philosophy points out that no distribution of worldly goods will quench our bitter complaints. "Wild greed," she says, "swallows what it has sought, and still gapes wide for more." Those of us who think a meritocratic system will bring us to a greater social comity and personal satisfaction are as deluded as those who seek a more egalitarian system, and the utopians who imagine a world of plenty in which none hanker for more are most deluded of all. "What bit or bridle," Lady Philosophy asks, "will hold within its course this headlong lust, when, whetted by abundance of rich gifts, the thirst for possessions burns?"[4] The answer is clear. As Dame Philosophy teaches throughout her conversation with Boethius, we can conquer vice only with virtue. Spiritual diseases require spiritual cures.

The wisdom of Dame Philosophy is simple, yet in so much of our thinking about wealth and its capacity to distort and destroy human life we ignore it. When Mammon beckons and controls, no social reform will do the trick. One needs little experience in life to see that few will be happy with what they have, whether distributed according to merit, equally, or according to need. Moreover, as we see every day, no matter how we construct our economic system, greed will find a way to cheat, steal, and murder its way toward wealth. To be sure, we can use fear as a tool for bridling greed's worst excesses. The threat of punishment can stay the thieving hand of a greedy man. And furthermore, the logic of the marketplace is based upon the skeptical suspicion of buyer and seller, and this can also check the destructive social consequences of greed. However, the vice itself is largely untouched. We can be scrupulously honest as we fill out our tax returns, and still find ourselves in the thrall of Mammon, compulsively checking our retirement accounts and indulging in the obscene complaint that, in this country

4. (New York: Modern Library, 1943), p. 24.

awash with wealth, we are not paid "enough." No matter how much our avarice is hemmed in by law and the competitive market, we will continue to burn with the lust for more. The eye of our desire remains transfixed; our mouth gaps wide.

By and large, therefore, the Christian tradition has not treated greed as a vice that stems from the social phenomena of money and the marketplace, and it cannot therefore be overcome by destroying those social practices. For example, Evagrius of Pontus, one of the first Christian thinkers to lay out a scheme of the deadly sins, does not think we can root out covetousness by renouncing private property. Evagrius reiterates the ancient ascetical commonplace that "it is impossible for charity to exist in anyone along with money" (*Praktikos* 18). Evagrius lived among the desert monks from whom Cassian drew his teaching, and like Cassian, Evagrius sees that spiritual perfection must renounce possessions. Yet, what is important about Evagrius is his awareness that greed continues to afflict us, even if we utterly impoverish ourselves. "Avarice," he writes of the internal struggles of the monk, "suggests to the mind a lengthy old age, inability to perform manual labor at some future date, famines that are sure to come, sickness that will visit us, the pinch of poverty . . ." (*Praktikos* 9). The monk, far removed from commerce, continues to be afflicted by tempting thoughts. He cannot live like the birds in the air or the lilies of the field, for he worries about the morrow and begins to think about laying up a treasure here on earth in order to defend himself against earthly ills such as old age, famine, and sickness. For Evagrius, giving up private property may be a necessary condition for overcoming greed, but it is not sufficient. Avarice can take the guise of prudence and insinuate itself under the cover of a seemingly virtuous and sensible course of thought.

These thoughts of the morrow and all-too-reasonable anxieties about old age, ill health, and famine show how greed can insinuate itself into what we imagine to be virtue. Avarice is not simply a product of money or the marketplace. Quite the contrary, as the Sermon on the Mount makes clear, Mammon is the god of worldly security, and he plays upon worries that afflict even those who have taken vows of poverty and fled into the desert. This is why, no matter how Fortune (or we) organize social relations, even if we socialize capital, ban usury, and redistribute wealth, we cannot escape the dangerous temptations of avarice. Mammon has many methods of temptation at his disposal. He is not limited to the lure of gold and silver coins, or the conventions of inheritance, or economies that protect private property and use markets to allocate capital.

II

What wisdom does the tradition offer for understanding the wider stratagems of Mammon? As Saint Augustine teaches, "vices have a flawed reflection of beauty" (*Confessions* 2.6). It is the flawed reflection of beauty that makes the seven deadly sins so dangerous. Anger is dangerous because fierceness in defense of the innocent and punishment of the wicked is a good thing. Lust tempts us because conjugal love is a genuine boon. Pride appeals because, made in the image of God, we rightly rejoice in our capacities. What, then, of greed? How does that false god, Mammon, exploit the goodness of wealth? As Evagrius hints, avarice can move under the guise of prudence, but his remarks are cryptic. The devices of Mammon are many, but I want to focus on two: family responsibility and social realism. In order to illuminate both, I turn to two poets, one ancient and the other medieval.

Prudentius was a contemporary of Saint Augustine, and he wrote an influential allegory of sin's temptations and our struggles called the *Psychomachia,* the battle of the soul. Few literary critics find the poem meritorious.[5] However, Prudentius organizes this battle according to the convention of the seven deadly sins, and when he turns to the onslaught of avarice, he adds useful nuance.

In the allegory, Avarice appears on the scene as a grasping, conquering fury, accompanied by her companions, Care, Hunger, Fear, Distress, Pallor, Fraud, Intrigue, Deceit, Craft, and Sleeplessness (ll. 465-66). Avarice is the source of civil strife, setting brother against brother, son against father: "If a soldier sees his brother's helm agleam with tawny gems, he does not fear to draw his sword and strike off his head that he may snatch the jewels from the crown" (ll. 470-73). Against the direct onslaught of Avarice, the warrior Reason success-

5. See C. S. Lewis's overall assessment, *The Allegory of Love* (Oxford: Oxford University Press, 1936; reprinted as a Galaxy Book, 1958), p. 68.

fully resists. The fell deeds of Greed are plain for the eye to see, and a righteous man recognizes and resists the most blatant temptations. Indeed, in the larger context of Prudentius's allegory, the emergence of Christianity has reinforced and extended natural virtue. The army of Avarice bemoans the rise of Christianity. "The yellow image of the gleaming coin is worthless to the followers of Christ, money and wealth are paltry in their sight" (ll. 526-27). Thus, the scene reflects much of what we experience. Like the monks who have retreated into the desert, most of us have renounced the most obvious and destructive worship of Mammon. We do not define our lives by our bank accounts. We discipline ourselves to give to charity. We raise our children to recognize "higher values." We heed Jesus' warning that we cannot serve God and Mammon.

Or do we? The battle of the soul does not end with Reason's resistance to the direct assaults of Avarice. She retreats and asks herself whether a direct conflict with Reason is the wisest course of action. We can see that wealth and worldly honor are not the highest good, so, thinks Avarice, better to advance by indirect means. With this thought, continues Prudentius, "She puts off her fiendish look and frightful arms, and puts on honest mien: she now becomes a Virtue, stern of face and dress, and called Frugality" (ll. 551-54). In this way grasping greed becomes thrift. Now, in a moment of poignant moral insight, Prudentius portrays the covert warfare of covetousness against charity, a warfare evident in most of us who are often found laying up a treasure in heaven, justifying it by the needs of our families. As Prudentius observes, Avarice can exploit a genuine virtue — "love of offspring" — to insinuate herself into our lives (l. 562).

When I think about my subservience to Mammon, I can recognize my own thoughts in Prudentius's allegory. How often do I justify my devotion to accumulation because of a perceived duty to family and children? It is a commonplace in patristic and medieval literature to personify Avarice as surrounded by wealth and yet haggard, hollow eyed, and threadbare. For example, in his *Faerie Queene* Edmund Spenser portrays a parade of the "six sage Counsellours" who follow the lead of the "gentle Husher, Vanitie by name." These figures personify the seven deadly sins. In this parade Avarice rides "vpon a Camell loaden all with gold" and on his lap is "an heape of coine." Yet Spenser describes Avarice as "nigh vnto deaths doore," wearing a "thred-bare cote" to cover his emaciated body, for "ne scarse good morsell all his life did taste."[6]

The conjunction of wealth and poverty is not contradictory. For the covetous heart surrounds itself with wealth while, slave to the need for more and more wealth, it denies itself and undertakes innumerable economies. As Spenser describes, the greedy soul is one "whose wealth was want, whose plenty made him pore." Many of are just such souls, and we justify our greedy poverty as a necessary duty, for the family. We surround our children with advantages and comforts — a good neighborhood and an excellent school, piano lessons and a computer, summer camp and opportunities to expand their horizons with travel. And at the same time we work ourselves to the bone to pay all the bills. So, we see the tragedy of parents whose zeal to provide their children with every opportunity so consumes their time and energies that they have nothing of themselves left to give. Thus does Mammon corrupt a well-meaning heart.

The image of the exhausted executive who comes home late at night in his Lexus, wearing his Armani suit, and kisses his already-asleep children good night is a vivid image that should give us pause. And we should be aware that the church fathers and medieval writers well knew that we can be greedy for achievements, recognition, and accomplishments as well, so that same father might be wearing a clerical collar and drive a modest Toyota — or I might add, a professorial tweed jacket. We can become slaves of many worldly rewards, not just money. Writing the next book can be a consuming desire as voracious and corruptive as the lust for stock options.

But can life be lived any other way? This is the question to which I now wish to turn. For a modern man or woman who has read a book or two in economic or political theory might well think that ambition and desire for reward are necessary for any society. So, like the disguise of frugality and love of offspring, avarice can cloak herself in the garb of social necessity. In fact, as Adam Smith suggests, the private vice of greed, when harnessed to the marketplace, has the paradoxical effect of contributing to the common good. In this way, private vice can put on the mien of public virtue.

6. The parade of the seven deadly sins occupies the greater part of canto III of book 1. The lines describing avarice are in stanzas xxvii-xxix.

William Langland, a late medieval poet and contemporary of Chaucer, wrote a strange and beautiful poem called *Piers Plowman.* That poem is preoccupied with the question of whether, as social beings engaged in economic relations, we can live without avarice. I cannot offer a systematic analysis of Langland's argument, for the poem is a complex series of allegorical dreams. One dream, however, is illuminating. It involves Lady Meed, and it represents the author's recognition that the promise of wealth seems an indispensable incentive for human societies.[7]

Lady Meed is the personification of earthly reward ("meed" is an old English word for "reward"). For Langland, who lived when the fluid money economy was rapidly replacing the static feudal system of wealth based upon land and social status, Lady Meed is predominantly associated with movable wealth. She is portrayed as very lovely and much sought after, but dangerous. Langland focuses on the way Lady Meed is used by Falsehood to corrupt just forms of social life (specifically by breaking the Ten Commandments — 2.87). Falsehood uses Lady Meed to bring knights, clerics, sheriffs, jurors, and clerks to betray their duties (2.55-60). In this dream the dramatic crisis comes when Falsehood prepares to marry Lady Meed and thus guarantee his full and complete control over her attractions. To prevent this, Truthful rushes to the King's court to tell Conscience, and then Conscience, in turn, tells the King to arrest Falsehood and Lady Meed. This is done, and the two are brought to the court.

Now we reach the most poignant aspect of the dream. As Langland observes, Lady Meed is "ever subverting the work of Conscience" (3.49). From the very moment she arrives, the clerks of the court begin to think of prebends and benefices she might give them. Knights waver and turn to thoughts of reward. In words that could be spoken to any cleric who wants to launch a capital campaign, Lady

7. My reading of *Piers Plowman* follows the helpful analysis found in chapter 4 of Donald R. Howard, *The Three Temptations: Medieval Man in Search of the World* (Princeton: Princeton University Press, 1966). See also David Aers, *Chaucer, Langland, and the Creative Imagination* (London: Routledge and Kegan Paul, 1980), especially chap. 1, "Imagination and Traditional Ideologies in *Piers Plowman*," pp. 1-37. Citation of the poem follows passus and line as found in the translation of the "C" text by George Economou (Philadelphia: University of Pennsylvania Press, 1996).

Meed sweetly promises, "I'll have your church roofed and build you a cloister" (3.64). The reaction is predictable — clergy swoon and are eager to serve her. Conscience and Truthful urge the King to expel Lady Meed, but the King wants to keep her. In fact, he tries to arrange for Conscience to marry Lady Meed. But Conscience refuses. No, he argues, we should live by duty and honor, not meed.

This refusal and alternative vision of social motivation leads to a trial of Lady Meed. In a key speech, she offers a defense of her indispensable role in any kingdom:

> It becomes a King that shall rule a realm
> To give meed to the men that humbly serve him,
> To honor with gifts all men, his own and foreign;
> Meed makes him beloved and taken for a real man.
> Emperors, earls, and all kinds of lords
> Pay servants to run and ride their errands.
> The pope and all prelates accept presents
> And give meed to men to maintain their laws.
> Servants expect meed for their services
> And their masters reward them as agreed.
> Both beggars and bondsmen want meed for their prayers;
> Minstrels ask for it for their minstrelsy;
> Priests that preach to the people and teach them
> Ask for meed, mass pennies, and their meals too.
> Craftsmen crave it from their apprentices;
> Merchandise and meed must go together.
> There is no living man that doesn't love meed
> And glad to grasp it, great lord or poor man.

(3.264-83)

The King, after all, must run the kingdom, and how is this possible without rewarding those who are loyal? A king must have meed to distribute; otherwise, the wheels of commerce and society will stop turning.

In the trial Lady Meed is condemned by Reason and Conscience, and the King pledges to rule without her. The dream ends. Yet, as the poem unfolds, it becomes clear that while Langland prefers a society based upon love of God and love of neighbor, he sees that a society designed along these lines will be subverted by a seemingly inevitable slide into vice.[8] In order to motivate the lazy and the greedy, we must deploy the attractions of Lady Meed. Furthermore, the only way to control violence and punish wickedness is to offer meed to knights, whose job is to drive away brigands. Thus, in the larger context of the poem, Lady Meed's speech wins the day. Servants will not serve, and minstrels will not offer their minstrelsy, unless motivated by rewards. In other words, it is not true that love makes the world go 'round. In general, love either makes the world stop in its tracks — or go off its rails. As this allegory of Lady Meed makes clear, Langland sees that among men and women tainted by original sin, meed makes the world go 'round.

If I am right about my interpretation of *Piers Plowman*, then it tentatively arrives at a conclusion we now widely accept. We cannot build a society based upon the ephemeral hope that men and women will act virtuously. We must shape our social policies in such a way that our all-too-real vices are restrained and disciplined to serve useful ends. As Chrysostom noted, avarice is a very powerful vice, even to the point of trumping lust. The desire to acquire and retain wealth, status, power, and position drives our social systems, whether capitalist or socialist, and at the level of social policy the only real decisions we have is how best to discipline and direct that desire toward the common good. Not only is it dangerously self-deceptive to seek social solutions to spiritual vices, it is also impractical. Truly, Mammon is the god of this world.

I have embarked on this long digression because the conclusion represents the single most powerful temptation of Mammon — a spiritual submission to his worldly dominion. This submission is based on the false inference from the inevitable and necessary role of avarice in worldly life to the conclusion that it is not a vice. We should resist this false inference with all our might, for at root, the conclusion is a transgression of the first commandment, because it presumes that the god of this world has the power to define good and evil.

How does this happen? It happens, to my mind, because we have trained ourselves to believe that there is no difference between spiri-

8. See passus VII and the social collapse of Piers's half-acre commune. Only the lashing discipline of Sir Hunger, the stick that matches the carrot of Lady Meed, saves the social order.

tual and worldly life. Because we find intolerable any suggestion that our social existence is vicious, we conclude that what is necessary must be virtuous. This happens in two ways. We can capitulate spiritually or we can rebel materially. We can redefine virtue to accommodate economic necessities, or we can insist that economic necessities must produce virtue. We can celebrate the dynamic and wealth-generating economies of democratic capitalism as providential gifts, or we can rally in the streets to smash capitalism and establish a social system in which it will be impossible to be greedy. In both cases, like the idol worshiper and the iconoclast, we want our decisions about political parties or social policies to be spiritually pure. In both cases, we raise the god of the worldly life — Mammon — to the level of the God of heaven and earth, either to insure comity or initiate combat. But I must break off here. I cannot allow myself to digress into the silliness of baptizing capitalism or the fantasies of those who decry private property — or the perhaps more common spiritual danger of progressive preachers who bring us to serve Mammon by using the Sermon on the Mount to critique American society rather than the hearts of Christians. I must say something, in conclusion, about how we might escape the clutches of avarice and avoid serving Mammon, the god of our world. For the wisdom of the tradition is not simply diagnostic; it is prescriptive.

III

I will begin with a simple inference. If Mammon is the god of this world, then we can escape his clutches only if we renounce the world. It turns out that the great bulk of the premodern Christian tradition, while not always formulating the antecedent (perhaps pride and not love of money is the root of all evil), consistently affirms the consequent. Consider the advice that Saint Paul gives to those of us whose duties and vocations necessarily involve us in the "necessities" of life — marriage and procreation, as well as commerce and governance. He tells us to "deal with the world as though [you] have no dealings with it. For the present form of the world is passing away" (1 Cor. 7:31). We may not be able to withdraw from the world. In fact, God may call us to an even greater involvement in the world. Yet, it should be an involvement as though it were no involvement, an acknowledgment of certain worldly necessities that is, at the same time, a recognition that such necessities are passing away.[9]

The implications for avarice are clear. One need not serve Mammon if one is willing to renounce citizenship in his kingdom and live as a resident alien. We can acknowledge the necessity of meed and yet escape the vice of avarice, if we will not define our lives in terms of the worldly affairs that Mammon inevitably dominates. For this reason, in one way or another, the Christian tradition has taught *contemptus mundi,* contempt for the world, as the basic strategy for overcoming avarice. To live a life of action and responsibility is the vocation of most Christians. Few of us are called into the desert or cloister. Yet such a life must be lived with the knowledge that this world we are called to serve, sustain, and improve is passing away.

This is easily said, but how can it be done? There are many strategies. One thinks, for example, of the haughty nobility of the chivalrous ideal in medieval poetry. The deep shame the poet ascribes to Sir Gawain when the Green Knight exposes his secret cowardice and covetousness, a cowardice and covetousness based on no shameful thing but rather on a love of life, testifies to the medieval ideal of contempt for the world.[10] But we do not live in a world in which chivalrous ideals can function (though the success of the Tolkien movies may suggest otherwise), so I turn to three other spiritual strategies for resisting greed, each of which is widely commended by the old writers of the tradition, and each of which creates a contempt for the world that allows us to develop a proper love for God.

In late medieval and Renaissance culture, contempt for the world is expressed in the popular image of the saint or nobleman contemplating a skull in order to overcome the bewitchment of the world by bringing to mind the reality of death. This contemplation of death — *memento mori* — remains an apt spiritual exercise. A common piece of contemporary wisdom reiterates this ancient truth. We are told that in our dying moments we will not regret that we did not work harder. To know the ubiquity of death makes us sensible of the absurdity of putting our trust and hope in wealth and worldly achievement. Is it an ac-

9. This is how I take Jesus' hard words in Luke 14:26.
10. See *Sir Gawain and the Green Knight,* lines 2374-75.

cident that our society, which so wants our loyalty, hides death from view and wishes to protect us from this harsh reality?

The image of the saint and the skull is a convention, but when I turn to Dante, I find the same dynamic of contemplation of decay and dissolution richly symbolized. In his *Purgatorio,* Dante depicts the Mountain of Purgatory with seven ledges, one for each of the seven deadly sins. On the ledge of avarice the souls lie, facedown, adhered to the pavement. Dante stoops down to speak with one. He explains to Dante his punishment: "Even as our eyes fixed upon earthly things, were not lifted on high, so justice here has sunk them to the earth" (canto 19.118-20). When I first read these lines, I was perplexed. Dante always envisions the punishments on the Mountain of Purgatory as purifying and transformative, and I could not see how the downward gaze of the greedy could cure them of their lust for worldly good. Should they not be purified by the upward vision of God? Then, when I thought of *memento mori,* I recognized Dante's genius. The avaricious sin because they love too much the finite beauty of worldly things. A pious soul — the person who explains the punishment is a long-dead pope who meant well — can become a slave to Mammon when he makes an idol of worldly wealth and power. The eyes are forced downward in punishment so that the penitent soul can watch the objects of worldly greed rust and molder. To see the truth about Mammon's kingdom releases one from his thrall.

In our own time and place, we do well to fix our eyes downward and onto the affairs of the world. Go to funerals and be reminded that from dust we have come and to dust we shall return. Attend city council meetings and learn that while the meek may inherit the earth, it is currently run by the real estate developers, lobbyists, and ill-informed elected officials. Read the *Wall Street Journal* and enjoy the absurdity of current efforts to ensure that stock analysts are not influenced by the investment bankers who pay their salaries. This is not to say that love, dignity, and honesty do not shine through worldly affairs. The point of Dante's poetic image of the punishment of the avaricious is not to instill contempt for humanity or a hatred of finite existence. Rather, the point of contemplating the world is to recognize the utter absurdity of imagining that anyone other than God himself could fashion it into a heavenly kingdom. God may call us to become doctors and fight to snatch a few more years out of death's grip. He may call us to political action or economic responsibility. But anyone who imagines that such vocations are intrinsically divine, and that one's successes and failures are freighted with transcendent significance, will fall victim to avarice and will serve Mammon in order to serve God — something Jesus refused to do when tempted by Satan in the wilderness when he renounced the offer of worldly power.

I must leave off the path of contemplation and turn to the way of action. The old writers consistently advocate charity as the great bulwark against greed. Langland's allegorical dreams again and again emphasize that giving money to the poor is the direct route to defeating the dominance of Lady Meed. She may rule society, but she need not rule our hearts. Evagrius tells the story of a monk who epitomized this strategy for resisting temptation: "One of the brethren owned only a book of the gospels. He sold it and gave money for the support of the poor. He made a statement that deserves remembrance: 'I have sold the very word that speaks to me, saying, "Sell your possessions and give to the poor"'" (*Praktikos* 46). Whatever the context, we must part with something in order to drive a wedge in our hearts between God and Mammon. Giving away money is a crucial step in breaking off our adulterous romance with wealth.

Yet in my experience most contemporary Christians, especially sensible and responsible American Christians, fail to understand and practice the ancient idea of charity. From Saint Augustine to William Langland, Christian writers have urged the wealthy and powerful to take responsibility for the common good. We are called to support projects and programs that ameliorate poverty, promote education, and support public institutions. However central to Christian responsibility and justice, this form of charity does not adequately address the temptations of avarice. For this reason, one consistently finds that the old writers endorse forms of personal and to our minds "irresponsible" charity. The nobleman is not just to set up a poorhouse. He is to throw a springtime banquet for all. The former involves an attempt to work within the constraints of worldly affairs, because it seeks to do a good that will endure. The latter is an act of contempt for the world, for it is an act of celebration that cares not for the morrow.

We should take up a discipline of "irresponsible" or "foolish" charity. Give and do not try to control the outcome of your giving. Give with a careless attitude that trusts in the providence of God rather than the ways of the world. Do not say, "He will only use the money to buy another bottle of booze." Do not say, "Why throw good money after bad?" Do not say, "How can I be sure the resources are being used well?" Show contempt for the world with an act of charity that does not simply take from the right hand of Mammon to give to the left, from your mutual fund to a foundation's mutual fund. For a well-meaning and philanthropic American Christian, an act of charity that has no promise of bearing worldly fruit may be a very important way of escaping from the subtle insinuations of avarice.

I have briefly developed two strategies for overcoming the temptation to worship Mammon: contempt for the world and wanton charity. I wish to end with a third, for we cannot overcome sin by recognizing its ugliness and perversity. We can free ourselves from lower loves only by a higher love. Contemplation of the rusting and moldering structures of worldly life frees us from fantasies about our lower loves. Foolish acts of charity help us free our souls for the foolishness of the gospel. But in order to escape from Mammon, we must turn our eyes upward. We can resist a finite beauty only if we allow ourselves to be ravished by infinite beauty. Thus, only if we nourish a love for the kingdom of God can we develop and sustain a contempt for the world that does not decay into despair or cynicism.

This exchange of loves is directly related by Saint Augustine to the sin of avarice. Commenting on the final verses of Psalm 90, he urges us, "If we are greedy, we should be greedy for eternal life. Yearn for the life that has no end. That is where our greed should stretch. Do you covet endless money? Then desire eternal, endless life. Do you hope for possessions unlimited? Seek eternal life."[11] Concretely, Saint Augustine's advice entails developing a greedy love of prayer. The discipline of prayer is a stick in the eye of worldly necessity. The morning and evening offices are pure and perfect opportunities to waste time. The sacrifice of praise and thanksgiving involves a spiritual contempt for the world, because it snatches our lips and hands from the maw of Mammon and redirects them toward God.

The absorptive waste holds for the study of Scripture. It is not a curse that the languages are ancient, the idiom foreign, and the content hopelessly complex. God has blessed us with a word that is such a

---

11. *Exposition of the Psalms*, Exposition 2 of Psalm 90 [12].

puzzle and challenge that one would have to give over one's entire life to trying to understand it. Take this blessing to heart. Pile up the commentaries and lexicons. If we will exhaust ourselves in the study of Scripture, *then nothing is left to be consumed by Mammon.* Thus does the psalmist petition God: "Incline my heart to thy testimonies, and not to gain" (119:36). The psalmist is confident that contempt for the world will not evacuate us and leave us with a thin whisper of mere spiritual existence. A contempt for gain does not impoverish. It frees us to be filled with far more than we can ever digest or understand, for the Lord promises, "Open your mouth wide and I will fill it" (Ps. 81:10).

If we turn toward the beauty of holiness, then we can see how Jesus' law is also a promise. His moral demands are a species of his gospel, always circling back to the first commandment, which is itself more declaration of truth than moral imperative. This is clearly evident in Jesus' teaching on wealth. We cannot, as he tells us, serve God and Mammon. The logic of the disjunction is pure grace. If we will but serve God, then we *cannot* serve Mammon. The sword that divides us from the world is the sword that delivers us from our own grasping desire to hold on to the many finite loves that cannot save us. The first commandment tears us from the grasp of all the other false gods of this world, and in so doing sets us free. Our jealous God, his consuming love, leaves nothing to be subjugated in the rotting, rusting kingdom of Mammon.

236

IV. THE DIVINE COMMAND

Keeping the Commandments

Robert Louis Wilken

Given the contentiousness of public life in the United States today, it was inevitable that the bulky stone monument inscribed with the Ten Commandments and placed in the rotunda of the Supreme Court of the State of Alabama would provoke controversy. When Judge Moore commissioned Richard Hahnemann to sculpt the monument, he surely knew it would be provocative, though perhaps even he did not foresee that it would culminate in his suspension and the removal of the monument under court order. Not long ago the Decalogue was a venerable public standard of morality, but in recent decades the relentless levelers who would scrape clean American life of anything that bears the marks of religious particularity have mounted an aggressive campaign to depict the Ten Commandments as the arbitrary preferences of Jews and Christians, and hence to confine the Decalogue to the private world of religious communities.

The Ten Commandments do of course have their origin in a particular religious tradition, Judaism, and the text printed on the monument comes from a Protestant Bible, the King James Version. It is inscribed on two tablets that may remind many viewers of the account in the book of Exodus of the giving of the "Ten Words" to Moses. "The Lord said to Moses, 'Cut two tables of stone like the first and I will write upon the tables the words that were on the first tables, which you broke.'" The tablets rest on a kind of craggy rock that recalls the jagged peaks of the mountain range of which Mount Sinai is a part. On first viewing, the monument seems to present the commandments given by God to Moses and written down for later generations in the biblical book of Exodus, that is, in the Jewish Torah, the Pentateuch of the Christian Old Testament. Some have complained that the sloping top of the monument and the two tablets lying open like a book call to mind a Bible lying open on a lectern. Judge Thompson ruled that Alabama Chief Justice Roy S. Moore had created "a religious sanctuary within the walls of a courthouse."

Yet on the monument the commandments do not stand alone. They are flanked by a series of inscriptions on the four sides of the rock. These statements are taken not from the Bible, nor from Jewish or Christian sources, but from the Declaration of Independence, the Judiciary Act of 1789, the National Motto of 1956, writings of the founding fathers, the words of a Supreme Court justice, and other historic documents.

Here are some of the citations:

Front Panel:

One nation, under God, indivisible, with liberty and justice for all. (Pledge of Allegiance)

Can the liberties of a nation be thought secure when we have removed their only firm basis, a conviction in the minds of the people that these liberties are the gift of God? (Thomas Jefferson)

Left Side Panel:

So help me God. (Judiciary Act of 1789)

Along with this oath one finds a statement of George Washington: "Let it simply be asked, where is the security for property, for reputation, for life if the sense of religious obligation deserts the oaths which are the instruments of investigation in the courts of justice?"

Right Side Panel:
Here one finds phrases from the Declaration of Independence, e.g., "laws of nature and of nature's God," surrounded by citations of George Mason, James Madison, and Justice William Blackstone.

George Mason: "The laws of nature are the laws of God; whose authority can be superseded by no power on earth." And Blackstone: "This law of nature, being co-eval with mankind and dictated by God Himself, is of course superior in obligation to any other. It is binding over all the globe, in all countries, and at all times: no human laws are of any validity, if contrary to this; . . . upon these two foundations, the law of nature and the law of revelation, depend all human laws; that is to say, no human laws should be suffered to contradict these."

On the Alabama monument the Ten Commandments are self-consciously interpreted within the context of American life. Although the text of the Decalogue is taken from the Bible, it is presented neither as Jewish nor as Christian teaching. The setting is not religious but civil and public, and the commandments are understood to codify in brief and memorable axioms a morality, in Blackstone's phrase, "binding over all the globe, in all countries."

The statements on the side panel also call attention to the relation between the Decalogue and the codified laws of the land. At the trial Judge Moore testified that he had installed the monument to express his belief that the Ten Commandments are the "moral foundation of American law." Even Judge Thompson, in ruling that the monument be removed, acknowledged that the Ten Commandments are "one of the most important sources of American law."

Further, the supporting quotations highlight the divine origin of the precepts found in the commandments, but ground them in the laws of the God of nature, not in the biblical revelation given to Moses. On the front panel, for example, are inscribed the words of founding father James Wilson: "Human law must rest its authority ultimately upon the authority of that law which is divine."

Finally, to impress on the viewer that what is engraved on the monument has been embodied in the actual laws of the state, it features a passage from the Constitution of Alabama: "We, the people of the State of Alabama," look to the "favor and guidance of Almighty" God in establishing the "constitution and form of government for the State of Alabama."

In placing the Decalogue on a monument in the rotunda of the Supreme Court of Alabama, Judge Moore wished that the Ten Commandments be seen as the form in which a universal code of law has been promulgated, handed on, taught, and codified in the traditions of this country. Its source is nature's God, the creator and lawgiver, the transcendent author of moral wisdom. When men and women pass through the rotunda, whether Jewish or Christian, Muslim or Buddhist, agnostic or atheist, they are reminded that the laws of the land are guided by a moral law grounded in something other than convention, caprice, or imperiousness.

The same text of the Ten Commandments can be found in a wholly different setting. In many Episcopalian churches built in the nineteenth century, for example, the Cathedral of St. Luke and St. Paul in Charleston, South Carolina, the Decalogue is inscribed on the walls of the apse. In this setting the commandments are presented and interpreted not as the work of the God of nature, but as the ordinances of the God of Abraham, Isaac, and Jacob, the God of biblical revelation, and their source is identified as chapter 20 of the biblical book of Exodus. Understandably, they are flanked not by quotations from Thomas Jefferson or William Blackstone — as in Judge Moore's monument — but by the Apostles' Creed and the Lord's Prayer. For those who read the words of the commandments on the wall of the cathedral in Charleston, sometimes while kneeling, the Decalogue is presented not as a universal moral code but as the Law given to Moses and an exhortation to Christians. So important is the Decalogue that it is given prominence by being placed in the chancel facing the altar where the Eucharist is celebrated and the cathedra, the chair of the bishop, the successor to the apostles, is found. The 1928 *Book of Common Prayer* also prescribed that the Decalogue be read in the service at least one Sunday a month.

Though the text of the Decalogue in the rotunda of the Alabama Supreme Court and in this cathedral is the same, those who turn their eyes to the commandments as they receive Communion will have a different sense of what the commandments require of them than will those who stop to read them in a state building.

The distinction between these two uses of the Decalogue may seem obvious, but not to Americans United for Separation of Church and State. Executive director Rev. Barry Lynn fumed and fretted that the monument endangers our civil liberties: "It is not the job of government to single out one religious code and hold it up as the state's favorite. Promoting the Ten Commandments is a task for our houses of worship, not government officials," Lynn said. "It's high time Moore learned that the source of U.S. law is the Constitution, not the Bible." Predictably he was joined by the Anti-Defamation League (ADL): "We are gratified that the federal court agreed with our position that true religious liberty means freedom from having the government impose religion on its citizens," commented Deborah Lauter, Southeast Regional Director of the ADL. Others were more shrill: Judge Moore had turned a hall of justice into a religious sanctuary where people drop on their knees to pray.

The Ten Commandments are traditionally divided into two "tables," the first including the invocation of God, "Thou shalt have no other gods before me," and the injunction to keep the Sabbath day holy, and the second the prohibitions against stealing, adultery, false witness, murder, et al. The secular critique of the Ten Commandments turns in large measure on the first table, whose commandments apply, in the condescending words of Lynn, to "one religious code." The second table is less controversial, though given the strident screeching tone of the critics and their eagerness to vandalize anything that has the authority of the past or of religious tradition, they would no doubt find some of the other commandments an affront as well (consider, for example, the prohibition against adultery).

The distinction between the two tables of the law, the first that enjoins duties to God and the second that sets forth responsibilities to our fellow human beings, is very ancient and has been the staple of Christian instruction and exposition for centuries. In the *Institutes* John Calvin said that "we ought to ponder what the division of the divine law into two Tables meant. . . . God has so divided his law into two parts, which contain the whole of righteousness, as to assign the first part to those duties of religion which particularly concern the worship of his majesty; the second, to the duties of love that have to do with men."[1]

For most of the church's history the distinction between the two tables was largely catechetical. During a brief period in British ecclesiastical history, however, the classical division between the two tables came to define two parties within the church, the Puritans, on the one hand, and the Anglicans, on the other. Although Anglicans and Puritans agreed on the authority of the Decalogue, and both parties

---

1. *Institutes of the Christian Religion* 2.8.11.

thought all the commandments were binding, they nevertheless dis-
agreed as to where the accent should lie. Each accused the other of being "carvers," that is, of carving out of the Ten Commandments what
did not suit the interests of their party. The knife was applied at the
cleavage between the first and second tables of the law. Puritans emphasized the commandments of the first table, duties toward God, and
Anglicans the commandments of the second table, duties to neighbor.

At first glance the controversy is puzzling. Neither Puritans nor
Anglicans rejected the other table. The Anglicans were no less committed to the worship of the one true God, nor did Puritans eschew the
prohibitions against adultery or stealing or murder. They too recognized the duties to one's fellow man. Where one placed the accent defined what each party considered the "bosom sins." Yet there was a
genuine fault line, and it turned on the "natural" morality embodied
in the second table. The moral code in the second table, it was argued,
could be deduced by the use of natural reason.

The difference between Puritans and Anglicans is nicely illustrated in sermons from the period. In a funeral sermon preached in
1659, Thomas Pierce (Anglican clergyman who rose to prominence after the Restoration) said, "Give me leave to tell you, what is not every
day considered. The most material part of godliness is moral honesty. . . . The Second Table is the touchstone to our obedience to the
First." Speaking of the deceased, Pierce said he had been "sober and
righteous," hence he was also "godly" and put the lie to those who
have only the form of godliness but lack its power. In the state of "civil
righteousness," wrote Richard Hooker, one who lives peaceably with
one's neighbors would not "hurt so much as his neighbor's dog, pays
every man his own, . . . no drunkard, adulterer or quarreler." Such a
person takes pride in his dealing with his fellow men.[2]

In turn the Puritans responded that the Anglicans practiced an
external virtue while ignoring the genuine worship of God. A good example is Richard Sibbes, master of St. Catherine's Hall, Cambridge.
The "rise of all sin against man is our sinning against God first. . . . The
breach of the First Commandment is the ground of the breach of all the
rest." For some the commandments were divided not so much into

---

2. See J. Sears McGee, *The Godly Man in Stuart England: Anglicans, Puritans,
and the Two Tables, 1620-1670* (New Haven, 1976), pp. 70 and 95.

two tables but into a single first commandment, worship of the true God, followed by the other nine. William Perkins said that "the ground of the nine later commandments is the first, 'Thou shalt have no other gods before me.'"[3]

This controversy within the English church, one of the few instances in the history of Christianity when there was a dispute over the Ten Commandments, shows that Christians have a stake in *two* different ways of interpreting and using the commandments. On the one hand the Decalogue can be viewed as a universal law applicable to all human beings, the norm for "civil righteousness," in the language of the seventeenth century, and on the other hand as a guide for the Christian life, a set of precepts to lead the faithful into a more intimate relation to God. Neither excludes the other, yet each has its own distinctive character, logic, and application. Both can be traced back to the New Testament and the early church.

Already in the second century Tertullian, the North African theologian who first wrote in Latin, addressed the topic: "Why should God, the creator of the universe, the governor of the whole world, the fashioner of human beings, the world, the producer of all peoples, be believed to have given a law through Moses to one people and not to have assigned it to all people?" A reasonable question. Why should a law for all peoples be transmitted through Moses to the Israelites? Tertullian's answer is that the giving of the law to Moses was only one instance of promulgations of a universal moral law. According to the Old Testament, the law was given not once but many times and to different people, first to Adam and Eve (do not eat of the tree planted in the midst of paradise), and later in specific precepts written down by Moses on Mount Sinai. However, before the law was given to Moses there was an "unwritten law" which was "understood naturally."[4] As examples of those who knew the law before it was promulgated, he mentions Noah, who was "found righteous," Abraham, and other figures in the Old Testament who lived before Moses. He might have included Job, who was "blameless and upright" yet did not know the laws of Israel. In his view the Law of Moses is not the original law from which all others derived, but the form in which the universal law

3. McGee, p. 71.
4. *Against the Jews* 2.

was proclaimed to the Jewish people at a particular time. This is an argument with legs that could be put to work in the present situation: even something that claims universality will inevitably have a particular origin.

Augustine makes a similar point, but his argument moves more along natural law lines. The law has been "written in our hearts" by our "fashioner," he says. Even before the law was given to Moses, human beings were not ignorant of it, because they were able to distinguish right and wrong and knew they were responsible for their actions. That is, an implicit ethical standard was built into human nature. At the same time, it is not insignificant that the law was promulgated. "To take away from human beings any grounds for complaining that they had not been provided for, a law written on tablets was given. It stated what was already written in their hearts."[5] Though the law was always there, written on the heart, people could willfully ignore it or claim it did not exist. However, when it was promulgated, it stood before them as a reproach that could not be ignored and men and women were forced to attend to its precepts.

The appearance of the phrase "written in their hearts" in Tertullian and Augustine is noteworthy. It is of course a reference to Romans 2, the most explicit statement of the authority of the natural law in the Scriptures. Paul writes: "When Gentiles who have not the law do by nature what the law requires, they are a law to themselves, even though they do not have the law. They show that what the law requires is written on their hearts, while their conscience also bears witness" (Rom. 2:14-15).

Biblical scholars debate whether Paul is speaking here of the natural law, but Paul's argument is so similar to what one finds in other ancient sources, e.g., Philo or Cicero, that resistance to such an interpretation seems to stem more from willfulness, the reluctance to acknowledge the presence of natural law in the Scriptures, than from careful exegesis. In any case, whatever the view of contemporary biblical scholars, Romans 2 was taken by the church fathers and the medievals to refer to the natural law.

Thomas Aquinas cites Romans 2 in his discussion of the moral precepts of the old law in the *Summa*. The question was "whether all

---

5. *Exposition of Psalm* 57.1.

the moral precepts of the old law belong to the law of nature." Thomas responds, "On the contrary, the apostle says that the Gentiles, who have not the Law, do by nature those things that are of the Law."[6] His argument is that human morals are not arbitrary but depend on their relation to reason. Those acts we call good are in accord with reason. In some cases the precepts are self-evident, in other cases judgment and deliberation are required, and in others one needs to be helped by divine instruction. Nevertheless, all the moral precepts belong to the law of nature, "but not all in the same way." Significantly Thomas does not draw a sharp line between things that are known by reason and those arrived at with the help of tradition or revelation, a point that is relevant to the use of the Decalogue in a pluralistic society. That something took form in a particular religious tradition does not place it beyond the bounds of reasonable discourse.

From earliest times, then, Christian thinkers acknowledged that the law of Moses is not a law for the Jewish people alone, nor solely for Christians, but for all men and women. It is the form in which a universal law has been promulgated among the Jews and received later by Christians. In the present debate this would suggest that interpretation of the Decalogue in the rotunda of the Alabama supreme court is not alien to Christian tradition or thought, but one Christians of all confessions should applaud and step forward to defend.

Even though the law is written on the hearts of human beings, its promulgation in a specific code forces people to attend to it, reflect on it, and, one hopes, act on it. It is unrealistic to think that any society can rely solely on the law written on the heart or relegate moral exhortation to the inner life of religious communities or to the conscience of the individual. The sentiments we read on public buildings or find inscribed on monuments and memorials are not abstractions, but concrete testimonies to the lives and convictions of those who have gone before us. As John Lukacs has reminded us, there is a "recorded" history and also "remembered" history. The things we remember in our common life quietly convey a precious inheritance that helps us keep faith with the dead and form, in unspoken ways, the sensibilities and attitudes, not to say hopes and dreams, of those who will follow us. There is no greater betrayal than to impoverish a generation yet un-

6. *Summa theologiae* IaIIae Q100, art. 1.

born by willful acts of amnesia. What we honor in our public life has a bearing on how we live as individuals.

In his testimony at the trial in the federal court in Alabama, Rabbi David Novak argued that we should not succumb to the argument that secular and religious are mutually exclusive terms. Maimonides distinguished between those who accept commandments because of "natural inclination" and those who accept them because of divine revelation. Maimonides went on to say that whether for religious reasons or secular reasons, all persons, religious or not, can affirm the practical authority of the same commandments.

It should not be overlooked that the claim that the Decalogue is universal is not simply grounded in the argument that one can make a case from reason that stealing, adultery, or murder is wrong. Its precepts are also universal in that they reflect moral codes found in other religions. The most striking case is Buddhism. Within Buddhism there are lists of virtues and prohibitions that are remarkably similar to what is found in the Ten Commandments: do not take life, do not take what is not given, practice sexual purity, speak the truth, speak gently, guard one's word, refrain from slander, restrain covetous thoughts of another's wealth, avoid thoughts of doing harm to others, sustain the perfect vision. Negatively they could be stated as follows: abstain from killing, stealing, sexual misconduct, lying, slander, idle talk and cursing, coveting, and opinionated thoughts. Buddhist kings made these virtues the center of political law.

The correspondence between this Buddhist list and the Ten Commandments gives strong support to the Christian and Jewish contention that the Ten Commandments are not simply the arbitrary and accidental preferences of the religious traditions of the West. Even in particulars they represent a broad moral consensus that embraces both West and East.

Nevertheless, one might argue that the particularity of the commandments of the first table makes the Decalogue unsuitable for our pluralistic society. The offending commands are "Thou shalt have no other gods" before me and "Remember the Sabbath day to keep it holy."

The Sabbath command seems to me to pose the more difficult case. Though some would purge the name of God from our public life, the invocation of God is deeply rooted in our history, from the Declaration of Independence, to the oaths in court, to our coinage, to the Pledge of Allegiance, to proclamations on Thanksgiving, to Memorial Day celebrations, and to the religious language used by all our presidents to this day. Because the Decalogue begins with a command to worship God, it appeals to a higher law than convention, to a standard that is beyond the power of states and people to abrogate. In the words of George Mason on the monument: "The laws of nature are the laws of God; whose authority can be superseded by no power on earth." Elimination of references to God in our public discourse is alien to American experience and the convictions of most Americans.

The command to remember the Sabbath is of a different order. Of course, one might make the argument that any society needs a day of rest, a day unlike other days of the week, when schools and public offices are closed and life moves at a slower pace. How sweet it is to drive city streets on a Sunday morning. The command to keep the Jewish Sabbath could then be taken metaphorically to refer to any day of rest, and because of the history and customs of this country, that day is Sunday, the Christian sabbath.

That argument strikes me as strained and artificial. I think it better to acknowledge that every nation or people has a particular history, and the form in which the universal moral law comes to us is derived from Christian and Jewish tradition, that is, from the Bible, the Christian Old Testament, the Jewish Torah. The fact that some wish to put distance between themselves and the beliefs that formed us as a nation does not mean that all references to the particularity of our traditions must be wiped clean. Why should this history be considered offensive? To brand it as arbitrary is a haughty act of intellectual hybris, thin in substance and contemptuous of our ancestors. It also cuts against the grain of common sense. We are who we are because of our history. In *Henry V* Shakespeare said: "There is a history in all men's lives."

We do not come at anything of worth except through history, and that applies as much to matters of morality as it does to convictions about representative government, human rights, religious freedom. What is to be gained by willfully afflicting the society with forgetfulness? A moral code constructed solely on the basis of our own reasonings without foundation in history would be abstract and antiseptic, and in the present cultural climate a fantasy. Agreement could never be reached. The Ten Commandments are unique, a gift of our history, that anchors our moral world more convincingly than anything that would be created anew. That the Decalogue is linked to a particular tradition with a specific historical origin is an argument in its favor, not against it. For Americans the Decalogue is not just "one religious code."

Which brings me to the use of the Ten Commandments within the churches. Christians (and Jews) recognize that the civic righteousness of the second table is hardly sufficient as a goal for the Christian life. The substance of the Decalogue is presented in the New Testament, and in its particulars. For example, Romans 13:8-10: "Owe no one anything, except to love one another; for he who loves his neighbor has fulfilled the law. The commandments, 'You shall not commit adultery, You shall not kill, You shall not steal, You shall not covet,' and any other commandment, are summed up in this sentence, 'You shall love your neighbor as yourself.' Love does no wrong to a neighbor; therefore love is the fulfilling of the law."

Though Paul knows and recalls Jesus' summary of the law, he is not content with generalities. He spells out in some detail the specific commands that belong to the Decalogue. In Ephesians he mentions honor your father and mother and adds the interesting commentary that this is the first commandment with a promise, "that it may be well with you." In 1 Timothy Paul, or one of his disciples, refers to the "law," by which he means the Ten Commandments, as the list that follows makes clear. Most of the commandments can be identified by the catalogue of sinners, the unholy and profane, murderers of fathers and mothers, manslayers, sodomites, perjurers, et al., or the works of the flesh, fornication, impurity, idolatry, enmity. When complemented by the gifts of the Spirit, love, joy, peace, patience, kindness, the commandments become a positive program rather than a simple list of prohibitions.

Following the New Testament, Christian writers in the second century took for granted that the commandments inscribed in the Decalogue are authoritative for Christians. The apologist Aristides, for example, presents the ideal Christian life by reference to the commandments of the Decalogue. Later Augustine (who was the first to treat the Decalogue systematically in the context of Christian catechetics) brought the commandments into intimate relation with the life in Christ. In one sermon he refers to the Decalogue as God's harp, citing Psalm 144: "O God, I will sing you a new song, on a harp of ten strings I will play to you," and urges his congregation not to get the harp out of tune.[7] Elsewhere he interprets the Ten Commandments as tablets given by Christ to his bride the church.[8] They are not the ordinances of a stern and distant judge but the loving gift of the bridegroom to his beloved. Given in love, they are not to be feared but embraced.

For Christians the Ten Commandments are much more than prohibitions imposed from without, negative commands having to do with what should be avoided in our external actions. They have to do not only with behavior but with attitudes and dispositions, that is, with the interior life. Recall the great meditation on the law, Psalm 119, a psalm Christians often ignore, partly because of its length, partly because of its repetitiveness, and partly because it has to do with law. What it says about law, however, is quite unconventional, one might even say unlawlike. I am thinking not only of such verses as "Oh, how I love thy law! It is my meditation all the day" (not the kind of thing one is likely to hear from a law student) or "I long for thy commandments," but also of its accent on interiority: "I incline my *heart* to perform thy statues," a verse that occurs in several forms in the psalm. Psalm 119 forms a fitting backdrop to the words of Jesus: "You have heard that it was said, 'You shall not commit adultery.' But I say to you that every one who looks at a woman lustfully has already committed adultery with her in his heart.'"

When we think of observing the law, of keeping the commandments, it is the will that first comes to mind. The psalmist surprises us by making our actions dependent not only on the will or the intellect but on the heart, the affections. Only when the heart is inclined to God's law, only when we love God, can we make the commandments our own.

But perhaps the place to end is with Luther, from whom I first learned the commandments and their "explanations." Luther does not cite Psalm 119 in his two catechisms, but he prefaces his explanation of each commandment with the phrase "We should fear, *love* and trust in God above all things," sentiments that are found in the psalm. After

---

7. *Sermon* 9.6-7.
8. *Against Faustus* 15.4.

each commandment is recited he asks: What does this mean? and re-peats the introductory formula. At "You shall not kill" he says, "We should fear and love God, and so we should not endanger our neigh-bor's life." For Luther the commandments have to do with a total transformation, a change of "thought, word and deed," in his words, not only doing no harm to our neighbor, but treating him with pa-tience, love, and kindness. Only when the heart "clings" to God and "entrusts" itself to God, says Luther, can we live as the command-ments direct us. That, finally, is why the first and greatest command-ment in the Scriptures is one that has no place on a public monument, but is to be burned into the hearts of each generation of the faithful: "You shall love the Lord your God with all your heart, and with all your soul, and with all your mind."

Hearts Set to Obey

Gilbert Meilaender

At least since the seventh century, and no doubt even earlier, Christians have been praying, in the words of the Collect for Peace, used in vespers: "O God, from whom come all holy desires, all good counsels, and all just works: Give to us, your servants, that peace which the world cannot give, that our hearts may be set to obey your commandments. . . ." Any theological system or construct that, in effect, subverts such a prayer or, even if only implicitly, suggests that we might be wrong to pray in this way invites our attention. And we know that — of all the trajectories within the history of Christian thought — it is Lutheran theology that has perhaps most often been suspected of undercutting such a prayer. Not that Lutherans have ceased to pray it, of course. To that degree, perhaps, their practice has sometimes been better than their theory.

I want to examine critically a certain understanding of Lutheranism, which (whether our language is that of paradox, of the law-gospel distinction, of the law as always accusing, of dialectic, or of freedom from law and critique of any third use of the law) eventually arrives at a kind of practical antinomianism — which is, alas, all too readily accompanied by a strident moralism — but which, were it consistent, would have no reason to pray that our hearts may be set to obey God's commandments.[1]

1. I have taken up this issue at various times in various works; indeed, it has in a sense been the most abiding preoccupation of my writing. See, for example, the

It is important to observe at the outset, however, that the problem I examine is not simply a Lutheran problem. The tension between two understandings of the person — as one whose self is shaped by what he does, or as one whose deeds reflect the person he is (declared by God to be) — goes deep into the heart of the Christian tradition more generally. It is fair to say, though, that this tension has been more pronounced at some places within the tradition, and Lutheranism has been such a place.

The Command of God and the History of Redemption

Whether we prefer the language of law, of command, or of evangelical imperative, our concern is to examine the place within Christian life of "the unchanging will of God, according to which human beings are to conduct themselves in this life," as the Formula of Concord defines the "one single meaning" of the word "law."[2] This will of God that is to structure the conduct of our lives is made known to us in several ways. The God of Abraham, Isaac, and Jacob binds himself to his people in covenant fidelity, and that covenant, in turn, calls for their responsible obedience. The will of the covenanting Lord is given to Israel in the commands of Sinai — which, in the simplest sense, call for avoidance of any idolatry and for structures of life that honor the neighbor and bind human lives together in community. The gift of the Sinai covenant is honored time and again by the great prophets of Israel, whose focal point is often Israel's failure to be faithful to her covenant obligations.

One encounters the will of God not only in the covenant but also in the structure of creation itself. The God who commands at Sinai has created a world with a morally coherent shape and form — a shape

---

following: *The Limits of Love* (Philadelphia: Pennsylvania State University Press, 1987), chap. 3; *The Theory and Practice of Virtue* (Notre Dame: University of Notre Dame Press, 1984), chap. 5; *Faith and Faithfulness* (Notre Dame: University of Notre Dame Press, 1991), chap. 4; "Grace, Justification through Faith, and Sin," in *Ecumenical Ventures in Ethics,* ed. Reinhard Hütter and Theodor Dieter (Grand Rapids: Eerdmans, 1998), pp. 60-83.

2. Formula of Concord, Solid Declaration, VI, 15, in *The Book of Concord,* ed. Robert Kolb and Timothy J. Wengert (Minneapolis: Fortress, 2000).

that is knowable, at least in part, also by those who have not yet bound themselves in covenant with Israel's God. And indeed, the wisdom traditions recorded in the Bible must be the fruit of long reflection on this moral form of the created order.

These two revelations of God's will — the commandments of Torah and the structure of creation — cohere, as is nicely illustrated, for example, in Psalm 19. The psalmist affirms that "the heavens are telling the glory of God." Without speech or words in any ordinary sense, the creation does not confront us with the personal address of one who commands. Yet the firmament proclaims its Creator's handiwork in its coherent moral order which "Day to day pours forth speech / and night to night declares knowledge." Israel's God does not, however, leave his people to their own inadequate attempts to discern this order embedded in the creation. He is gracious enough to speak, to command, as the psalmist also recognizes. "The law of the LORD is perfect, reviving the soul."[3] Not without good reason, therefore, does Bonhoeffer write, referring to this psalm and several others that make God's law the object of praise, "It is grace to know God's commands."[4]

We know, of course, that in the history of redemption the incarnate God himself must finally vindicate the moral order of creation in the face of human failure and disobedience. Moreover, we who in our baptism have come to name Jesus as Lord, are now called not just to discern the shape of creation or listen for the commands of Torah, but also to understand the moral life as discipleship, as following Jesus in his obedience to the Father. "Have this mind among yourselves, which is yours in Christ Jesus," Paul writes in Philippians. Or, as the hymn puts it: "Let us ever walk with Jesus / Follow his example pure. . . . / Let us do the Father's bidding."

Romans 6 sets the terms for our discipleship. As we seek daily to creep ever more fully into our baptism, we struggle to distinguish between those actions that follow Christ and those that do not.

3. The brief summary in this and the two preceding paragraphs of what we might call Old Testament ethics relies on Walter Brueggemann, *Reverberations of Faith: A Theological Handbook of Old Testament Themes* (Louisville: Westminster John Knox, 2002), pp. 66-69.

4. Dietrich Bonhoeffer, *Psalms: The Prayer Book of the Bible* (Minneapolis: Augsburg, 1970), p. 31.

When we encounter the will of God in the moral order of creation or in the commands of Torah, we quickly realize that — because we have not yet come to the end of the history of redemption or to the end of our own personal way as followers of Jesus — the new life into which we are baptized must sometimes be believed more than seen. Hence, the note of eschatological reservation, the sense that we are only on the way, in Romans 6: "For if we have been united with him in a death like his, we shall certainly be united with him in a resurrection like his." We remain both sinner and saint as long as we are in this life, but ours is not a static condition. The grace of God enables us, along the way, to make progress in the life of discipleship.

For something decisive has happened. "We were buried therefore with him by baptism into death, so that as Christ was raised from the dead by the glory of the Father, we too might walk in newness of life." We are no longer "enslaved" to sin. In Christ Jesus we are "alive to God" — desiring to know his will and learning to delight in his commands. And, although as followers on the way we sin daily, we are no longer in bondage to that sin. Something has happened. There is movement in this story that is the history of redemption. "For sin will have no dominion over you, since you are not under law but under grace." Our hearts are now set to obey the commandments of the God whose face we have seen in the crucified and risen One.

To be sure, it is also true that at any moment we may experience ourselves as caught between the continuing hold of sin and our liberation in Christ. We may experience our condition as both saint and sinner in a more static way. In those moments the history of redemption may seem to be less a story with movement and direction than a never ending battle between the powerful grip of sin and the new life under grace into which we have been baptized. I would never wish to deny the importance of this recurring experience in the life of disciples. It is of enormous significance for pastoral care in ways to which I shall return below, but it should not be the chief structuring principle of Christian ethics — as if the only issue for theology were to understand the indefinitely repeated, momentary *transition* from fallen to new creation, or as if the whole of our theological attention should be focused on those who find themselves in situations of extreme temptation and anxiety.[5] Rather, although theologians must be constantly alert to the possibility of such extremity of despair, they need not do their work under a kind of self-denying ordinance that forbids attention to anything other than the transition from sin to grace, from despair to faith.

How, then, should we respond in the face of that recurring experience of the power of sin? Part of the answer, of course, is that these are the moments in Christians' lives when the language of faith is a necessity: we *trust* that the grace of God in Christ has pardoned our sin and set us free for discipleship even in those moments when we cannot experience it happening. But there is still more to be said. We not only trust that God has done this — as if we could simply rest content in simultaneously experiencing our enslavement to sin and our trust in a pardoning God, as if we could simply salute the grace of God and go on our way. We not only trust; we also pray. We pray that, by the grace of God, the new life in Christ — the new thing that has happened, whether it is for the moment apparent or not — would, day by day, take an increasingly firm hold upon our hearts, that they might be set to obey God's commandments. It is in no way contrary to the life of discipleship that we should, again and again, experience ourselves as simply caught in the tension between the reality of our sin and the reality of God's forgiveness. What *is* contrary to the path of discipleship is that we should rest content in that static condition, that we should not in prayer strain against it as we ask Christ's Spirit to make the history of redemption an ever more effective reality in what we think, say, and do. "Strive," says the Letter to the Hebrews, "for the holiness without which no one will see the Lord." To this also I will return below.

5. This is the issue explored in helpful detail by Robert P. Scharlemann, *Thomas Aquinas and John Gerhard* (New Haven and London: Yale University Press, 1964). Scharlemann characterizes Gerhard's theology as one that focused on situations of extreme anxiety. He notes, however, that Gerhard himself saw a possible "way out" of this narrow focus, but it was a way that he did not finally take. He might, Scharlemann writes, have regarded "the extreme situations of which he speaks as universally possible but not necessarily universally actual" (p. 240).

A Dialectical Lutheranism and the Loss of Ethics

I said at the outset that Lutheran theology has sometimes been suspected of undermining this striving for holiness — "[s]lackness is the hereditary sin of Lutheranism," as Einar Billing put it[6] — and we need now to examine more systematically why this has been the case. Certainly there are important strands in Luther's thought which, seeming to divorce theology from ethics and faith from life, might, as John Witte has noted, "lead an earnest Evangelical follower straight into antinomianism."[7] Of course, even were this true of everything that Luther wrote — as it is not — it would still be true that Luther is not Lutheranism, and Witte's work makes clear how quickly Lutheran jurists in Germany began to fashion "reformation laws" that gave moral form and social shape to the life of their duly reformed cities. "When properly understood and applied," they believed, "the law not only coerced sinners, it also educated saints."[8]

What the jurists thought it necessary to do, and what they thought perfectly continuous with Luther's theology, others have viewed as a betrayal. Lutheranism can be depicted as having a kind of allergy to law, and the characteristically Lutheran distinction between law and gospel can be presented not as a corrective to abuses that had arisen within the church but, rather, as the basis for an entirely new system of theology. Rather than being a distinction important for pastoral care of believers who are "on the way" in the midst of the history of redemption, it becomes, as David Yeago observes, "the prime structuring principle" of all Christian theology.[9] We should note, in passing, the peculiarity of this tendency. After all, the Lutheran confessional writings begin with the ecumenical creeds, and the first three articles of the Augsburg Confession simply reaffirm received Christian teach-

---

6. Einar Billing, *Our Calling* (Philadelphia: Fortress, 1964), p. 35.

7. John Witte, Jr., *Law and Protestantism: The Legal Teachings of the Lutheran Reformation* (Cambridge: University Press, 2002), p. 92. We should note that these are by no means the only strands in Luther's thought. Of the works cited in n. 1, see in particular *The Theory and Practice of Virtue* (chap. 5) and *Faith and Faithfulness* (chap. 4).

8. Witte, p. 170.

9. David S. Yeago, "Gnosticism, Antinomianism, and Reformation Theology," *Pro Ecclesia* 2 (winter 1993): 38.

ing about the triune God, about sin, and about Christ. This does not suggest an attempt to develop a theology structured in an entirely novel way. Peculiar or not, however, the claim of novelty is dear to the hearts of many Lutherans, and it therefore needs our examination.

One of the most straightforward developments of this view of Lutheranism — as a "dialectical" theology that separates theology from ethics — can be found in a recent book by Daphne Hampson, *Christian Contradictions: The Structures of Lutheran and Catholic Thought.*[10] Perhaps because she no longer regards herself as a Christian and thinks the basic framework of Christian theology must be discarded in the modern age, Hampson is unusually free to think through the implications of a dialectical Lutheranism, which, though it does not persuade her, she has often found attractive.[11]

She contrasts Lutheranism's "dialectic" framework of thought with Catholicism's "linear" framework. For Catholicism, that is, the Christian life is understood as a *via,* a journey (destined ultimately to end in the vision of God). At least at its non-Pelagian best, Catholicism emphasized prevenient grace, understanding it as the justifying power that made possible gradual progress toward a holiness that was fit to stand before God. Hence, the Catholic understanding of righteousness is substantive (a quality that inheres in the person) and quantitative (achieved bit by bit, a matter of more and more). Our sinful nature is gradually transformed and perfected along the way. One can even use the characteristically Lutheran formula of *simul justus et peccator,* but in this framework the formula must be understood quantitatively. Divine grace is a power that gradually makes us "more and more" righteous — less sinner, more saint, to put it a bit too crudely.

10. Cambridge University Press, 2001. Citations of *Christian Contradictions* will be given by page number in parentheses within the body of the text.

11. Anthony Lane says of Hampson's work: "Her approach would be followed by many, but by no means all, Lutherans." *Justification by Faith in Catholic-Protestant Dialogue* (London and New York: T. & T. Clark, 2002), p. 3 n. 1. In the same context, however, Lane writes: "Reading the *Formula of Concord* on this topic [i.e., justification] I am struck by how much common ground there is with Calvin's exposition and how relatively marginal are the differences" (p. 4). This suggests what is, I think, the case — that those Lutherans who take an approach something like Hampson's are drawing on certain aspects of Luther's theology, but that a wider sample of both Luther and Lutheranism would demonstrate how unstable is any theology built on those aspects alone.

"This way of thinking," Hampson writes, "is to have far-reaching implications for the whole of Catholic life. It will mean that all kinds of matters, whether euthanasia or questions of sexual ethics, are of fundamental concern to the church. By contrast, . . . for Protestants the world is a secular sphere, in which humans make their own arrangements according to their own lights" (pp. 86f.). A more succinct — and telling — characterization of where many Protestant churches find themselves today would be hard to write.[12]

The dialectical framework of Lutheran theology, by contrast, dispenses entirely, at least on Hampson's telling, with such linear notions of gradual growth in righteousness. Indeed, "the whole thrust of the Lutheran tradition is," she writes, "against self-perfection" (p. 51). Stronger still, even if in some tension with Jesus' words in Matthew 5:48, she writes: "The Christian is free not to be perfect" (p. 287). We accept — perhaps, in subtle ways, we even delight in — our condition as simultaneously saint and sinner. The only righteousness of concern to the Christian is extrinsic, the righteousness of Christ. Hence, the Lutheran understanding of righteousness is relational (rather than being a quality that inheres in a person). Grace is in no sense a power that enables us to become "more and more" what God wills we should be; rather, grace is pardon that announces God's acceptance of the sinner and thereby elicits the faith that puts sinners in right relation with God.

That grace having been announced, there is no more to be said — other than to say it "again and again."[13] That is, any serious struggle to

12. Lest we think these issues too simple, we should note that Roman Catholic moral theology may face the opposite problem. Having for so long focused its attention on ways in which character is formed by (right or wrong) acts, the tradition of Catholic moral theology has struggled to articulate a sense in which the person as a whole stands before God as saint or sinner and is not just a collection of acts. See John Mahoney, *The Making of Moral Theology* (Oxford: Clarendon, 1987). For an argument to the effect that this problem has not been entirely overcome in the moral teaching of Pope John Paul II, see Meilaender, "Grace, Justification through Faith, and Sin." For a perceptive articulation of how "revisionist" trends in Roman Catholic moral theology may go too far and — like dialectical Lutheranism — lose the importance of particular acts in the moral life, see Darlene Fozard Weaver, "Taking Sin Seriously," *Journal of Religious Ethics* 31 (spring 2003): 45-74.

13. The contrast between a righteousness that is, under grace, gradually acquired "more and more" and a righteousness that is simply given "again and

grow in righteousness, to obey God's commands more fully, will be understood as sin, since it may direct one's attention inward in a self-preoccupied way rather than outward to the extrinsic righteousness of Christ. From such self-perfecting tendencies one must simply flee again and again. Christians make no progress in righteousness; they simply return time and again to the word that announces pardon, a word that invites and elicits faith. They continually reclaim their starting point.

There can be no room here for ethical reflection. There is room for preaching, but perhaps not for catechesis. It is hard to know exactly how one who lived solely within this framework of thought could raise children or pass on the church's way of life. According to this dialectical framework, the church must strictly separate faith from life. It should confine itself to preaching the gospel that frees us from self-preoccupation. Again and again. If it talks of God's commandments, it does so in order to see how they condemn us and how we must — again and again — flee from that condemnation to the gospel's announcement of pardon.

In short, the central element in Hampson's analysis can be stated simply and clearly: For Luther or Lutheranism, righteousness is in no sense substantive; it is not a quality that — even by God's grace — inheres in believers. Hence, there is no sense in which righteousness can grow, in which one can become more and more holy, in which the grace of God should be understood as a power that makes possible the Christian's journey toward holiness. On the contrary, righteousness is entirely a relation. To have faith in Christ is to have his righteousness and, therefore, to be right with God. What more could be needed? Having that, we have no need for growth. There is need only to return again and again to the promise that elicits faith in Christ as our righteousness. Christians are not on the way. The Christian life goes no-

---

again" as one returns to the starting point, to the pardoning word of grace, is not specifically Hampson's language. It is, however, helpful for clarifying the two frameworks of thought. I have appropriated this language from George Hunsinger's essay, "What Karl Barth Learned from Martin Luther," in *Disruptive Grace: Studies in the Theology of Karl Barth* (Grand Rapids: Eerdmans, 2000), pp. 279-304; cf. especially pp. 299-300. In some of the other writings cited in n. 1 I have — to make much the same sort of point — contrasted the Christian life as "journey" with the Christian life as "dialogue."

where. Rather, it returns — again and again. It starts over. It is a constant return to the promise, a constant struggle to trust that Christ is indeed our righteousness. Moreover, serious attention to the moral life and to God's commands, serious ethical reflection about the sort of acts we should do and the sort of persons we should be, must be renounced as temptation. Expressing a sinful preoccupation with self, such concern simply demonstrates that, in ourselves, we are indeed wholly and entirely slaves to sin.

Before turning to more systematic examination of the adequacy of this characterization of Lutheran theology, it may be worth making a passing observation about the system of thought Hampson depicts. This approach to theology — important for pastoral care as it sometimes is — narrows our range of vision considerably. We can put this point in terms used by Robert Scharlemann in his comparative study of the theology of Aquinas and Gerhard. The object of Gerhard's theological attention — in characteristically dialectical fashion — "is not the whole picture of man as he is by nature and by grace, but the picture of man precisely at the point of transition between the two states."[14] Consequently, what one should say theologically always depends on the state of the person to whom one speaks, and there seem to be only two such states that play a determinative role in a dialectical theology: the person addressed is either "complacent man" or "despairing man." If complacent, he must be brought to despair; if despairing, he is ready to hear the gospel.

But are these the only two sorts of people we might address? Are there none who, neither complacent nor despairing, are simply baptized Christians who know they are no longer in bondage to sin but are still sinners who need to grow in grace? How ought one speak to them? Or must we tacitly assume that they are really complacent and must be moved to despair before we have anything else to say to them? A theology that puts the language of "paradox" front and center, once we start to press upon it, is likely to leave us with such questions.[15]

14. Scharlemann, pp. 226-27.

15. Of course, characterizing Lutheran theology as fundamentally "paradoxical" is, to some degree, a rather recent phenomenon — fruit of the enormous influence of H. Richard Niebuhr's typology in *Christ and Culture* (New York: Harper and Row, 1951). Interestingly, however, Scharlemann notes a sense in which Gerhard's narrowed focus actually removes from Aquinas's view what is "genuinely paradox-

Having been more or less trained in such an approach to Lutheran theology, I recall that I sensed there was something wrong with
it long before I began to be able to say what that might be. I first
thought that what was mistaken about this way of structuring a theological system was that it lacked a doctrine of creation. Unwilling to
talk of a moral order embedded in the creation, it seemed unable to say
that our action should conform to that order. I still think there is something to that first thought of mine; that is, there are moments when an
incipient Marcionite tendency makes its presence felt in this version of
Lutheran theology. But I now wonder whether something almost the
opposite might not come even closer to the truth, whether it might not
be more accurate to say that this approach has *nothing but* a doctrine of
creation.[16] It is just creation and new creation "again and again." Nothing else ever happens. There is no movement, no *history* of redemption. There is only the moment of transition from sin to faith, returned
to time and again. No person whom God has created is set on the way
toward progress in the new life — only created again and again.

Obeying God's Commandments: A More Expansive Lutheranism

Not without good reason, therefore, has Niels Henrik Gregersen argued that "Luther's dialectic of law and gospel should not be elevated
into a theological principle that structures the interpretation of Christian faith from beginning to end." When that is done, Gregersen notes,
we end with a theology that "cannot express the extent to which the

---

ical" (p. 154). Gerhard will not puzzle with Aquinas over the paradox of how divine
and human agency somehow interpenetrate and cooperate in human action; agency
must belong to one or the other, and the movement of the will in conversion is "either of God or of man" (p. 159). This suggests to Scharlemann that "the concept of
free will has, in Gerhard's thinking, lost virtually all of the dialectical and paradoxical functions which it had in the Thomistic use" (p. 159). Although Scharlemann
also notes (p. 182) a way in which paradox reappears in Gerhard's thought, this is
indeed an interesting subversion of our normal characterizations.

16. Cf. Oliver O'Donovan, *The Problem of Self-Love in St. Augustine* (New Haven and London: Yale University Press, 1980), p. 158. Cf. also Hampson, p. 35: "Salvation and the doctrine of creation are one and the same thing, to be placed on one
side of what I have called the 'dialectic.'"

New Testament constantly instructs the believer to act according to his or her belief: 'Let the same mind be in you as was in Jesus Christ.'"[17] We need to do better than this dialectical Lutheranism. We need a theology that does not invite us to forget that "the grace of God has appeared for the salvation of all men, training us to renounce irreligion and worldly passions, and to live sober, upright, and godly lives in this world, awaiting our blessed hope, the appearing of the glory of our great God and Savior Jesus Christ, who gave himself for us to redeem us from all iniquity and to purify for himself a people of his own who are zealous for good deeds" (Titus 2:11-14). We need a theology that does not invite us to act as if the incarnation, cross, and empty tomb have done nothing new and transforming in human history. In short, we need to be able to say, as Luther does in thesis 23 of the Heidelberg Disputation, "The law brings the wrath of God, kills, reviles, accuses, judges, and condemns everything *that is not in Christ.*"[18]

Fortunately, we do not have to create or invent this ex nihilo; to some degree there is already such a Lutheran theology. We may, however, be ill prepared to recognize it since, for the last quarter-century, the baptized people of God have been invited to confess in the words of the "Brief Order for Confession and Forgiveness" in the *Lutheran Book of Worship,* that "we are in bondage to sin."[19] But resources for this better theology exist, for example, in Article IV of the Apology of the Augsburg Confession. It has always been something of a mystery that Article IV, simply because it refers regularly to the formula that the "law always accuses," should be read in a static, wooden fashion that ignores its own equally regular affirmations that the grace of God is a power that has accomplished something within the history of redemption in the lives of the baptized. The Apology teaches, of course, that the "fulfillment of the law, which follows our renewal, is scanty and impure," and that "the remnants of sin still cling" to us in this life

17. Niels Henrik Gregersen, "Ten Theses on the Future of Lutheran Theology: Charisms, Contexts, and Challenges," *dialog* 41 (winter 2002): 268.

18. *Luther's Works,* 31:41. This thesis was called to my attention by Yeago, p. 48 n. 22.

19. See the "Brief Order for Confession and Forgiveness" printed with settings 1, 2, and 3 of the liturgy (pp. 56, 77, and 98) in the *Lutheran Book of Worship* (Minneapolis: Augsburg; Philadelphia: Board of Publication, Lutheran Church in America, 1978).

(159). But it never denies that something decisive has happened. Indeed, it affirms that renewal has begun and that, therefore, these remnants of sin "always accuse us unless by faith in Christ we take hold of the forgiveness of sins" (159).

To be sure, Article IV does not answer all the questions that need to be answered. In considerable measure, it simply sets two understandings of the Christian life side by side, leaving us with the task of bringing them together in a coherent whole. There are, for example, places where Article IV clearly thinks of the Christian life as a constant return — again and again — to the promise of grace which faith grasps. "[W]hen we say that faith justifies, some will think that it refers to a foundational principle, namely, that faith is the beginning of justification or the preparation for justification. As a result, it is not by faith itself that we are accepted by God, but by the works that follow. . . . We do not think of faith in this way. Instead, we maintain that, properly and truly, by faith itself we are regarded as righteous for Christ's sake, that is, we are acceptable to God" (71-72). Here, it is clear, the Apology depicts our righteousness as relational rather than substantive, as an either/or condition. Either one is wholly and entirely righteous because he has taken hold of the righteousness of Christ, or one attempts to stand before God simply on one's own — in which case, however good many of our actions may be when taken piecemeal, the person who does them is only a sinner, wholly under condemnation. And for the justified sinner who is right with God, good works are said to follow spontaneously, as the good tree produces good fruit. Moral reflection or instruction is really beside the point.

But there are also places — quite a few, in fact — where Article IV thinks of the Christian life as gradual growth in a righteousness that is acquired "more and more" as the Spirit of Christ empowers us. Thus, for example: "[W]e ought to begin to keep the law and then keep it more and more. Now, we are not talking about ceremonies, but about that law which deals with the impulses of the heart, namely, the Decalogue" (124). Or again: "We openly confess, therefore, that the keeping of the law must begin in us and then increase more and more" (136). Here, it is clear, one must go to work pruning and fertilizing the tree if one hopes for good fruit. Reflection, instruction, direction, and inculcation may all be needed. This kind of righteousness is not imputed but imparted. Not a matter of either/or, but a matter of bit-by-bit and more-and-more. It grows as the renewing power of Christ's Spirit begins to transform the impulses of our hearts. Something new has happened in the baptized. They are no longer in bondage to sin, and a new power is at work in their lives, setting them on the way toward the holiness Christ not only asks but also promises.

Having placed these two understandings of the Christian's righteousness side by side, the Apology left to later generations the task of thinking through precisely how we are to use and do justice to both. Article VI of the Formula of Concord ("Concerning the Third Use of the Law") attempts just this. Some have read it as, in effect, failing really to affirm any distinctive third use, and we can understand how that argument goes. Because Article VI acknowledges — as we all should — that Christians are not perfectly renewed in this life, we are bound, at least sometimes, to experience God's law as prodding or admonishing us, and we will then be unlikely to delight inwardly in that law. One might argue, therefore, that our experience of the law will always constitute an accusation. The very realization that it prods us forces us to flee — again and again — to the gospel that promises Christ's righteousness to all who trust him. Thus, on this reading, Article VI offers no way to move beyond that essentially static tension in which we are (in ourselves) wholly and entirely sinner, and (in Christ) wholly and entirely saint — struggling to trust that it is as saint that God really sees us.

This is, I think, far too wooden a reading of an article which does, after all, say that Christians "should daily practice the law of the Lord, as it is written in Psalms 1 and 119, 'Blessed are those . . . whose delight is in the law of the Lord, and on his law they meditate day and night'" (Formula of Concord [FC], Solid Declaration [SD], VI, 4). Acknowledging that until the last day the sinful flesh retains its hold even on renewed Christians, who will therefore feel the prodding of the law, Article VI nevertheless distinguishes between "two different kinds of people" who may do what God requires (16). Those who have not been reborn are in bondage to the law and condemned by it even when they keep it in part. But those who have been born again and set free from bondage do what God commands — moved not simply by the law's prodding (or even by a sense of the majesty of the moral law) but by the power of Christ's Spirit (16-17). These Christians are on the way toward the holiness God promises to work in them. Along the way, of course, they will often stumble — and hence will need to return time and again to the word of promise that constitutes their recurring starting point. But they are not like Sisyphus, and they do more than just begin again and again. Article VI is clear that the last truth about God's promise is that he will bring them ever more fully — and substantively — into Christ's righteousness "until the sinful flesh is completely stripped away and people are perfectly renewed in the resurrection" (24).[20] That is the end of the history of redemption, and movement toward that end has already begun in the lives of believers.

Article III of the Formula of Concord ("Concerning the Righteousness of Faith before God") comes at similar issues from a slightly different angle, and it articulates what has been, I think, the standard alternative to a dialectical Lutheranism. Concerned to distinguish between justification and regeneration, it asserts that there must be a "proper order" between them — according to which order, renewal follows justification, not temporally but conceptually (FC, SD, III, 40-41). This formulation, though not mistaken, turns out to be of relatively little help. Once again in Article III, however, we find a clear recognition that there are two equally legitimate ways of speaking about our righteousness before God, the one relational and the other substantive. It distinguishes between the righteousness imputed in the gospel's promise of forgiveness and "being made righteous in fact and in truth on account of the love and other virtues infused into us through the Holy Spirit" (62).[21]

Of course, had the Formula of Concord offered a fully satisfactory resolution to the problem of the place of the law — and of the rela-

---

20. Cf. Luther's remarks in his commentary on Rom. 4:7: "This life, then, is a life of being healed from sin, it is not a life of sinlessness, with the cure completed and perfect health attained. The church is the inn and the infirmary for those who are sick and in need of being made well. But heaven is the palace of the healthy and the righteous. As blessed Peter says in his Second Epistle 3:13 that the Lord will build 'new heavens and a new earth in which righteousness dwells.' Righteousness does not yet dwell here, but it is preparing a dwelling place for itself here in the meantime by healing sin." *Luther's Works*, vol. 25 (St. Louis: Concordia, 1972), pp. 262-63.

21. Thus, commenting on Rom. 4:7, Luther says of those whose sin is forgiven: "They are actually sinners, but they are righteous by the imputation of a merciful God. . . . [T]hey are sinners in fact but righteous in hope." *Luther's Works*, 25:258.

tion between a righteousness acquired "more and more" and a righteousness reclaimed "again and again" — we might not still be troubled by this issue today. Indeed, although I shall shortly attempt to formulate the issue in a way that seems to me more satisfactory, perhaps there is no perfect way to sort out a question that — at the level of our own being and doing — must ultimately be sorted out by God when he makes these two sorts of righteousness one. Some have attempted terminological solutions, but I doubt whether they can get to the heart of the matter. Thus, for example, William Lazareth wants to eschew the language of a law's third use but get much of the same traction by speaking of a "second use" of the gospel.[22] This sort of terminological stipulation often goes hand in hand with what we might call a "Luther positivism" — for which the legitimacy of a third use of the law depends entirely on whether we can find it in Luther. That very search is often obscured, of course, by a failure to distinguish between the presence of a term and the presence of a concept.

The deeper problem with terminological solutions is that they are likely to leave untouched the inability of dialectical Lutheranism to speak of the law as the law of that one God who simply *is* gracious. That is, they do not address the incipient Marcionism that turns the distinction between law and gospel into a division within God's own being and thereby makes the normative will of God of purely passing significance. In practice, this dualism is tempted to treat the content of the moral life as a purely secular matter. So long, then, as the surrounding culture is relatively "Christianized," that culture does the work of carrying and transmitting Christian wisdom about how to live — thereby enabling the church to hide from herself the fact that she no longer has any moral guidance to offer. It is only when "times change" and the culture no longer seems reliable as a transmitter of Christian virtue that we suddenly realize the church has lost the ability to shape lives. This does not mean, of course, that the church ceases to speak about moral law; it means simply that what the church has to say increasingly mimics the secular sphere both in what it accepts and in what it rejects.

So long as this ontological dualism, together with its disastrous

---

22. William H. Lazareth, "Antinomians: Then and Now," *Lutheran Forum* 36 (winter 2002): 21.

effect on the church's ability to transmit a way of life, is renounced, there may be no need to quibble over preferred terminology. Because the New Testament often uses the term "law" to refer to the command of God when experienced as burdensome by sinful human beings and contrasts that experience with the liberation given when one hears and believes the word of promise, it may be that thinking in terms of an "evangelical command" captures well the sense that something new has occurred in the history of redemption when God gives the Christ.[23] Nevertheless, even if we avoid the language of law, we must still be able to speak of a command of God that is not oppressive. "[E]very creative and redemptive summons from God" must not, to use Oliver O'Donovan's searching formulation, "be introduced, as it were, with an apology for the fact that it is not good news." The command of God "is not a crutch; it is a life-giving command, 'Rise, take up your bed and walk!'"[24]

Putting an End to the "Simul"

Recall, now, where the Lutheran confessional writings — and Lutheranism — may leave us: with two contrasting depictions of the way grace works in our lives to make us righteous before God. According to one formulation, God's grace is a power working within us, bringing us ever more fully into that holiness of life without which no one will see the Lord. This holiness is not a *condition* for communion with God; rather, it is simply a *description* of what we must become before we can really want to be in God's presence. According to the sec-

---

23. Oliver O'Donovan, *Resurrection and Moral Order* (Grand Rapids: Eerdmans, 1986), p. 152. O'Donovan makes this connection to the history of redemption clear: "The law was thus a particular historical phase of Israel's experience of God; but the Jewish experience of history is seen [by St. Paul] to represent a universal existential situation in which an individual at any point of history may find himself before Christ has become a saving reality in his own experience. To experience moral command as 'the law,' then, is to encounter it *as though* from a point in the history of salvation at which God has not yet given the total blessing which he has promised his people. Law [in this universal existential sense] supposes that God's complete saving purpose is still an object of hope" (p. 152).

24. O'Donovan, *Resurrection and Moral Order*, p. 154.

ond formulation, grace is not power but pardon. It is the word of forgiveness and acceptance to which we must return in faith again and again.

When Lutherans have asked themselves about the relation between these two kinds of righteousness — at least whenever they have not, in dialectical fashion, simply eliminated entirely the depiction of grace as a power making us holy — they have generally tried to say, as in Article III of the Formula of Concord, that sanctification follows justification, not temporally but conceptually, and that the proper order between the two must be maintained. The problem has always been that a strong commitment to the language of justification seems to undercut any need for the language of sanctification.[25] If grace has really pardoned the sinner, clothing him in the righteousness of Christ than which there can be nothing more righteous, there seems little need any longer for grace to empower a journey toward holiness. We're already there! That holiness has already been given in Christ. What more could be needed? All that is left is for these good trees to bring forth good fruit, leaping in joyful spontaneity to the side of needy neighbors, and needing no instruction or guidance — or, alas, sinning contentedly in the sweet assurance that grace will abound.

We always seem to arrive at this same dead end, with these same alternatives, neither of which has any place for obeying the commandments. And this produces a church entirely captive — both in what it affirms and in what it rejects — to the terms of the moral life prevailing in the surrounding culture. Hence, the formula "justification followed by sanctification," accurate though it may be, never gets us very far. In making place for sanctification, we seem to make justification a fiction. In emphasizing the reality of justification, we make it hard to explain what still needs doing in sanctification. We are always seeming to endanger the reality of one or the other.

Can we do better?[26] In an article titled "What Karl Barth Learned

25. Cf. Hampson, p. 62: "By their very nature imputation and transformational change would seem to obviate the need for the other."

26. I am not so foolish as to suppose that what follows is a new creation. When we work on a problem that has engaged so many serious Christian thinkers over the centuries, our first concern should hardly be creativity. The approach I take in the following paragraphs bears at least some resemblance to what has sometimes been called the "double justification" formula on which (some) Catholics and Protestants

from Martin Luther," George Hunsinger, using language I appropriated earlier, depicted two ways of thinking about the relation of grace and the Christian life — contrasting the "again and again" motif with the "more and more" motif. He did this in order to argue that Barth had in fact deliberately revived and reemphasized the "again and again" motif that had been pronounced in Luther's own understanding. "Nothing is more characteristic of Barth's soteriology than the thesis that grace is new to us as sinners each morning, . . . and that it does not arrive by portions and pieces, but comes to us again and again in the perfection of the finished work of Christ."[27] But Hunsinger also noticed an important respect in which Barth nevertheless differed somewhat from Luther, and it is our clue to the way forward. In contrast to Luther, Hunsinger wrote, Barth "elevated reconciliation to preeminence so that justification became a subordinate concept which described reconciliation as a whole — as also did sanctification, justification's simultaneous counterpart."[28] That is, these theological constructs give us two different languages with which to describe God's work of reconciliation.

The terms "justification" and "sanctification" point not to different works of God but to two different angles — pardon and power —

(including Melanchthon) reached agreement at the Regensburg Colloquy in 1541. That colloquy was the last serious attempt to avoid a permanently divided church before the Council of Trent made such a hope futile. See Steven Ozment, *The Age of Reform, 1250-1550* (New Haven and London: Yale University Press, 1980), pp. 377-78, 405-6. (We should note that Anthony Lane [p. 58] denies that the Regensburg formula is properly characterized as "double justification." Rather, its references to imputed and inherent righteousness are, according to Lane, "simply ways of describing justification and sanctification.") My own approach differs, I think, from the "double justification" formula (if we wish to call it that) in that (1) I leave any final reconciliation of these two "languages" to God and accept the need to distinguish their use in pastoral practice; (2) I emphasize (following Barth) that this final reconciliation must somehow involve the fact that these are simply two different angles on the one reconciling work of God, even if the angles must remain somewhat distinct in Christian experience in this life; and (3) I am clear that the Catholic emphasis on internal transformation points to the *reality* that God is accomplishing, even while the Lutheran emphasis on an extrinsic righteousness which must be grasped by faith is (at some moments) essential for Christians who are only on the way toward the reality God has promised to accomplish.

27. Hunsinger, p. 300.
28. Hunsinger, p. 304.

from which to describe the one work of God in Christ, reconciling the world to himself. These are different ways of describing how God's Spirit draws our lives into the story of Jesus. The language of pardon addresses a truth of our experience — the continuing lure of sin. The language of power articulates the truth of reality — that God is at work, fulfilling his promise to turn sinners into saints. Our concern, therefore, should not be that justification must always precede sanctification, that a word of pardon precede a word of power. The distinction between these works of the Holy Spirit lies not in their order but in the circumstances in which these different words of grace are needed and appropriate. To those who are troubled in their hearts and tempted to despair, God's word of grace must be spoken as sheer pardon, free of any demand that might be heard as accusation. Only grace as pardon can draw the despairing out of themselves, teach them not to look inward (which is, after all, their problem), but outward to the righteousness of Christ. To those who trust that by God's grace they are no longer in bondage to sin and who seek, however haltingly and imperfectly, to bring their lives into obedience to his will, the gift and guidance of God's empowering grace should be offered. Thus, the distinction between justification and sanctification lies not in some wooden order of priority, but is a pastoral art, the skill of discerning whether grace as pardon or as power is needed. And the distinction between these languages is not the chief structuring principle of theology; it is, rather, the pastor's art.[29]

How these two languages — these two understandings of our righteousness before God — can themselves be united or reconciled is God's own eschatological mystery.[30] We may be confident, however,

29. Anthony Lane has made a similar point in describing the differing "concerns" with which Protestants and Catholics come to a discussion of sanctification. "Protestants are concerned to emphasize our continuing need of mercy and the assurance that comes from the imputed righteousness of Christ and fear anything that detracts from the finished work of Christ on the cross. Catholics are concerned to emphasize the reality of the transformation that Christ brings and fear the idea of a purely external righteousness and anything that detracts from the effective work of the Holy Spirit in our lives" (Lane, p. 12).

30. This, in fact, is the most important way in which the "simul" must retain a place in Christian theology. Until the end of the age, Christians will need to talk of God's gracious work in two — different but equally essential — ways: as both pardon and power.

that the one God — in whom it is always yes — who has graciously pardoned us, is himself committed to empowering us for holiness of life and will one day complete that task, as Luther himself makes clear in a wonderful extended metaphor:

> It is similar to the case of a sick man who believes the doctor who promises him a sure recovery and in the meantime obeys the doctor's order in the hope of the promised recovery and abstains from those things which have been forbidden him, so that he may in no way hinder the promised return to health or increase his sickness until the doctor can fulfil his promise to him. Now is this sick man well? The fact is that he is both sick and well at the same time. He is sick in fact, but he is well because of the sure promise of the doctor, whom he trusts and who has reckoned him as already cured, because he is sure that he will cure him; for he has already begun to cure him and no longer reckons to him a sickness unto death. In the same way Christ, our Samaritan, has brought His half-dead man into the inn to be cared for, and He has begun to heal him, . . . but in the meantime in the hope of the promised recovery He prohibits him from doing or omitting things by which his cure might be impeded. . . . Now, is he perfectly righteous? no, for he is at the same time both a sinner and a righteous man; a sinner in fact, but a righteous man by the sure imputation and promise of God that He will continue to deliver him from sin until He has completely cured him. And thus he is entirely healthy in hope, but in fact he is still a sinner; but he has the beginning of righteousness, so that he continues more and more always to seek it.[31]

Christians may often experience their life as a daily return — again and again, new every morning — to the word of pardon that gives them hope. But the report of that *experience,* crucial as it is, must not subvert the truth of *reality* — that within the inn of his church, God is at work forming people whose hearts are set to obey. These are not people who suppose that they can ever face the judgment of God secure in their own deeds and character; rather, these are people in whom there has begun to be, as Paul Ramsey put it, "a combination of

31. *Luther's Works,* Volume 25: *Lectures on Romans,* p. 260.

increasing humility and increasing achievement."[32] The more God's grace empowers their lives, the more they know their need of his pardon. And the word of pardon carries with it God's commitment to make us people who will want to live in his presence — to make us what he says we are. Hence, God's promise is embedded in his command: "You shall be holy."

Until that day, of course, we continue to exist within the "simul" — as simultaneously saint and sinner. We dare not, however, contentedly accept this as our normal and appropriate condition — as if God did not intend one day to have done with the "simul," and were not already at work on that project here and now. As Barth says, the people of God, as the "living community of the Lord Jesus," must be "horrified by the dishonor that is done to God in that *simul* relation."[33] We should therefore pray that the power of God's perfecting grace may day by day, more and more, have its effect in our lives. Not to pray that seriously is not to take seriously God's own commitment to make us holy. "The wakeful church and its wakeful members pray 'Hallowed be thy name,'" Barth writes, "even though all around them, uttered even by themselves sometimes in their waking dreams, there continues the apathetic and monotonous murmur: 'At one and the same time both righteous and sinner, world without end. Amen.' No, the living community and its members cannot say Amen to this."[34]

We should pray God to put an end to the "simul," that our hearts may be set to obey. The command of God, which calls for our obedience, comes to us day by day as the command of the One whose grace has been revealed in the face of Jesus Christ. And because that is true, because we can and must say "Amen" to him, we should listen for the promise in the commands of the Decalogue: You *shall* love the Lord your God with all your heart, soul, and mind. You *shall* become a child who loves the Father, a bride eager to greet her bridegroom, a creature who loves the Creator from whom comes life and every good thing, a lover of God in whose speech the praise of God resounds. All this . . .

32. Paul Ramsey, *Basic Christian Ethics* (New York: Charles Scribner's Sons, 1950), p. 200. Ramsey adds: "This has been the hall-mark of Christian character in all ages."
33. Karl Barth, *The Christian Life* (Grand Rapids: Eerdmans, 1981), pp. 153-54.
34. Barth, p. 154.

you *shall* be. And to trust that promise — the promise that we shall become people whose hearts are set to obey God's commandments — is both our duty and our delight.